ASIAN PERCEPTIONS OF NATURE

NORDIC INSTITUTE OF ASIAN STUDIES

Studies in Asian Topics

ASIAN PERCEPTIONS OF NATURE

A CRITICAL APPROACH

edited by
Ole Bruun
and Arne Kalland

CURZON
PRESS

Nordic Institute of Asian Studies
Studies in Asian Topics, No. 18

First published 1995 by Curzon Press Ltd.,
St. John's Studios, Church Road
Richmond, Surrey TW9 2QA

Reprinted 1996

ISBN 0-7007-0301-2 [Hardback]
ISBN 0-7007-0290-3 [Paperback]

British Library Catalogue in Publication Data
A CIP catalogue record for this book
is available from the British Library

Printed in Great Britain by Antony Rowe Ltd, Chippenham, Wiltshire

GE
190
.A78
A85
1995

Contents

Illustrations

In the chapter, *Japanese Advertising Nature*, a number of advertisements are reproduced to illustrate the argument of the text. Every effort has been made to trace the copyright holders of these illustrations. Unfortunately, in some cases, this has proved to be impossible. The authors and publishers would be pleased to hear from any copyright holders they have been unable to contact and to print due acknowledgements in the next volume of the book.

Ole Bruun and Arne Kalland

Images of Nature
An Introduction to the Study of Man–Environment Relations in Asia

Growing concern for the natural environment has opened up a new field of inter-disciplinary studies of relations between man and nature. The ensuing intellectual debate has spread internationally and has nourished cross-cultural communication on environmental issues. The intentions behind this volume are implicitly to provide studies on specific topics related to Asian perceptions of nature and explicitly to provide a perspective on the cultural communication between Asia and the West in regard to our natural environment.

In environmental studies it has commonly been assumed that there exists a fundamental connection between a society's management of natural resources and its perception of nature. For instance, ecological and environmental problems in the West have been accredited to the Judaeo-Christian cosmology of man's mastery of nature.[1] Within this tradition, perhaps nobody has claimed man's mastery over nature more successfully than Descartes. One of the roots for the present deep concern for nature in the western world is apparently the growing awareness of the inadequacies of the Cartesian world-view, in which an intensified dichotomy of reality separated subject from object, culture from nature, and cultural sciences from natural sciences. More precisely, both sciences and popular ideologies have come to question the division between 'science for people (social sciences) and science for nature' (Dickens 1992:3). With the challenged – some would say crumbling – western paradigms, an entirely new ecological paradigm is frequently called for (e.g. Dunlap and Catton 1980), a paradigm where 'man' and

---

[1] See Lynn White 1967/1973; Callicott and Ames 1989:1c. as prominent examples; from a theological stance see John B. Cobb 1972, and for the argument that western ideas are equally harmful in the East see, for instance, Eugene C. Hargrove 1989.

'environment' no longer are seen as separate and opposite entities but where 'organisms and environment form part of one another' (Dickens 1992:15).

Scientists and laymen alike have searched for new inspiration to correct these ills from outside western traditions. A large body of literature offers alternative world-views to the prevailing western ones: usually depicting man as an integral part of nature instead of being separated from it and trying to dominate it. They portray man and environment as a harmonious unity of mutual respect, complementarity and symbiosis; their views are holistic-organic rather than atomistic-mechanistic as in the industrial West (Callicott and Ames 1989:5).

The perceptions of nature found among indigeneous peoples and tribal societies have provided us with rich notions of alternatives. These are, however, commonly marketed in a specific ideological pursuit and thus entangled with a continuing critique of western culture. Native American beliefs and myths, for instance, have greatly inspired radical environmentalists; the founders of Greenpeace saw themselves as the *Rainbow Warriors* who, according to a Cree myth, would come to the Indians' rescue and 'teach the white man reverence for the earth' (Brown and May 1991:13).[2]

By the same token, Asian perceptions, particularly as they are articulated in Daoism, Buddhism and Hinduism, have been extensively used for similar purposes. In popular literature on ecology, allusions to Asian philosophies as a remedy for environmental ills are widespread. While natural scientists have repeatedly pointed to parallels between the new physics and biology, on the one hand, and eastern philosophies on the other, others – from rebellious youths with only a rudimentary understanding of Oriental cultures to more sophisticated proponents of 'deep ecology' – have incorporated Asian ideas more or less critically into their world-views. An underlying assumption in much of this work is that Asian cosmologies have made Asian peoples more successful than others in taking care of nature, and Hargrove (1989) therefore laments that we have not given Asian perceptions the attention they deserve.

However, many anthropologists, geographers, sociologists and others doing fieldwork in Asia have noticed that Asian philosophies and cosmologies seem to have had little effect in preventing over-

---

[2] See Buenfil (1991) for an insider's vision of a new environmental awareness based on Native concepts.

exploitation of soils, over-grazing, erosion, deforestation, pollution of waters and other environmental disasters – by which a number of Asian societies are acutely threatened. Nor can it be claimed that environmental degradation is a new phenomenon in Asia (cf. Simmons 1989; Totman 1989). It was against this background that we wanted to take a closer look at Asian attitudes to nature. The studies presented here address a series of issues related to perception of nature, attitudes to environmental change, and the use of natural metaphors across the Asian world. The collection of essays jointly promotes a more critical approach to the study of perceptions of nature in general. We wish to provide a new perspective to the myths of western dominance of nature; particularly, we wish to confront what has become established as the counter-myth of a prevailing Asian ecology-mindedness. However, it is beyond the scope of this collection of essay to analyse the processes behind the construction of such myths and their function in the western debate on man and environment. Nor is it our aim to depreciate Asian philosophy and thought; intellectual production in all parts of the world are valuable in redefining the man–environment relation.

Instead, this volume will concentrate on a selection of Asian societies, from which such myths may draw their material. The contributors to the volume, anthropologists, historians, geographers and sociologists – all competent area specialists drawing on original research and recent fieldwork – will portray perceptions of nature in their local arena of thought and action: their sociology, articulation, proponents, audience and function. The papers show the creativity and richness contained in local perceptions of nature as well as the uniqueness that each area attaches to its relation between man and environment. Thus our collective contribution to the debate on Asian ideological alternatives is to provide a tool rather than a conclusive argument.

We are not the first to question the 'Oriental' solution; John B. Cobb (1972) and John Passmore (1980), for example, have both argued against turning to eastern philosophies to find remedies for environmental problems. Hargrove (1989:xviii), on the other hand, argues that such criticism is rooted in the belief that insidious eastern ideas will destroy western civilization, or in the belief that eastern environmental attitudes are either too incompatible with western traditions to be assimilable or too ineffective in the East to be of any use in the West. However, our critique is not based on a belief that Asian influence is dangerous to western civilization, nor do we subscribe to the myth of the inscrutable Orientals. Furthermore, that eastern ideas have been ineffective in the

East is not *a priori* any reason why they should not be effective in the West.

In order to lead the debate beyond such trivialities we shall focus on some interrelated themes, crucial to both localized and cross-cultural studies of perceptions of nature.

- Firstly, this collection of papers shows a profound variation and continuous change in regard to perceptions of the natural environment. There is no such a thing as *the* Asian perception of nature, nor is there a universal western one. Perceptions of the natural environment are often contested within a given culture and they are subject to essential change along with natural and man-made changes in the environment itself.

- Secondly, an issue of great concern to a number of the contributors is the cross-cultural significance of the concept of nature as well as of classifications of natural objects and phenomena. Several papers show the mutual interlocking between the understanding of natural objects and natural processes, on the one hand, and social institutions and specific behaviour on the other (e.g. Bruun; Eisenstadt; Kalland). How these go together to form the prevalent cultural orientations and have specific social implications at the local level are essential topics in the study of man and environment.

- Thirdly, the use of natural metaphors as a common frame of reference in Asian agricultural societies pervades most papers and is of particular concern to several (e.g. Bruun; Clarke; Pedersen; Sparkes; Sperber). Natural processes provide a rich resource for the construction of meaning and expression of feelings, as well as for the interpretation and manipulation of social relations, both between the sexes and in the political and economic spheres.

- Fourthly, man and environment bound together in a moral order is an issue of historical significance (Boomgaard; Kathirithamby-Wells) as well as of current value, not least in Buddhist societies. Frequently, the notion of a moral universal order implies a strongly personified natural environment, in which a variety of beings react to undue human interference (Sandell; Sperber).

- Finally, the commonly assumed link between a society's prevalent perception of nature and its actual human behaviour is questioned either explicitly (e.g. Boomgaard; Kalland; Pedersen) or implicitly. Several papers question the widely held notion of benign Asian attitudes toward nature. They argue that sensitivity to nature does not necessarily indicate love for, showing respect for or living in harmony with the natural environment (Bruun; Kalland; Moeran and Skov; Sparkes). Likewise, management of natural resources probably owes more to local power relations than directly to perceptions (Boomgaard; Knudsen; Sandell; Sperber).

Diversity in time and space

Considering the sheer size of Asia it is, of course, deceptive to talk about an Asian conception in the singular. Nonetheless, this is often what popular writings on attitudes to nature tend to do. When large parts of Asia are indiscriminately embraced in simple terms like the 'Orient', the 'East' or just 'Asia' – equipped with properties produced for western consumption (Savage 1984) – we maintain that this is merely a rhetorical device to define 'the other' through juxtaposing 'we' and 'them'. In our often sweeping generalizations we tend to forget the extent of the concepts we use, in this case 'Asia'.[3] In the history of western travel, discovery and expansion, the idea of relativeness created the mythical and glamorous East, notions later to be strengthened in the romantic opposition to the rationalism of the industrializing western societies. The rise and function in the West of notions concerning eastern, Oriental and Asian nature perception, environment protection, social harmony, human satisfaction, ecological consciousness and so on are then crucial topics for understanding our own culture and as our own culture changes so do our images of the other. We have to look beyond such popular visions of 'Asia' – visions that are often strongly endorsed by some Asian writers themselves as shown by Poul Pedersen – if we are to understand the complexities and the true processes shaping Asian societies' attitudes to nature.

---

[3] As expressed by Jamie Mackie (1993:155), 'Use of the blanket term "Asia" to cover all those countries ... carries an implication that they are all much the same, or have something in common that differentiates from us. That is not only untrue, but positively misleading – and harmful to our understanding of that part of the world'.

People in Asia have adapted to a wide range of different environments, having made their homes on small tropical islands and arctic
tundras; extensive plains and steep mountains and hills; dense rainforest
and arid deserts. The present volume reflects some of this diversity.
Geographically, the papers deal with people from Pakistan in the west
to Japan in the east and from the Indonesian archipelago in the south to
the Himalayas and China in the north. The contributors have used
ethnographies of agro-pastoralists in remote Himalayan villages (Clarke;
Knudsen; Sperber), wet-rice cultivators in Southeast Asia and Sri Lanka
(Boomgaard; Sandell; Sparkes) and urbanized societies (Bruun;
Eisenstadt; Kalland; Kathirithamby-Wells; Moeran and Skov). It can
hardly be taken as an expression of environmental determinism to point
out the unlikelihood that people so dispersed in space and with such
different modes of adaptation should share one perception of their
environments.

That perceptions can vary greatly even within limited geographical
areas is indicated by Peter Boomgaard in his paper on tree spirits in
Indonesia. Whereas sandal trees have been regarded as sacred and
inhabited by spirits on Java and to a lesser extent on Sumba until
recently, there exists no indication that people on Timor ever held such
beliefs. If they ever did, Boomgaard argues, these beliefs have long been
lost perhaps because extraction of sandalwood on Timor was, unlike on
the adjacent islands, a corvée duty ordered by an aristocracy that was
also held responsible if disasters struck.

Neither in Asian societies, nor in others, are attitudes to nature
static. For millennia, Asia has seen the rise and fall of large civilizations
which throughout their entire history have been in contact with each
other and even with cultures of the West. All the 'great religions' –
Hinduism, Buddhism, Judaism, Christianity and Islam – were founded
in Asia and they have all put their strong marks on the continent.
Nevertheless, 'native' thought – or 'folk religion' – has survived the
pressure from these great religions to an extent seldom seen in Europe.
Rather than eradicating earlier beliefs and practices, the great religions
added new dimensions to existing cosmologies. At the same time, the
great religions have in many places been influenced by native concepts
and values to such an extent that it is meaningless to distinguish
between 'Great' and 'Little' traditions (cf. Redfield 1955). Thus, Graham
E. Clarke argues that the dominant world-view in highland Nepal may
draw from both populist, natural models and the codified literate worlds
of the great religions, as well as from the modern discourse of progress

and development, but may not be classified as either of them. Rather, it represents a routine, vernacular world, in which individuals think through their own daily experience – a field often neglected by research. The resulting 'folk wisdom' embodies both open-minded empiricism and a certain scepticism, which have wide applications to social, political and religious life, linking both the natural and the cultural spheres to the same cyclical processes.

Asian societies are in a process of change, and the aspirations of the Asian governments are commonly large-scale industrialization and rapid modernization. The economic and political systems of a number of Asian societies move in the direction of western standards, involving democratization, emphasis on market relations and increasing awareness of international society. In terms of mode of life, the modern Asian world is embracing the extremes. Huge world financial centres with highly sophisticated life styles are often surrounded by simple peasant economies, and the growing number of Asian cities with a million-plus inhabitants are often geographically close to vast areas occupied by tribal societies.

Typically, the city serves as an entrepôt for foreign ideas which are only slowly disseminated through its hinterland – creating tensions between the centre and its periphery. Moreover, conflicts over control of natural resources have intensified in the industrializing society: between industry and agriculture, between large- and small-scale economies, between centre and periphery, and between ethnic groups. Although imported ideas and technologies may give different messages to people's perceptions of nature, they together produce a larger possible repertoire, opening the field for manipulation to a degree hitherto unknown. Not least, the international nature conservation idiom has provided those in power with a new, potent weapon, accentuating the conflict between centre and periphery. One example of this is, as shown in Are Knudsen's paper, the conflict between the propagators of western environmentalism and the farmers in the Hunza Valley in northeastern Pakistan, where the national government inspired by a western environmental discourse and encouraged by NGOs established the Khunjerab National Park.

However, responding to western discourses does not necessarily mean that they are copied in the East. Like foreign ideas in the past, they might be adjusted to the host culture's values and perceptions, but in the process also contribute to cultural change. That western discourses are being 'Asianized' is shown by Poul Pedersen in his paper on environmentalism in Asia and by Brian Moeran and Lise Skov in their paper on ecological advertising in Japan. Being a part of a worldwide trend, the Japanese advertisements nevertheless take on a special flavour with a widespread use of women-nature metaphors where 'ecology' and 'nature' contribute to a cultural discourse on modernity. It remains to be seen how ecological advertisements in the long run will also contribute to changes in Japanese perceptions of nature.

The concept of nature

Throughout this century the natural sciences have indicated the cultural bias and shortcomings of our view of nature, and have incorporated a host of new concepts incompatible with previous paradigms. Unquestionably, the twentieth-century scientific revolution, with the break-up of the mechanistic paradigm which has seen the whole as the sum of its constituent parts, demands a stronger response also outside the natural sciences; perhaps even 'a return to the kind of philosophical reflection, clarification, and generalizations, in the grand manner of Plato, Descartes and Kant, that had been the hallmark of western philosophy for nearly two and a half millennia' (Callicott and Ames 1989:x). In this process the natural and moral philosophies may reintegrate and synthesize to form a new 'environmental philosophy', which ostensibly has much in common with the Asian traditions (ibid:xi).

Perhaps as an independent trend our relation to the physical environment is changing. It may be argued that the western view of nature is currently in a state of transition, expressed by a propagating ecological awareness and practice: a switch from unbound expansion to a tentative beginning of withdrawal. Concomitantly spreading in the western world is the naturalist view that 'our survival lies in the protection of wilderness'.[4]

In anthropology, the assessment of the inadequacies of the western dualistic thought nevertheless goes on, stressing, for instance, the conceptual prison of the nature–culture dichotomy and in its stead introducing the 'mutualism of person and environment' (Ingold 1992:40).

---

[4] This is a common stand taken by environment groups in the protection of the rainforests and the oceans, thereby questioning the utilitarian approach to nature. Instead they advocate 'rights' of nature (Regan 1984; Nash 1989; Benton 1993).

It is true, of course, that people do not just adapt to their environment, but also tend to shape it from materials and possibilities they see in the surrounding habitat and life forms (Croll and Parkin 1992:16). Man makes the environment and is simultaneously influenced by it. Nature and culture, in their countless variants and sub-categories, form key distinctions in most cosmologies, allowing for constant dissolving, reconvening and recombining (ibid.). A crucial theme in the interpretation and negotiation of meaning then becomes the constitution of power and hierarchy in society. Among the questions to ask are which groups possess the authority to formulate the central distinctions and what are the respective interests of state versus locality, elite versus folk culture, collective versus private, clergy versus commoners and male versus female?

In discussing 'nature' we are dealing with maybe the most complex concept in western languages, that in common usage has a complicated repertoire of meanings (Lewis 1960; Williams 1976).[5] On the basis of complex Greek and Latin roots, it has been moulded into a single multifaceted concept which finds a variety of uses and which, moreover, is still in a process of change. Recurring intervals of romanticism have given it much of its flavour.

Testifying to the powerful abstractions of the western philosophical tradition is the strictly substantive definition of a physical world which has given rise to metaphysics or 'ultimate reality' – through the history of western thought in the form of ideas, magic, the perfection of God, vitalism, structures, signs or final goals. The notion that nature is not the full description of reality is apparently shared by Platonian, Aristotelian and Christian thought: these are the roots of an intense dualism, or dichotomization of existence, expressed in idealism, metaphysics and transcendence.

Therefore, if we investigate a number of western concepts such as 'nature' and 'landscape' they reveal reference not only to the physical aspects of earth, but also to an abstract space containing a variety of ideas and principles, defying easy definition (Williams 1976:184; McArthur 1986:14). Even if we define a common core of meaning in the term 'nature', it does not permit us to place it definitely in any of

---

[5] Raymond Williams (1976) gives 'nature' three basic meanings: (i) the essential quality and character of something, (ii) the inherent force which directs either the world of human beings or both, and (iii) the material world itself, taken as including or not including human beings, i.e. the 'not culture' category.

Popper's (1972:ch.4) three worlds of reference.[6] The qualities of our environment, conceived by such concepts, are products of the human consciousness as much as they are universal and objective. We differentiate 'nature' by means of accurate definitions, classes and systems, including shapes and colours, but attribute to it meanings and emotions, thus turning the environment into landscapes. Accordingly, concepts like 'nature' and 'landscape' may be seen as anthropocentric and subjective-sophisticated tools of the mind in the pursuit of order among apparent chaos.

As this collection of papers demonstrates, the Asian concepts are no less complex than their western counterparts.[7] Those papers defining local concepts of nature (i.e. Bruun; Kalland; Moeran and Skov; Sandell) show that these share at least one meaning with western uses of the concept; 'that which comes of itself', stressing spontaneity in the natural surroundings, frequently expressive of an immanent cosmological order, as opposed to a transcendent order.

A second complex of meanings embedded in western concepts of nature is 'not culture'. This usage is not unknown in Asia. Among the Kalasha in northwestern Pakistan, for example, nature (*kalibana*) is 'everything which is not cultivated'; Birgitte Sperber shows that a basic distinction between *onjesta* (pure) and *pragata* (impure) denotes a cosmological duality encompassing both the physical environment and human relations in sets of binary oppositions, pure–impure, man–women, goat–cow, mountain–valley. Stephen Sparkes also deals with dualities in his paper on the Isan in Northeast Thailand. Following Ortner's (1974) model that nature relates to female as culture to male, he goes on to analyse gender in terms of culture and nature, the latter being metaphors of the former. This strikes at the very centre of the debate about the relationship between culture and nature.

A number of papers in this volume stress the unity of man and

---

[6] As put by Tom McArthur (1986:9): 'The lines that you are reading belong to World 1, part of the general worldscape. How you process them is World 2, your mindscape. Their message or content, however, is part of World 3, which has independent value and, ..., make libraries and databanks far and away more important than the knowledge that is in any one person's head at any one time. What we call the 'oratures' of pre-literate peoples belong also in World 3, but they are far less efficiently housed and safeguarded than the 'literatures' of literate societies.'

[7] An indication of this complexity is provided by Klas Sandell who lists no less than six Sinhala words for 'nature', none of which are completely corresponding to the English term.

nature or of culture and nature. The nature–culture distinction may be less categorical in the East than in the West and both S.N. Eisenstadt and Arne Kalland stress that the Japanese do not distinguish sharply between nature and culture. To Kalland they are located along a continuum where tamed, or cooked, nature conflates with culture at one extreme and with raw nature at the other, whereas Eisenstadt in his paper shows how the Japanese approach to nature is essentially dualistic, but with a high degree of mutual embedment of nature and culture and a strong pragmatic–activist trend. Thus reality is structured in shifting contexts and even in discrete ontological entities, as opposed to the absolutist Western approach.

Man and environment as a moral unity

Since some variety of the nature–culture distinction is found everywhere – although the distinction might be contextual and relative rather than absolute – the real question is how the two spheres are combined and what systems of transformation allow people, things and concepts to travel from one to the other. Rituals may satisfy spirits abiding in trees thus permitting Indonesian villagers to fell the trees and cut them up for boats or boards (Boomgaard); 'taming' practices may accommodate nature to cultural norms (Kalland; Sperber); Chinese geomantic principles may draw universal forces into auspicious bearing on houses and graves (Bruun); and sophisticated symbolism may reintroduce 'nature' into Japanese city dwellers' consumption patterns (Moeran and Skov).

Contrary to western tendencies to dichotomize the universe and stress the absolute, many Asian cultures contextualize the oppositions between nature and culture, the wild and the tame, humans and deities, purity and impurity, good and evil, and so on. This contextualism frequently applies to the concept of morality. Nature and morality are closely linked in many Asian cultures, man and environment forming a moral unity. Yet, as there is no absolute good or evil, there is no absolute morality, at least not for commoners. Thus, people's moral obligations towards nature are contextual.[8]

---

[8] Sandell provides us with a telling example of this pragmatic contextualism when in his paper he discusses the contradiction between the Buddhist prohibition against taking life and modern agricultural practices. To many of the Sri Lankan farmers this

In, for instance, Sinhalese Buddhist cosmology, nature is believed to be illusory, passing away like everything else in existence, sharing with man the experience of destruction and death. Separate levels of existence are found in nature, just as the view of it varies with positions in the social order from monks to commoners. Since there is no clear-cut distinction between man and nature, virtuous acts and moral gestures are not only aimed at fellow humans but are properties of fundamental ethics. Farming from a Buddhist perspective, Klas Sandell argues, implies linking changes in the physical environment to changes in society, and vice versa. Inadequate rainfall and poor harvests may result from bad behaviour, for instance felling the forest or neglect of rituals. Nature is therefore affected positively by the observation of rituals. Boomgaard, on the other hand, argues that in general the influence of religious conceptions is merely postulated and he sees in Indonesian history no evidence confirming clear links between belief systems and ecological change.

Being contextual implies that concepts must repeatedly be defined or redefined and thus be subjected to competition and manipulation. The actors must continuously establish a framework for the interaction taking place and this is frequently done by ritual means. This also applies to the concept of 'nature' and in several Asian cultures this ritualization implies sanctification of nature. Parts of nature – particularly trees, mountains, caves, rivers and lakes – are regarded as sacred abodes of a variety of spirits. Mountain gods and water spirits are essential elements of Southeast Asian ritual (Kathirithamby-Wells), Isan villagers in northeastern Thailand believe that their ancestors live in trees (Sparkes) while the Kalasha fairies prefer mountains (Sperber). Frequently it is taboo to approach these sacred dwelling-places and approaches must at least be done under strict observation of purity. Sacrifices and prayers are offered to the spirits residing in nature in order to gain their support and avoid disasters. In can be argued, as Kalland does in his paper, that this ritualistic approach to nature is one way to come to terms with the 'nature in the raw' and 'tame' it.

Similarly, Jeya Kathirithamby-Wells argues that Southeast Asian perceptions of nature through history recognized resource exploitation as part and parcel of the political process, and that the mandate for

---

was not a problem because the killing was not 'intentional' but a 'by-product of the agricultural practices'. By the same token, most people hold the view that once an animal has been killed, there is no harm in eating it.

political authority was contingent upon the harmonious management of spiritual and material affairs within the cosmological unit, congruent with the ecosystem. Being the divine mediator with the entire living universe, the ruler would lose his mandate if calamity struck.

Nature as metaphors

Both East and Southeast Asian cultures are known for a customary usage of natural metaphors in social classifications and morality. Although used by imperial courts and local aristocracies they are equally common in ordinary peasant societies, where they form a ready-made vocabulary for a wide range of purposes.

We can certainly recognize common features of a number of Asian societies. Asian reality is often one of large political structures in both time and space, incorporating the individual into a type of social organization firmly linking the local community to the world outside. Moreover, these large political structures may be reflected in some Asian cosmologies, emphasizing the higher value of a larger unified world as compared to fragmentation. In Japanese Confucian society, this larger polity is often likened to the human body: each class of people playing different roles yet being dependent on each other in the same way as feet, hands and head play different but interdependent role. In Chinese imperial society ideas about nature were taken from the macro-cosmos and used to explain social relations at the micro level. Natural metaphors are apparently crucial in the constitution of political authority, for which the example provided by Kathirithamby-Wells also serves – the Southeast Asian ruler was the lord of 'land and water', effectively including control over manpower within the *mandala*, or 'area of influence'.

On the local level, biological universals such as plant growth cycles and land use typically form a holistic model for both natural and cultural domains, where they juxtapose the 'natural' and the 'normal' and even conflate them. Clarke, for instance, focuses on how biological universals become models for politics and society where ideas of the natural environment are extended outwards through the construction of images and metaphors to be used as general life models explaining success and failure in daily life routines.

Like the Confucian political ideology, Chinese geomancy (*fengshui*) operates by the extensive use of cosmological analogies. Geomancy has been applied to Chinese settlements for centuries, and even in the modern city it has adapted its practice to circumstances. Ole Bruun argues in his article that behind the reference to natural forces, *fengshui* serves as an outlet for culturally debased feelings and motives and in that sense it conspicuously runs counter to high Chinese culture. By searching for auspiciousness in all human affairs it attempts to encircle and define the 'world that matters' for ordinary people, placing the family dwelling in a meaningful local context and placing the local area as an integral and important part of the larger world. Bruun thus argues that *fengshui* can be seen as a social discourse drawing heavily on natural metaphors.

Another common theme is nature–culture symbolism being applied to gender relations (Moeran and Skov; Sparkes; Sperber). Women are extensively associated with life-giving nature as opposed to the cultured, but more aggressive male-universe, on which foundation a rich symbolism is constructed. Such symbolism is not specifically Asian, of course, since it belongs to the archetypal images, but it is certainly prevalent among the Asian societies described in this volume, including the Chinese *yin–yang* pair, the natural beauty and capacity attached to Japanese women, the Kalasha analogy between female, impurity and wilderness, and the Isan fertility rites linking women to Mother Earth.

Being a part of a worldwide trend, Japanese advertisements, for example, take on a special flavour with a widespread use of women-nature metaphors where 'ecology' and 'nature' contribute to a cultural discourse on modernity. Further, Moeran and Skov note that the discourse in Japanese advertising is double-edged: on the one hand, nature is used to establish an ideal of universal harmony among all human beings on earth and, on the other, nature is a symbol of Japan's exploitation of resources and people in its endless search to create new markets and thereby maintain an unchallenged economic power. In her paper, Sperber – drawing on local myths – argues that the Kalasha conceptualize gender in terms of topographical features and domesticated animals, the basic distinction being made between *onjesta* (pure) and *pragata* (impure) where men tend to be regarded as cleaner than women. To maintain the hierarchical ordering of male over female, which some see as the primary motive, the frame of reference must, however, be constantly shifted. Thus both the nature–culture distinction and the related gender distinction tend to be soft and dynamic – or contextual – rather than dichotomous. Sparkes also discusses gender relations in his paper on the Isan, and he suggests that the villagers anthropomorphize nature 'by giving it the characteristic of gender', with all important nature spirits being female: Mother Earth, Mother Rice, Mother Water and Lady of the Wood. Male spirits are less important, but more aggressive and demanding of offerings. Rites and ceremonies frequently invert male and female principles, but the aim underlying such crossing of symbolic boundaries is to maintain gender categories and ultimately the hierarchical ordering of male over female.

The socio-centric use of natural models for society, for instance in defining social harmony or preserving power and hierarchy, may at its extreme imply seeing the natural environment as merely a resource potential to be converted into usefulness. Of all the natural resources, forests are among those encompassed by the greatest tensions. They are of prime concern to both the world community, the national economies and the people traditionally depending on them fully or partially for their livelihood. Forests are an ultimate resource to native peoples, but also often symbolize the untamed nature that houses the spiritual world as, for example, in Java where the trees represent, as pointed out by Boomgaard, the universe or chaotic nature.[9] At the same time they mark – as they do in the Kalasha Valleys (Sperber), Northeast-Thailand (Sparkes) and Japan (Kalland) – the opposition to village, field and domesticated animals.

Perception versus behaviour

In general terms, Asian perceptions of nature have not operated in prevention of massive pollution, destruction of natural resources and environmental disasters. The economies of Japan, South-Korea and Taiwan have, with their formidable growth rates, played the role of pace-setters for Asian development, but their industries were simultaneously producing toxic wastes now causing political problems both at home and abroad. Japan has already experienced major pollution crises affecting tens of thousands. India is experiencing a disastrous laying waste of land due to state exploitation of forests and uncontrolled gathering by the rural poor. China's booming economy has driven the

---

[9] It must be stressed that this approach is not unique to Asian cultures. Quite contrary it is an approach that often bedevils the environmental debate in the West; environmental movements turn elements of nature – certain landscapes, rainforests and animals – into metonyms for the whole of nature.

natural environment to the edge of disaster, the extent of which can only be concealed by a heavy state monopoly on information. In the Indonesia-Malay region the land is being stripped of its rainforests at an alarming rate with prospects of large-scale climatic change. Even in the scarcely populated mountainous territories of inner Asia, countries like Nepal, Tibet and Mongolia are facing deforestation, ecological degradation and pollution. Today, a great number of Asian societies share a common destiny in terms of population pressure, rapid environmental change, resource scarcity and frequent environmental crisis.[10]

Such reality is obviously out of tune with notions of the 'ecological Oriental'. This seeming paradox has been explained in various ways. Some want us to believe that environmental disasters are new to Asia and a consequence of western colonialism or growing populations – itself an effect of industrialization along western lines. But whereas shifting cultivators can be said to imitate nature in their agricultural practices (Geertz 1963), wet-rice cultivation, which has been practised in some Asian societies for more than two thousand years, means radical alternation and even total destruction of pre-existing ecosystems. Realizing that environmental degradation is not a new phenomenon in Asia, Hargrove (1989:xix) suggests that such degradation might be 'the result of empirical ignorance ... rather than the pragmatic inefficacy of eastern environmental attitudes and values'.

However, theory and practice may be far apart. Discussing the relation between nature thinking and concrete action, several authors tend to agree in emphasizing the need to tread cautiously when inducing ecological practices from philosophical traditions. Referring to Holy and Stuchlik (1983), Pedersen argues that it is too simplistic to assume that values and norms work directly on the individuals. Rather, they should be seen as rhetorical devices which are utilized in order to achieve a specific goal or legitimize an action. Therefore, he continues, we cannot take environmental behaviour as evidence of specific values.

It can even be argued that the notion of a connection between people's perceptions of nature and the ways they manage the natural environment is a western one, not necessarily shared by people in Asia. The very question regarding this relationship might turn out to be based

---

[10] Under the caption 'False economies', the Far Eastern Economic Review (19 September 1991) paints a gloomy picture of both the environment in Asia and the attempts of reversing past degradations and preventing future ecological disasters: 'In the case of Asia, present efforts must – for the most part – be judged harshly' (p. 37).

on the western dichotomy between theory – or ideology – and practice. Although the conflict between ideology and practice is by no means absent in Asian cultures – Japan comes immediately to mind – it may be solved through, for instance, contextualism (Berque 1986; Eisenstadt; Kalland). This contextualism implies not only that there are no clear-cut distinctions between nature and non-nature or between man and other satient beings but also that people's approach to nature tends to be particularistic, or pragmatic, rather than governed by absolute principles.

Infusing nature with spirits or using nature as a repertoire for metaphors is no assurance for the well-being of the environment. Through rituals, spirits can be removed from locations which developers want to use for other purposes. Thus, Boomgaard investigates the power of animistic spirit beliefs commonly thought to be favourable to conservation, finding that the impact of western enterprise on the peasantry, the state and the need for land was stronger than the fear of tree-spirits; such beliefs tended to diminish along with the forest. Sparkes makes a similar point in his paper; Kalland argues that in Japan metaphorical use of nature might depend more on the quality than the quantity of nature and that turning natural elements into metonyms for the whole of nature may downgrade the rest, thus making it more vulnerable to neglect and destruction.

There is hardly any evidence that one religious creed protects nature better than others. Other factors seem to be far more important to people's treatment of nature than religious beliefs and practices. Boomgaard points out that when people did not destroy nature this was more the result of low population density compared to resources available than of conscious resource conservation. Sandell argues that 'ecostrategies' are limited by economic factors rather than by religion, whereas Kathirithamby-Wells argues that Southeast Asian perceptions of nature recognized resource exploitation as depending on political authority. As we have already seen, however, Pedersen rejects the notion that there is a direct relationship between values and behaviour.

Ideological factors obviously manifest themselves in environmental exploitation, albeit tenuously and often contradictorily. Over-exploitation of resources is maybe modified by the commoditization of nature, by new disputes over rights to nature, and by the emerging definition of independent rights of nature. Environmental degradation seems in many cases to be more the outcome of a change in power relations than of a collapse of old values. Local peoples in Asia, as elsewhere, are not only facing increasing competition from the state and its agencies but also from urban elites who want to use the countryside for hunting and other forms of recreation, from businessmen who see great profit from turning nature into commodities for tourists and from domestic and international environmental and animal welfare organizations which might be more concerned with the survival of animals than of people. Rural people are to an increasing extent losing influence over the natural resources on which their way of life depends. The establishment of the Khunjerab National Park in Pakistan is a case in point. The state's appropriation of forest and wildlife resources has not led to conservation but has alienated local farmers from their resources and the conservationist cause. Knudsen argues that the native hill farmers are the best custodians of the forests, a point which is increasingly being recognized by international bodies.[11] What is needed when it comes to management of natural resources is therefore management bodies through which local interests, customary law, perceptions of fairness and knowledge of the environment can be articulated.

Conclusion: The comparative dilemma

Ideological responses to environmental change should be measured on a number of levels. In both Asia and the West, informal groups are often conspicuous pace-setters in changing environmental attitudes: grassroots organizations, women's organizations, environmentalist volunteer groups, political sub-groups, religious organizations and so on. A number of environmentally oriented groups have emerged in Asia; among the best known are the Chipko movement in India and the student-led Tokyo Narita Airport protest, but many more are appearing with their own local characteristics, for instance the Buddhist environmentalists in Thailand and the green movement in Hong Kong. For the moment, such groups tend to address local issues specifically

---

[11] Recognizing that the people who are most likely to protect the environment are those with vested economic interests in it – such as fishermen, farmers, loggers and the tourist industry if nature is turned into a commodity for their use – the report *Caring for the Earth* (IUCN, UNEP and WWF 1991) strongly advocates local participation in resource management. This is also the main message in the 'Brundtland Report' *Our Common Future* (The World Commission on Environment and Development 1987) and WWF's position paper on sustainability (WWF 1993).

rather than linking them to regional or global ones.[12] Again we see a tendency to contextualism in some Asian cultures as compared with a western tendency towards universalism.

In the western world ideological factors may operate in favour of environment control. Developing from the early idealistic naturalism of the 1960s and 70s, environmentalism through the 80s became increasingly institutionalized and broadened. Huge dedicated organizations now work for nature preservation: wildlife, rainforest and sea protection; whales, seals, birds and butterflies guardianship; invalidation of decisions concerning the construction of airports, bridges, waste depots and nuclear testing grounds. In the western economies we even spot a new eco-commercialism, the commercialization of environmental considerations, urging both producers and retailers to integrate such considerations as a matter of marketing. Although in a narrow sense capitalism and environmentalism are contradictory, ecology-mindedness has entered production, not least through fashion (Yearley 1991; Moeran and Skov). Companies and advertisers are forced by the public to follow suit, although this is frequently done with a calculated cynicism (Yearley 1991:100). Similarly, political climates are strongly in favour of environmental consciousness, making political extremes compete over greenness to catch up with the still more strongly articulated demands from pressure groups and, to a certain degree, the general population. Some would argue that there is an intermediate level between philosophical ideas and everyday practice that tends to be ignored: the socially prevalent tastes, preferences and desires that control the marketplace: a level between the objective and the subjective, which, if to a greater extent it involved the appreciation of quality, durability, aesthetics, health, not to speak of social relations, arguably would be of more relevance for effecting change (Elvin 1991:192).

---

[12] One may ask whether it is inherent in some Asian traditions that such large-scale issues as global environmental monitoring are a responsibility of the state covered by its mandate to rule rather than being the interest of individuals or groups without formal authority. This seems to be the case in China where the huge 'Chinese Ecological Research Network' (CERN) has been established. An outside observer may comment that 'not surprising is how well CERN manifests the Chinese institutional trait of seeking to maximize capabilities internally that minimize the need to work with outside institutions' (CEN, Vol.18,4:23). Or it might be, as it is in Japan (McKean 1981), that people tend to look upon the world in relational rather than in absolute terms. People care less about abstract ideas of mankind than about concrete social relations, which also influences the attitude towards the environment.

But how do Asian cultures react to environmental change? Is the transformation from natural to cultural landscape less problematic within the context of dynamic philosophies or Buddhist cosmology, where the world's present forms are illusive rather than manifest? And further, how do ideological factors operate in those Asian societies, where both 'man' and 'nature' tend to be vaguely defined in terms of abstract entities with separate, ultimate rights and requirements? Do we in some Asian cosmologies find only an elastic, relativistic naturalism, linking the physical environment to the demands of society rather than dichotomizing nature and culture? We should, perhaps, not be deceived by people's alleged sensitivity and love of nature but rather see this as a commonplace use of natural metaphors, metonyms, analogies and euphemisms, serving the needs of the social order rather than addressing the physical environment. It may be argued that 'nature' in this sense is an aesthetic abstraction with little relationship to the nature of a real ecosystem. The papers included here seek to provide material for further debate on such issues, each from their locality, without necessarily giving definite answers.

The idea that there is a continuous interaction between man and his environment – man changing it and being influenced by it – may be traced from western antiquity. As tied to ideas about order and purpose, man's role increased until finally Man became 'an epoch in the history of nature' (Glacken 1967). Ideas of environmental determinism have been persistent in western thought, not least with reference to the 'uncivilized' peoples. In the environmental debate some have used the ecosystem approach in order to escape the nature–society dichotomy of western thought, and in the social sciences the ecological approach has been attempted specifically in rejection of earlier environmental deterministic explanations (e.g. Geertz 1963; Moran [ed.] 1984). Even though such attempts are aimed at generating universally applicable concepts, the approach must recognize that the major influence on the environment is now humans and their institutions, without which aspect any knowledge of an ecosystem is of little meaning.

As already indicated, the quality of public debate in both East and West deserves attention. What is born out of a critical approach to western civilization in the form of notions of Asian alternatives may be seen to acquire a quite different role in some Asian societies, where public expression tends to be confirmatory to civilization and power. Notions that are held up against power holders in the West are soon adopted by some writers in the East in indicating superiority of their own culture and thus implicitly supporting tradition and even justifying present power relations. Pedersen argues that by expressing their concern about the environment in religious terms – in what he calls the 'religious environmental paradigm' – local people appear as stewards of profound ecological knowledge and thus acquire cultural significance. Speaking of nature becomes for them a way of speaking about themselves, a way of defining their identity.

A number of people inhabiting mountain and forest areas across Asia are in some way affected by the environmental discourse. Although some, who have been facing unconcerned regimes for decades (as in the case described by Sperber), may in the long run benefit from linking their claims to the type of argument now ruling the international organizations, others might feel the new environmental discourse as a threat to their customary access to natural resources (as in the case described by Knudsen). We may then ask how modern internationalism is reflected in the environment issues and whether an international response to regional environmental degradation is justified by such discourse. Or is the western perception in this field another example of western universalism, projecting its own shortcomings onto the developing world, spotting solutions there to problems already causing resignation among ourselves? Some people would argue that this is the case.

We should be aware of the risk of an ethnocentric bias in all comparative research, not least in the field of nature: our means of comparison are to some extent limited by culturally specific notions. A central theme of this volume is how our cultural biases distort the process of transferring ideas from our own social reality to an Asian one, or of translating elements of Asian cultures into our own. Distortion is likely to occur if we fail to specify the basis of the concepts we use when analyzing other cultures' relation to 'nature'.

Scholars have far too often compared western realities with eastern ideals. It is time to look at eastern realities as well, although it may eventually lead to the dethronement of the 'oriental ecologists', in much the same way as the 'savage ecologist' has already been dethroned (cf. Ellen 1986). In line with the purpose of this volume, we can conclude this introduction by issuing a warning: statements on the natural environment differ dramatically from region to region, not only by the 'natural' and 'cultural' context in which they are expressed, but also in terms of their technique, audience and aim. There is no exclusive 'nature' that justifies the unreflected transferring of a nature-related discourse and ideology across cultural borders, let alone across civilizations. If statements of this kind are transferred, they appear as purely abstract thought patterns – that demand to be recontextualized to become meaningful.

References

Benton, Ted. 1993. *Natural Relations. Ecology, Animal Rights and Social Justice.* London: Verso.

Berque, Augustin. 1986. 'The sense of nature and its relation to space in Japan'. In Hendry, J. and J. Webber (eds), *Interpreting Japanese Society – Anthropological Approaches.* Oxford: JASO.

Brown, Michael and John May. 1991. *The Greenpeace Story.* London: Dorling Kindersley.

Buenfil, Alberto Ruz. 1991. *Rainbow Nation Without Borders. Toward an Ecotopian Millennium.* Santa Fe: Bear and Company Publishing.

Callicott, J. Baird and Roger T. Ames (eds). 1989. *Nature in Asian Traditions of Thought: Essays in Environmental Philosophy.* Albany: State University of New York Press.

CEN (*China Exchange News*). 1990, 18(4):2–33. 'Perspectives on Environmental Sciences in China'. National Academy of Sciences, Washington.

Cobb, John B. 1972. *Is It Too Late?: A Theology of Ecology.* Beverly Hills, Calif: Faith and Life Series.

Croll, Elisabeth and David Parkin. 1992. *Bush Base: Forest Farm. Culture, Environment and Development.* London: Routledge.

Dickens, Peter. 1992. *Society and Nature. Towards a Green Social Theory.* London: Harvester Wheatsheaf.

Dunlap, W. and R. Catton. 1980. 'A new ecological paradigm for post exuberant sociology', *American Behavioral Scientists* 24(1):15–47.

Ellen, Roy F. 1986. 'What Black Elk left unsaid. On the illusory images of Green primitivism'. *Anthropology Today* 2(6):8–12.

Elvin, Mark. 1991. Book Review (Callicott and Ames 1989). *Asian Studies Review* 14(3):191–93.

FEER (*Far Eastern Economic Review*). 1991. September 19, p. 37–57. 'Environment in Asia: False Economies. Wasted resources, environmental damage threatens growth across Asia'.

Geertz, Clifford. 1963. *Agricultural Involution*. Berkeley: University of California Press.

Glacken, Clarence. 1967. *Traces on the Rhodian Shore*. Berkeley: University of California Press.

Hargrove, Eugene C. 1989. 'Foreword'. In Callicott, J.B. and R.T. Ames (eds), *Nature in Asian Traditions of Thought: Essays in Environmental Philosophy*. Albany: State University of New York Press.

Holy, L. and M. Stuchlik. 1983. *Actions, Norms and Representations: Foundations of Anthropological Inquiry*. Cambridge: Cambridge Studies in Social Anthropology.

Ingold, Tim. 1992. 'Culture and the Perception of the Environment'. In Croll, E. and D. Parkin (eds), *Bush Base: Forest Farm. Culture, environment and development*. London: Routledge.

IUCN, UNEP and WWF. 1991. *Caring for the Earth – A Strategy for Sustainable Living*. Gland, Switzerland.

Lewis, C. S. 1960. *Studies in Words*. Cambridge: Cambridge University Press.

McArthur, Tom. 1986. *Worlds of Reference*. Cambridge: Cambridge University Press.

McKean, Margaret A. 1981. *Environmental Protest and Citizen Politics in Japan*. Berkeley: University of California Press.

Mackie, Jamie. 1993. 'On the Question of Asia'. *Asian Studies Review* 17(1):155.

Moran, Emilio F. (ed.). 1984. *The Ecosystem Concept in Anthropology*. Boulder: Westview.

Nash, Roderick Frazier. 1989. *The Rights of Nature. A History of Environmental Ethics*. Madison: The University of Wisconsin Press.

Ortner, Sherry B. 1974. 'Is Female to Male as Nature is to Culture'. In Rosaldo, M. Z. and L. Lamphere (eds), *Woman, Culture and Society*. Stanford: Stanford University Press.

Passmore, John. 1980. *Man's Responsibility for Nature*. London: Duckworth.

Popper, Karl. 1972. *Objective Knowledge: An Evolutionary Approach*. (Reprint 1989). Oxford: Clarendon Press.

Redfield, R. 1955. 'The Social Organisation of Tradition', *Far Eastern Quarterly* 15(1):13–21.

Regan, Tom. 1984. *The Case of Animal Rights*. London: Routledge and Kegan Paul.

Savage, V. R. 1984. *Western Impressions of Nature and Landscape in Southeast Asia*. Singapore: Singapore University Press.

Simmons, I. G. 1989. *Changing the Face of Earth. Environment, History, Culture*. Oxford: Blackwell.

Totman, Conrad. 1989. *The Green Archipelago. Forestry in Preindustrial Japan*. Berkeley: University of California Press.

White, Lynn. 1973. 'The Historical Roots of our Ecological Crisis' (orig. 1967). In Barbour, I. G. (ed.), *Western Man and Environmental Ethics*. Reading, Mass: Addison-Wesley.

Williams, Raymond. 1973. *The Country and the City*. London: Chatto and Windus.

—— 1976. *Keywords*. London: Fontana Press.

The World Commission on Environment and Development. 1987. *Our Common Future*. Oxford: Oxford University Press.

WWF. 1993. *Sustainable Use of Natural Resources: Concepts, Issues, and Criteria*. WWF International Position Paper. Gland, Switzerland: WWF.

Yearley, Steven. 1991. *The Green Case. A Sociology of Environmental Issues, Arguments and Politics*. London: Harper Collins.

J. Kathirithamby-Wells

Socio-Political Structures and the Southeast Asian Ecosystem
An Historical Perspective up to the Mid-Nineteenth Century[1]

> '...[H]uman social systems and ecosystems have an interactive relationship, so that the structure of society is modified by its relation to the environment, just as the structure of the ecosystem is influenced by human activities.'
>
> (Rambo and Sajise 1984:6).

Ecological factors limited population growth and land use in Southeast Asia, in contrast to India and China. At the same time, inland forests were an outstanding repository of valuable and exotic gums, resins, aromatics and animal products. No less important were its gold and tin deposits and marine produce. The underpinnings of an East-West trade had, in fact, been firmly fixed in this strategically placed, environmentally rich region long before the age of European commercial expansion. With the dawn of the modern era it became an important area for the cultivation of cash-crops, having the necessary conditions of suitable climate and free land.

Unlike India or China, with a semblance of unity conditioned by a single landmass and the open plains of river systems, the intermediate region of Southeast Asia with confined river valleys, delta-plains and islands, is geographically segmented. Due to the peculiar features of the environment, riverine configurations with dendritic patterns of human settlement and urbanisation were the dominant characteristics of development.

At the same time, due to the shifting nature of capitals, arising partly from conditions of climate which gave rise to erosion and river-

---

[1] This tentative study was undertaken during a Visiting Fellowship at Clare Hall, Cambridge in 1991, with the support of a British Academy Visiting Professorship.

silting, centres of power were too transitory and localised to influence
the region as a whole. The absence of a single name for the region is, in
. fact, a feature of this phenomenon. Yet, any apparent disunity was
subsumed by a shared maritime tradition linking the region with the
wider world of the Indian Ocean and the South China Sea. Under the
stimulus of these connections, favoured coasts and fertile valleys
ceaselessly yielded city-states as of the first century A.D., engaged in
nourishing trade in the exotic produce of the hinterlands. As city-states
expanded their frontiers to carve out empires in the quest for resources,
geographical factors specific to the region influenced perceptions of
nature integral to the mechanics of the state and its political ideology.

This article will discuss, first, the importance of the integrated
riverine economy to the growth of international trade in Southeast Asia
during the pre-modern period. It will then trace the impact on it of
accelerated commercial growth, especially as of the seventeenth century,
with the entry of North European participation.

Early perceptions of nature and state

Until recent years, Southeast Asian perceptions of nature have been
viewed mainly in relation to religious ideology and animistic cults,
unrelated to the business of state and economy. The external provenance
of Hindu-Buddhist ideology, associated with statecraft, precluded ready
identification of commonalities with indigenous animistic beliefs,
evolved within the context of the local environment. Seen from this
perspective, the Southeast Asian culture and belief-systems were viewed
as syncretic layerings conditioned by space and time. Within this
conceptual famework, the early tribal and village cultures of the remoter
parts of the region were believed to be more closely drawn to the
natural world of wind, water and forest than the Indianized and later
Islamized urban, court cultures. Only in recent years has there been
greater appreciation of the direct association between Southeast Asian
spirit cults and the assimilation of Hindu-Buddhist religious beliefs (see
Mabbett 1985:22-3). The resulting corpus of Southeast Asian ideology,
seen in the light of the region's political economy, reveals the society's
integral links with the natural world.

The fish, crane-egret, deer, toad and tiger motifs of the early
Dong-Son period during the late centuries B.C., symbols of a rain-fed
agricultural economy (Davidson 1979:110; Von Devalle 1979:110),

preceded the *naga* imagery of the river-irrigated, early Hindu-Buddhist states of Funan and Srivijaya. The *naga*, the water spirit, and thus symbol of fertility and the earth, was a recurrent motif in Angkorian art and mythology. The *naga* mythology was no less important for the ideology of the maritime kingdom of Srivijaya. Chiefs of the realm are believed to have taken the oath of loyalty by drinking the water poured over the imprecatory seven-headed *naga* stone of seventeenth-century Telagabatu in Palembang (De Casparis 1956:28-9, 36-47). The sanctity of the *naga* for the commercially-oriented Srivijaya may be attributed to the equal importance there, as in agrarian kingdoms, of propitiating and winning favour from the spirits of fertility. These were perceived to reside in the forested uplands, a region which was the source of rich soils for lowland agriculture. The same hinterlands were the repositories of food and exotic fauna and flora, on which hunter-gatherers and swidden cultivators were dependent.

The fusing of the Indian concept of Mount Meru, the *axis mundi* of the universe, with the indigenous animistic worship of mountains as abodes of ancestral souls and the bountiful spirits of nature, provided the cosmological foundations for Southeast Asian statecraft (Aeusrivongse 1976:111-12, 120). Central to this was the cult of Siva, 'King of the Mountain' (Wheatley 1980:2-4), strengthened through its integration with particular elements of local animistic beliefs. Java saw the adoption of the indigenous 'rice goddess', Dewi Seri, as Giriputri, the life-giving force, or *skti*, of the mountain god, Mahendradeva or Siva (Van der Meer 1979:102-4; Danandjaja 1972:16). The rich volcanic mountains of the central and eastern regions of the island became potent symbols of the creative and destructive forces of nature and, thus, the seat of the gods. The vital symbol of the *gunung* as the all pervading life-force is epitomized in its central and indispensable position in the Javanese *wayang*. Reconciling animistic beliefs in mountain spirits with the Hindu-Buddhist ideology of Mount Meru as the abode of the gods and their point of interaction with man, Southeast Asian rulers established themselves as manifestations of Siva, the 'Lord of the Mountain'. They saw themselves effectively as embodiments of supernatural power for harnessing the natural forces for common prosperity within the *mandala*, or circle of divinely ordained influence. With no defined boundaries, the limits of influence which faded out at the fringes, varied with the moral and physical strength of individual rulers at the centre. But its optimum size, consistent with political viability was, as I shall proceed to argue, synonymous with the riverine exchange system.

Rulership and the riverine ecosystem

In Southeast Asia, as in monsoon Asia, wet-rice or *sawah* cultivation in the river valleys and deltas provided the economic foundations for state formation. Within such a system, the need for water management contributed to the emergence of leadership and hierarchical authority deriving from 'eco-units' evolved during the pre-Hindu period (Van Naerssen 1977:297-8). From Funan's genesis as a polity in the lower Mekong during the first centuries A.D., through to the founding of Ayudhaya by Uthong (r.1351-1369) and Bangkok by Rama I (r.1782-1809), land-drainage constituted a preliminary task of leadership. The construction by the Khmer ruler, Yasovarman I (r.889-900), of a *bayon* (lake), symbolised the importance of irrigation maintained through a simple system of dykes and bunds, essential for managing the waters of the Tonle Sap as it seasonally rose and fell (Hall 1985:147). In East Java, Airlangga (r.1019-1049) is believed to have initiated the building of dams to control the annual flooding of the Brantas which brought rich volcanic soils from the interior to the east Javanese plain (Van der Meer 1979:23, 34; Hall 1985:129-30, 134-5). For his contemporary, King Aniruddha (r.1044-1077) at Pagan, situated in the dry central plain of the Irrawaddy, political power was contingent upon irrigating Kyauk-hse and Maribun (Minbun) through a system of tanks. The resulting two-to-three crops, annually, proved a boon to his political authority (Aung-Thwin 1985:22, 97). Similar attention to irrigation by King Thiluin Man (r.1084-1112), who constructed a tank and reservoir, contributed to the prosperity of his reign (Than Tun 1988:10). During the fifteenth and sixteenth centuries, the construction by various Burmese rulers of irrigation systems, with the reclamation of jungle and 'wasteland', assisted the expansion of cultivation (Lieberman 1991:5-6).

Closely related to water control was management of manpower. The additional labour this involved, with increased production of food to meet labour services, obliged movement of population by the ruler from peripheral areas to the centre. Such population movements which occurred, as from the Mon areas to Pagan during the reign of Aniruddha, provided supplementary manpower for military service, as well as skilled artisans for building activity and crafts surrounding the court (Aung-Thwin 1985:22).

The perception of the Southeast Asian ruler as lord of 'land and water' effectively included control over people, as evident in the Malay term *tanah air* ('land and water'), embodying the concept of 'country' or 'nation'. The spiritual ties and patron-client relations which subsisted between rulers and subjects were more binding than legal contracts. The ruler, as 'lord of land and water', and as mediating agent with the natural forces, was perceived to be in ultimate control of the environment. With no fixed boundaries, the physical limits of the state, effectively the 'area of influence' or *mandala*, were determined by the extent of resource control exercised by the ruler, through a chain of loyalties spreading outwards from the centre and fading out gradually towards the fringes. In Southeast Asia, where the river systems served as the main means of communication, the network of loyalties and commercial exchange within the valley configuration of the *mandala* converged at the riverine or coastal capital.

Morphology and the configuration of river systems, dictating the degree of inter-valley communication via footpaths over watersheds and mountain passes, conditioned patterns of political integration. On the mainland, the importance of valley configurations is demonstrable, for example, in Burma's eventual loss to Siam, in 1727, of Chiengmai, conquered during the reign of Bayinnaung (r.1551-1581). Her territorial control was by and large limited to the outlines of the Irrawaddy basin. In contrast, in Sumatra and the Malay Peninsula, relatively smaller river courses flowing from the interior highlands, with lower watersheds, facilitated inter-riverine communication accounting for the integration, at various times in pre-colonial history, of multiple rivière systems under a single political authority. These conditions allowed, however, for competition between adjacently located larger river systems. In east Sumatra, communication by footpaths between the adjacent headwaters of the Palembang, Jambi, Inderagiri and Siak provided alternate outlets to the coast. This meant that a rival power within the neighbouring river system could be effectively undermined through tapping the resources of his *hulu* (Bronson 1977:39-52; Kathirithamby-Wells 1993a:81, 85-6, 88-9).

Early state and the forest economy

The riverine hinterland of the mainland and the western archipelago were the source of a rich variety of forest produce. Resins, particularly *ju*, a substitute for frankincense (*Boswellia*), camphor (from *Dryobalanops aromatica*); the aromatic benzoin (from *Styrax spp.*) and *gaharu-* (aloes-) or eagle-wood (*Aquilaria maleccensis*); dyes from sapan- or brazil-wood

(*Caesalpinia sappan*), *jernang* or 'dragon's blood' (*Dracaena draco*) and lac, from the female lac insect (*Tachardia lacca*); sandal-wood (*Santalum album*), and timber from teak (*Tectona grandis*) and 'Burmese rosewood' (*Pterocarpus indicus*) were products of the rich dipterocarp forests through which the rivers found their course. Also important were exports of rattan, alluavial gold, tin and animal products including the rare rhinoceros horn, elephant tusks and bezoir stones (*guliga*) originating from the stomachs of monkeys and porcupines, with the more abundant bird-feathers and deer-skins.

Though Southeast Asian riverine capitals developed within the focus of irrigated rice cultivation, an important ancilliary to the agrarian economy was long-distance trade, involved in the exchange of exotic forest produce for manufactured luxury goods, primarily Indian cloth, Chinese silk and porcelain, as well as currency and religious paraphernalia. The primary role of the trade in forest produce towards shaping Funan's emergence as a polity, integrating the lower reaches of the Mekong and the Isthmus, could have been of significance. There was the likely provision of *patchouli* (*Pogostemon cablin*) for perfumary from the Isthmus region and *gaharu*-wood and kingfisher-feathers from the Indochinese Peninsula for Funan's trade with China (Wheatley 1964:51; Wang 1958:34, 44). In addition, Kenneth Hall has postulated the conveyance by Malay traders of forest products from the Sunda region to Funan's port of Oc-Eo (Hall 1985:21, 70).

Because of their importance for international exchange, stipulated items of rarity and high value such as gold, camphor, bezoir stones, tusks and 'dragon's blood' invariably became a monopoly of the aristocratic chiefs and rulers. In Pagan, an edict issued in 1600 declared amber, gold, and gems, together with gums, a royal monopoly (Than Tun 1980:1, 9). Taxes levied on semi-exotic and bulk produce, such as pepper, benzoin, bamboo and tin, constituted a vital source of income, particularly to rulers and chiefs in the non-agrarian regions of Sumatra, the Peninsula and Borneo. By the seventeenth century, cash-crops and tin were added to the customary list of royal monopolies, with bulk goods superseding low-bulk forest products as primary sources of state wealth (see Kathirithamby-Wells 1990:3-6; 1993b:127-30). Nonetheless, till well into the nineteenth century forest produce continued to provide an important source of tribute goods to China, presents to European courts and valuable items of export in the form of woods, hides, aromatics, horn and ivory (Holleman 1981:68; Van Anrooij 1885:274-5; Mouhot 1864:276-7; Finlayson 1826:169, 179, 256-8). Reliance on forest produce was particularly significant during periods of political instability when cash cropping and taxation were disrupted in Sumatra for example (see Drewes 1979:13, 61, 63).

During the early centuries A.D. when trade beween the Indian Ocean and China was mediated via transit points such as Pan-Pan, Tun-sun and Langkasuka on the Isthmus of Kra, Funan was conveniently located to supervise the collection and exportation of forest produce from the surrounding region. Deriving its name from the Khmer word, *phnom (bnam)*, for mountain, Funan's evolution was closely linked with the forest environment. Funan's capital earned its name, Vyadhapura, 'the City of the Hunter', from its founder, known in second century Chinese annals as Hun P'an-huang (Wheatley 1980:2-3; 1983:124). According to the same annals of K'ang T'ai, the 'hunter-king' expanded his territories during the course of his elephant-hunting expeditions (Hall 1985:63).

With the decline of the Isthmus route in favour of the Straits of Melaka, Srivijaya superseded Funan in servicing the long distance trade in which the Arabs and Persians increasingly began to participate. The capital of the Srivijayan maritime kingdom was strategically located, first at Palembang and, later, at Jambi, commanding the extensive Musi and Batang Hari basins respectively. Only the commercial capital, and the surrounding area with some amount of wet-rice cultivation within the lower reaches of the river or *hilir*, were directly under the ruler's jurisdiction. More extensive were the up-river or forested *hulu* territories. These were administered through a system of reciprocity and redistribution by way of an exchange network, activated by alliances with coastal Malay chiefs at river mouths or *kuala*, and linked with interior chiefs administering exchange at collecting-points on river junctions and confluences. In the Straits of Melaka, the optimum limits of the circle of influence, as established by the Srivijayan Empire and, later, the Melaka Sultanate, remained within the confines of the river systems of Sumatra and the Peninsula draining into the Straits.

The success or failure of rulers and dynasties elsewhere in the region, as well, rested on maintaining hegemony over a comprehensive geographic area consistent with the river system. The power of Pagan, for example, was brought to a peak during the reign of King Narapati Cansu (r.1173-1210) when its borders encompassed the entire Irrawaddy basin and beyond, from Bhamo on the Chinese border in the north, to Tenasserim in the south. For Majapahit, during the fourteenth century, it meant effectively controlling the agricultural produce of the Brantas valley and the strategically located port of Ujung Galur near the coast, for collection of exotic produce from the Nusantara region (Van Naerssen and De Iongh 1977:67-8; Schrieke 1957:296-7). Here, as in other agrarian regions, spices, gold and forest produce, drawn from the peripheral and interior regions, provided the means for securing luxury goods through trade and tribute.

Beyond the irrigated valleys and alluvial plains of the Southeast Asian mainland, for example, the patchwork of tribal communities was dependent on a forest economy based on swidden agriculture and hunter-gatherer activities. As primary traders they exchanged marketable forest produce for salt, cloth and sometimes rice with secondary traders linked to tertiary feeder points along the river system which, in turn, serviced the court-centred commercial capitals. Ayuthaya and Qui Nhon (Hue), for example, tapped resources from the hill tribes through intermediate lines of exchange via Chiengmai and Kantum respectively.

Right up to the nineteenth century, ivory and cinnamon from highland Vietnam and the deer-skins and eagle-wood of Siam's interior were important to respective rulers in the rice growing deltas of the Red River and the Chao Phraya, as were spices and forest produce for the early maritime centres of Srivijaya, Melaka and Brunei. Reciprocal missions elicited from China, by the sending of tribute in the form of forest and marine produce, contributed to the political prestige of Southeast Asian rulers. Similar tributes in local produce were sent by less powerful states, like Cambodia, to Siam and Vietnam for winning patronage and security. Tributes in Cambodian forest produce were vital to Vietnam for regal prestige, as a source of valuable gifts for cementing internal networks of loyalties, and supplementing local goods for tribute to China. As late as 1807, the Vietnamese court at Hue fixed the triennial tribute from Cambodia at fifty *cau* or kilograms each of nutmegs, yellow wax, purple dye, cardamom, twenty jars of black lacquer, three rhinoceros horns, a pair of elephant tusks and two male elephants (Theam 1981:29).

Apart from accessibility to forest produce, the greater use of timber than stone for buildings, the indispensability of elephants to provide labour for monumental constructions, and materials for boat-building made forest hinterlands a vital part of urban conurbations. These depletions and the hunting traditions, particularly of the mainland Buddhist states, were offset by the preservation of royal parks and extensive tracts of woodland and parkland reserved for meditation and retreat within *sanga* property. It would seem that indigenous traditions, religious philosophy and concepts of *realpolitik* were influenced to a large extent by the peculiar features of the Southeast Asian environment.

Urban development

Early settlements in Southeast Asia, as demonstrated by the pre-historic sites of North and Northeast Thailand (Bayard 1980:95) appear to have favoured areas of lower rainfall, away from the wet and swampy deltaic and coastal areas requiring more advanced techniques for drainage, water control and rainfall distribution (Demaine 1978:49-50). Thus, early historic capitals selected elevated or inland locations away from the coast. In time, however, a number of factors contributed to the movement of principal population centres down-river: from Pagan and Ava to Rangoon on the Irrawaddy; from Chiengmai and Sukothai to Ayudhaya and Bangkok on the Chao Phraya; and in east Java, from Canggu to Ujung Galuh and Surabaya on the Brantas (Schrieke 1957:297-8). Cultivation of higher-yielding wet-rice did not extend inland on to the hillslopes in the absence of terracing technology. In such areas, as for example Thailand and south Vietnam, a repository of swidden cultivation and forest hinterland was maintained but agricultural expansion and population growth was generally towards coastal valleys and the estuarine marshes (Kasetsiri 1976:37-8).

Improved techniques for water control, drainage and irrigation (Ng 1979:778) and the growth of international trade were fundamental to new initiatives in the direction of coast-oriented developments. But also encouraging the coastward trend was the gradual silting of rivers and marshes through denudation of the fragile tropical environment. In all probability, the process could have been significantly assisted by urban development and agriculture during peak periods of royal activity. The 3-4,000 temples estimated to have filled some twenty-five square miles of the capital city of Pagan (Aung-Thwin 1985:169) represent, like the monumental temple complexes in Angkor and Borobudur, an enormous outlay in resources (Schrieke 1957:298-9). Apart from exploitation of the environment for building materials, it involved intensified cultivation and irrigation for the upkeep of manpower to generate labour. It has been argued that escalation of building activity stimulated internal lines of market exchange through attracting population and the clustering of settlements around the capital (Aung-Thwin 1985:170; Kasetsiri

1976:102). Nonetheless, such activity strained manpower resources and took a heavy toll on lives. Captain Henry Burney on his 1825-6 mission to Siam reported that, '... No less than 500 men had died last year in the labour of transporting to Bangkok from the interior, an enormous tree intended for a large boat for the present king' (Burney 1971:52). Evidence of abandoned city complexes suggests the cumulative effects of unrestrained building activity and urban development on climate, irrigation systems, river navigability, health and human resources.

The dictates of the riverine ecosystem on the development of commercial centres and capital cities of mainland Southeast Asia were also evident in the non-agrarian coastal cities of the Malay world. While these have retained their coastal positions, often in the general area of their original location, as in the case of Palembang or Brunei, long term survival necessitated the building of impermanent structures of wood and thatch, often on stilts, in adaptation to the aquatic environment. The environmental vulnerability of Southeast Asian capitals may indeed have contributed to the general fragility of political power, undermining the sustained physical development of capital cities common in Europe such as in the case of Rome, Venice, Paris and London.

Commerce and environment

The impact of early commercial exploitation of Southeast Asian natural resources on the environment and hinterland populations is difficult to establish. It would appear, however, that despite growth in the demand for forest produce, the diversity of the tropical biome and collection of specific items of fauna and flora, by small forest communities of overall low density, imposed in-built checks on the activity. Even in areas where communities such as the Kenyah and Dayak operated in restricted zones, determined by distance from markets, hunter-gatherer specialisations and territorial restrictions, tribal mores regulated economic activity to guarantee sustainable yields till well into this century (Lian 1988:110-20). All the same, expansion of international commerce meant a commensurate increase in market-oriented hunter-gatherer activities with the greater availability of salt imports and food supplements. These circumstances would have contributed to a steady rise in population, offsetting disease. Conditions were hereby established for the transition to mixed hunter-gatherer and swidden activities which, as Karl Pelzer points out, 'may well be the oldest system devised by man for the use of the ecosystem' (Pelzer 1979:271).

Ideally speaking, swidden cultivation in Southeast Asia, aptly termed 'forest farming', is based on a harmonious relationship with the environment. The swidden cultivator imitated the forest environment of species-rich vegetation by planting a mixture of grain, root-crops, shrubs, vines, herbs, trees and grasses such as maize (Pelzer 1978:273). This practice and strict maintenance of crop-rotation were inherent features of the system, ensuring the regeneration of vegetation and soil fertility. For beyond a certain point in shortening the period of fallow, clearance could outpace forest recovery, reducing the output of forest-derived goods and inflicting long-term environmental damage, with detriment to cultivation.

The introduction of cash-crops, principally pepper, to the drier slopes and upper valleys unsuited to *sawah*, and its ideal adaptation to swiddens, determined an important phase in Southeast Asian development. It marked the integration of the traditional river-based structure of settlement, exchange and political control with the modern international market economy. The black pepper (*Piper nigrum*) of Malabar, the cultivation of which in west Java is recorded in the twelfth century, became, like the spices of eastern Indonesia, an important item of international commerce. The coming of the north Europeans brought a spectacular expansion in the pepper trade centred at Aceh and Banten (see Kathirithamby-Wells 1987:27-36). Pepper was initially planted by swidden cultivators, strategically located to service the Indian Ocean trade, in the coastal areas of Sunda, south and west Sumatra. Planted on newly cleared forest soils or good soils originating from secondary growth, it allowed for swidden paddy and other food crops to be cultivated during the first one or two years of the thirteen to fifteen year cycle of vine-holdings.

Forced cultivation introduced by the British in the narrow coastal strip of west Sumatra during the seventeenth century caused greater attention to be drawn to pepper, with increased reliance on imported rice (see Kathirithamby-Wells 1977:131-2; *passim*). A different situation pertained in areas such as Lampung and east Sumatra, with larger river systems providing access to extensive swidden land. Here *ladang* cultivation was successfully maintained with cash-cropping. In Lampung, usually, after one harvest of paddy, the best *ladang* were planted with pepper (Lebar 1972:36). Mainly populated by the Orang Abung, the valleys of the Tulang Bawang, Seputih, Sekampung and Semangka rivers were the main areas of pepper production. Mangala, Tiabong,

Jebong and Betung, focal points on the respective rivers, provided the chief supplies for the sultanate of Banten (Breugel 1856:328-29; Marsden 1830:4-6).

Banten's imports from Lampung were supplemented, till well into the nineteenth century, by produce from swiddens of the interior Sunda region. The Sundanese were, however, estimated to be producing less than half their potential in pepper. This was not surprising in view of the poor prices paid by the Bantanese chiefs who then delivered the produce to the Sultan for up to a hundred per cent profit. Further, in view of the high prices extracted for imports, such as cloth and salt, self-sufficiency in grain was a prudent safeguard (Breugel 1856:342-3).

As well as proving economically and ecologically ideal, the integration of cash-cropping with swidden agriculure, ensured the retention of traditional structures of authority. Implicit in the system was the retention by coastal paramount authorities of the tribal *marga* structure, so essential for the administration of swidden land and for matters relating to the mechanics of land use and crop-rotation. *Marga* chiefs in Lampung were, for example, simply incorporated into the riverine exchange mechanism and their loyalties effectively won by the conferment of courtly Malay-Javanese titles, accompanied with the presentation of symbols of authority such as krises, pikes, *kopia* (badges) and *payong* (umbrellas).

The increased circulation of silver and Chinese *picis* as an important medium of internal market exchange for salt and Indian cloth proved a great incentive for swidden-based pepper cultivation. The large number of Minangkabaus it attracted to the upper reaches of the east Sumatran river systems, such as the Kampar and Inderagiri, meant that these areas became, effectively, the *rantau* or Minangkabau fringe areas. Their descent and settlement were most extensive down the Batang Hari, in Jambi, where they occupied the entire tributary system stretching from the Sungei Sumai, in the vicinity of the Inderagiri basin, to the Sungei Tembisi towards Palembang (Kathirithamby-Wells 1993a:82-3; Andaya 1993:99-101).

The Minangkabaus, who turned Jambi into a major producer of pepper, also planted swiddens, increasing food and rice production when prices for pepper were unfavourable. Although Jambi reputedly relied heavily on imports of rice from Java (Schrieke 1955:46-7), the up-river pepper areas would have been able to rely on the enfringing *sawah* hinterlands of Minangkabau and Kerinci for supplements during periods of shortage. In the main, swidden cultivation was integral to the ecological and economic sustainability of pepper production. Thus, any additional time and labour required for the upkeep and expansion of pepper holdings were, most likely, at the cost not of food production but of the strong, indigenous weaving traditions maintained, for example, by the cash-croppers of Jambi and Palembang (Andaya 1989:33).

Increased Minangkabau settlement in the *hulu* for the cultivation of pepper, pushed the autochthonous Kubu of Jambi, Palembang and Rawas coastwards but, at one and the same time, assisted in bringing them closer to expanding markets for exports, including forest produce (van Dongen 1910:204-5; Hasselt 1882 vol.3, pt.ii:40-41). The Kubu continued in their specialisation as hunter-gatherers of benzoin, 'dragon's blood' and rattan from forests fringing the coast, which they traded for rice, tobacco and salt with settled Kerinci, Minangkabau and Batak villages. Commercialisation amongst them was evident in their gradual abandonment of 'silent barter', whereby goods for exchange were left at specific points, avoiding direct encounter (Anderson 1826: 169-70; Tideman 1938:61-2; Sandbukt 1988:145-7).

A similarly successful interface between up-river swidden culti-vators and coast-oriented hunter-gatherers has survived into modern times in eastern Kalimantan. Here, the market-oriented nomadic Punan populate the middle Kayan, Segah and Kelai rivers, collecting camphor, bees'wax, rattan, dammar and other forest produce. This they trade for grain and other necessities with sedentary Dayak and Kayan agricultur-alists with whom they share 'a historical tradition of alliance and cultural affiliation' (Hoffman 1988:96, 110, 112-3; Bellwood 1985:134).

Integration of the cash-crop economy with swidden cultivation worked with equal, if not greater success, under indigenous entrepre-neurs at the turn of the eighteenth century in northeast Sumatra. Behind the coastal swamps, the lowland tropical rain-forest, stretching between Temiang in the north to Panai in the south, was intersected by short rivers, principally the Langkat, Deli and Asahan. A short distance from the river mouths, inhabited largely by Malays and other trading communities of Minangkabau, Bugis and Javanese origin, lived Karo and Simalunggan Batak communities who planted pepper in their *jaluran* or swiddens. Assistance from the coastal *orang kaya* in the form of advances in rice, salt and implements over an initial three-year period, drew large numbers from the densely populated Batak hinterland. In 1823 John Anderson, who made a survey of the coast for the Penang government, reported that at a distance of about a two-day journey from Sungghal

(Bulu Cina), no less than 20,000 Bataks were engaged in pepper cultivation. Not far away, at Kallumpang, he observed 'extensive and beautiful pepper plantations, paddy fields, and fruit-trees of various descriptions' (Anderson 1826:256-8). At Bulu China, 'there was an appearence of a very abundant crop both of grain and pepper; the former they were reaping, and the latter just beginning to pluck' (Anderson 1840:190). A number of environmentally related factors contributed towards structuring a viable economy. Foremost were: the availability of river transport for the collection and assembly of goods by small craft, a steady flow from the interior of a population not dependent on imports of grain, and the proximity of the coast to the markets of Penang and Singapore. It was estimated that Penang's imports of pepper from the east coast rose from 1,800 pikuls during 1817/18 to some 30,000 pikuls during 1822/23, with considerable returns in cash earnings and imports in salt, cloth and opium (Anderson 1926:262-3; 1840:184, 188).

Sufficiency of grain, produced in addition to pepper, allowed, in fact, regular exports. Furthermore, as both pepper and dry rice were not heavy on labour and time, the Batak successfully combined swidden cultivation with hunter-gatherer activities. Wax, rattan, and elephants' tusks supplemented benzoin, gold and camphor, brought down the valleys by the Dolok Bataks, the Alas and Gayo people for export from Langkat, Bulu Cina, Deli and Serdang (Anderson 1826:200-4).

Environmental degradation

As elsewhere in the region, successful adaptation of cash-cropping to traditional patterns of land use in east Sumatra soon came under the strain of European commercial expansion. During the two or three decades following the introduction of tobacco as a monoculture by European entrepreneurs in the 1860s, the abandonment of plantations after the first crop, led to invasion by *Imperata* grass or *alang alang* and concomitant soil degradation. This and the systematic laying out of plantations, pushing out *jaluran* and eradicating forest zones, brought radical changes to the landscape and a dependent community no longer in symbiosis with the environment. In an effort to check the effects of deforestation, the plantation community reverted, by the end of the century, to the integration of *jaluran* with cash-cropping and the introduction of fast-growing tree species. The interests of tobacco production continued, however, to be dominant, impeding regeneration of vegetation and soils. The long-term effects of soil erosion and silting in the terraced plantations was aggravated by intensive cultivation by the Batak of the highland interior to service expanding coastal populations and markets with provisions. Resulting river siltation brought problems of navigation and widespread floods, leading to planter-peasant tensions in the 1950s (Pelzer 1978:27, 49).

Long preceding symptoms of environmental degeneration noted in east Sumatra, similar problems were recognised from as early as the mid-nineteenth century in India and the Malay Peninsula (Grove 1988: 300; Logan 1848:534-6). These pointed largely to the ecological effects of timber felling. During the latter decades of the nineteenth century, for example, pronounced drought prevailed in the Dry Zone of Burma, attributed to deforestation of water catchment areas through the logging of teak (Keeton 1974:347).

Localised socio-economic and political problems, stemming from environmental denudation, have been long-standing. These result from the lack of appreciation of the interlocking eco-niches within the riverine systems, synonomous with Southeast Asian geo-political units. In the case of traditional swidden agriculture, adoption of cash-cropping of pepper in the late sixteenth century, like hunter-gatherer activities from early times, successfully integrated the indigenous state, via the riverine infrastructure, to the expanding world economy. However, subsequent efforts, under capitalist forces, to maximise productivity by pushing intensified monocultures beyond adaptable ecological frontiers, soon shifted swidden agriculture from core to marginal positions within the national economy (see Kunstadter and Chapman 1978:3). In the course of it, large tracks of land, in Kalimantan and south and east Sumatra, were withdrawn from minimal fellow cycles, impeding soil regeneration. The resulting invasion by *Imperata* grass (see, for example, Dove 1985:3; Potter 1988:129), posed severe problems to the peasantry, in an age of expanding populations and shrinking resources.

Sober appraisal of the double-edged thrust of natural denudation and accelerated human development through the course of time has in recent years given way to the desire for achieving a more even balance between the two forces. In a paper published in *Solidarity* (1987) entitled, 'Environment: Striking a Harmonious Balance,' Warief Djajanto of Indonesia draws attention to the five 'vulnerable problem areas in the country' as spelled out by the Minister of population and environment, Emil Salim. To the list of empirically established problems of deterioration of watershed areas, degeneration of coastlines, industrialisation and urbanisation, he added a fifth which influenced all the rest, namely, human outlook. 'The orientation that Indonesia has to develop now... is not that of man dominating the environment or letting the environment dominate man. The orientation is towards achieving harmony between man and the environment, as Emil Salim says,' urges Djajanto (1987:36).

Conclusion

Southeast Asian perceptions of nature, as articulated through religious traditions and belief systems, recognised resource exploitation as part and parcel of the political process. Implicit in the mandate for politictal authority was the harmonious management of spiritual and material affairs within the cosmological unit, defined as a *mandala* synonymous with the state. Contingent upon the role of the ruler as *dharmmaraja*, in the Buddhist mainland, and *klipatullah* in maritime Southeast Asia, was the successful and just management of material resources (Kathirithamby-Wells 1992:575-9; Koenig 1990:66-7). Calamities in the form of floods, famines, volcanic eruptions and disease were interpreted as symptomatic of the disruption in the harmony between the natural world and human affairs (see Ricklefs 1981:111; Ras 1987:xxxv, 7). In fact, environmentally related problems of drought, famine and disease contributed to a lesser or greater degree during the early nineteenth century to the escalation of political discontent, in many cases to rebellion (Koenig 1990:34-5; Kathirithamby-Wells 1992:591, 601; Carey, 1981: xliii, 5) and these remain to be more specifically identified and analysed. Resulting succession and dynastic conflicts were often meaningful expressions of the search for new leadership towards restoration of common prosperity within a managed environment.

Broadly speaking, the political economy of Southeast Asia, with associated resource utilisation, evolved within the riverine environment. In this context, the inherent tension between conservation and exploitation, and the concept of balanced development in the history of Southeast Asia gained optimum meaning. But increasingly intensive and altered systems of resource extraction, particularly during the nineteenth century, undermined this congruence of state and riverine ecosystem.

References

Aeusrivongse, Nidhi. 1976. 'Devaraja Cult and Khmer Kingship at Angkor'. In Hall, K. R. and J. K. Whitmore (eds), *Explorations in Early Southeast Asian History: The Origins of Southeast Asian Statecraft*. Michigan Papers on South and Southeast Asia, 11:107-48.

Andaya, B. 1989. 'The Cloth Trade in Jambi and Palembang Society during the Seventeenth and Eighteenth Centuries'. *Indonesia* 48:27-47.

—— 1993. 'Cash Cropping and Upstream-Downstream Tensions in the Seventeenth and Eighteenth Centuries'. In Reid, A. (ed.), *Southeast Asia in the Early Modern Era*. London: Cornell University Press.

Anderson, J. 1826. *Missions to the East Coast of Sumatra in 1823*. London: William Black and T. Caddell. (Reprinted 1971, intro. N. Tarling). Kuala Lumpur: Oxford University Press.

—— 1840. *Acheen and the Ports on the North and East Coasts of Sumatra*. London: William H. Allen and Co. (Reprinted 1971, intro. A.J.S. Reid). Kuala Lumpur: Oxford University Press.

Aung-Thwin, Michael. 1985. *The Origins of Modern Burma*. Honolulu: University of Hawaii Press.

Bayard, Donn. 1980. 'The Roots of Indochinese Civilization: Recent Developments in the Pre-history of Southeast Asia'. *Pacific Affairs* 53:89-114.

Bellwood, Peter. 1985. *Prehistory of the Indo-Malaysian Archipelago*. Sydney: Academic Press.

Breugel, J. de Rovere. 1856. 'Beschrijving van Bantam en de Lampungs'. *BKI* 5:307-57.

Bronson, B. 1977. 'Exchange at the Upstream and Downstream Ends: Notes towards a Functional Model of the Coastal State in Southeast Asia'. In Hutterer, K.L. (ed.), *Economic Exchange and Social Interaction in Southeast Asia: Perspectives from Pre-History, History and Ethnography*. Ann Arbor: Centre for South and Southeast Asian Studies, University of Michigan.

Burney, Henry. 1971. *The Burney Papers*. Bangkok 1910-1914. (Reprint, intro. D.K. Wyatt). Farnborough, Hans.: Gregg International Printers.

Carey, P.B.R. 1981. *Babad Dipanagara: An Account of the Outbreak of the Java War (1825-30)*. Monograph no. 9, Kuala Lumpur: Journal of the Malaysian Branch of the Royal Asiatic Society.

Danandjaja, James. 1972. *An Annotated Bibliography of Javanese Folklore.* Occasional Papers of the Center for South and Southeast Asian Studies, Berkeley: University of California.

Davidson, Jeremy H.G. 1979. 'Archaeology in Northern Viet-Nam since 1954'. In Smith R. B. and W. Watson (eds), *Early Southeast Asia: Essays in Archaeology, History and Historical Geography.* New York/Kuala Lumpur: Oxford University Press.

De Casparis, J.G. 1956. *Selected Inscriptions from the 7th to the 9th century A.D.* Bandung: Masa Baru.

Demaine, H. 1978. 'Magic and Management: Methods of Ensuring Water Supplies for Agriculture in Southeast Asia'. In Stott, P.A. (ed.), *Nature and Man in Southeast Asia.* London: School of Oriental and African Studies.

Djajanto, Warief. 1987. 'The Environment: Striking a Harmonious Balance'. In *Indonesia: Articles on Indonesian Politics and Culture. Solidarity.* 113:35–37. Manila: Solidaridad Publishing House.

Dove, R. 1985. 'The Agroecological Mythology of the Javanese and the Political Economy of Indonesia'. *Indonesia* 39:1-35.

Drewes, G.W.J. 1979. *Hikajat Potjut Muhamat.* Bibliotheca Indonesia. The Hague: Martinus Nijhoff.

Finlayson, George. 1826. *The Mission to Siam and Hue, 1821-22.* London: J. Murray. (Reprinted 1988, intro. D.K. Wyatt). Singapore: Oxford University Press.

Grove, R. 1988. 'Conservation and Colonial Expansion: A Study of the Evolution of Environmental Attitudes and Conservation Policies on St. Helena, Mauritius and in India'. Ph.D. thesis, Cambridge.

Hall, Kenneth. 1985. *Maritime Trade and State Development in Early Southeast Asia.* Honolulu: University of Hawaii Press.

Hasselt, A. C. van. 1882. *Volkbeschrijving van Midden-Sumatra.* Leiden: E.J. Brill.

Hoffman, Carl L. 1988. 'The "Wild Penan" of Borneo: A Matter of Economics'. In Dove, M. (ed.), *The Real and Imagined Role of Culture in Development.* Honolulu: University of Hawaii Press.

Holleman, J. E. (ed.) 1981. (Intro. H. W. J. Sonius), *Van Vollenhoven on Indonesian Adat Law.* The Hague: Martinus Nijhoff.

Kasetsiri, Charnvit. 1976. *The Rise of Ayudhya: A History of Siam in the Fourteenth and Fifteenth Centuries*. Kuala Lumpur: Oxford University Press.

Kathirithamby-Wells, J. 1977. *The British West Sumatran Presidency 1760-85): Problems of Early Colonial Enterprise*. Kuala Lumpur: University of Malaya Press.

—— 1987. 'Forces of Regional and State Integration in the Western Archipelago, c.1500-1800.' *JSEAS* 18(i):22-44.

—— 1990. 'Introduction: An Overview'. In Kathirithamby-Wells, J. and J. Villiers (eds), *The Southeast Asian Port and Polity: Rise and Demise*. Singapore: Singapore University Press.

—— 1992. 'The Age of Transition: The Mid-Eighteenth to the Early Nineteenth Centuries'. In Tarling, N. (ed.), *The Cambridge History of Southeast Asia*. Vol.1. Cambridge: Cambridge University Press.

—— 1993a. '*Hulu-Hilir* Unity and Conflict: Malay Statecraft in East Sumatra before the Mid-Nineteenth Century'. *Archipel* 45:77-96.

—— 1993b. 'Restraints on the Development of Merchant Capitalism in Southeast Asia before c. 1800'. In Reid, A. (ed.), *Southeast Asia in the Early Modern Period*. Ithaca: Cornell University Press.

Keeton, C.L. 1974. *King Thebaw and the Ecological Rape of Burma*. Delhi: Manohar Book Service.

Koenig, W.J. 1990. *The Burmese Polity, 1772-1819*. Michigan: Center for South and Southeast Asian Studies, The University of Michigan.

Kunstadter, Peter and E. C. Chapman. 1978. 'Problems of Shifting Cultivation and Economic Development in Northern Thailand'. In P. Kunstadter, E. C. Chapman and S. Sabhasri (eds), *Farmers in the Forest. Economic Development and Marginal Agriculture in Northern Thailand*. Honolulu: East-West Population Centre, University of Hawaii.

Lebar, Frank M. (ed.). 1972. *Ethnic Groups of Insular Southeast Asia*. Vol.1: '*Indonesia, Andaman Islands and Madagascar*'. New Haven: Human Relations Asia Files Press.

Lian, Francis J. 1988. 'The Economy and Ecology of the Production of the Tropical Rainforest Resources by Tribal Groups of Sarawak, Borneo'. In Dargavel, J., K. Dixon and N. Semple (eds), *Changing Tropical Forests: Historical Perspectives on Today's Challenges in Asia*. Canberra: Centre for Resource and Environmental Studies, A.N.U.

Lieberman, V. 1991. 'Secular Trends in Burmese Economic History. c.1350-1830'. *MAS* 25(i):1-31.

Logan, J.R. 1848. 'The Probable Effects of the Climate of Pinang of the Continued Destruction of its Hill Jungles'. *Journal of the Indian Archipelago* II:534–6. Singapore. (Nendeln, Liechtenstein: Kraus Reprint, 1970.)

Mabbett, I.W. 1985. 'A Survey of the Background of the Variety of Political Traditions in South-East Asia'. In Mabbett, I.W. (ed.), *Patterns of Kingship and Authority in Traditional Asia*. Sydney: Croom Helm.

Marsden, William (trans.). 1830. *Memoirs of a Malayan Family written by themselves*. London: Oriental Translations Fund.

McKinnon, Edward E. 1987. 'New Light on the Indianization of the Karo Batak'. In Rainer Carle (ed.), *Cultures and Societies of North Sumatra*. Berlin: Dietrich Reimer Verlag.

McNeely, J.A. and P.S. Wachtel. 1991. *Soul of the Tiger: Searching for Nature's Answers in Southeast Asia*. Singapore: Oxford University Press.

Mouhot, Henry. 1864. *Travels in Siam, Cambodia and Loas, 1858-60*. 2 vols. London: John Murray. (Reprinted 1989. Singapore: Oxford University Press.)

Ng, Ronald C.Y. 1979. 'The Geographical Habitat of Historical Settlement in Mainland Southeast Asia'. In Smith, R.B. and W. Watson (eds), *Essays in Archaeology, History and Historical Geography*. New York/Kuala Lumpur: Oxford University Press.

Pelzer, Karl J. 1978. 'Planter and Peasant: Colonial Policy and the Agrarian Struggle in East Sumatra'. *VKI* 84. The Hague: Martinus Nijhoff.

—— 1979. 'Swidden Cultivation in Southeast Asia: Historical, Ecological and Economic Perspectives'. In P. Kunstadter, E. C. Chapman and S. Sabhasri (eds), *Farmers in the Forest: Economic Development and Marginal Agriculture in Northern Thailand*. Honolulu: East-West Population Institute, University of Hawaii.

Potter, Lesley. 1988. 'Dutch Forest Policy in South and East Borneo (Kalimantan) 1900-1950.' In Dargavel, J., K. Dixon and N. Semple (eds), *Changing Tropical Forests: Historical Perspectives on Today's Challenges in Asia*. Canberra: Centre for Resource and Environmental Studies, A.N.U.

Rambo, Terry A. and Percy E. Sajise. 1984. *An Introduction to Human Ecology Research on Agricultural Systems in Southeast Asia*. Laguna: University of the Philippines, Los Bafios.

Ras, J.J. 1987. *Babad Tanah Djawi.* Dordrecht, Holland and Providence, U.S.A.: Floris Publications.

Ricklefs, M. 1981. *A History of Modern Indonesia.* London: Macmillan.

Sandbukt, O. 1988. 'Resource Constraints and Relations of Appropriation Among Tropical Forest Foragers: The Case of the Sumatran Kubu'. *Research in Economic Anthropology* X:117-56.

Schrieke, B. 1955/1957. *Indonesian Sociological Studies.* Pts.1 and 2. The Hague: Martinus Nijhoff.

Than Tun. 1980. *The Royal Orders of Burma, A.D. 1598-1885.* Pt.1. Kyoto: The Centre for Southeast Asian Studies, Kyoto University.

—— 1988. *Essays on the History and Buddhism of Burma.* Strachen, P. (ed.). Isle of Man, Scotland: Kiscadale.

Theam, B.S. 1981. 'Cambodia in the Mid-Nineteenth Century: A Quest for Survival, 1840-1863'. M.A. thesis, A.N.U., Canberra.

Tideman, J. 1938. *Djambi.* Koninklijke Vereeniging 'Koloniaal Instituut', Mededeeling No.42. Nederlandsch Aardrijkskundig Genootschap en het Zuid Sumatra Instituut. Amsterdam: Druk de Bussy.

Van Anrooij, H.A. Hijmans. 1885. 'Nota omtrent het Rijk van Siak.' *TBG* XXX:259-390.

Van der Meer, N.C. van Stetten. 1979. *Sawah Cultivation in Ancient Java: Aspects of Development during the late Indo-Javanese Period, 5th to the 15th Century.* Oriental Monograph Series 22. Faculty of Asian Studies in Association with A.N.U.: Canberra University Press.

Van Dongen, G.J. 1910. 'The Koeboes in de Onderafdeeling Koeboestreken der Residentie Palembang'. *BKI* 63:191-333.

Van Naerssen, F.H. 1977. 'Tribute to the God and Tribute to the King'. In Cowan C. D. and O. W. Wolters (eds), *Southeast Asian Historiography.* Ithaca: Cornell University Press.

Van Naerssen and R.C. De Iongh. 1977. *The Economic and Administrative History of Early Indonesia.* Leiden/Koln: E. J. Brill.

Von Dewall, Magdalene. 1979. 'Local Workshop Centres of the Late Bronze Age in Highland South East Asia'. In Smith, R.B. and W. Watson (eds), *Early South East Asia: Essays in Archaeology, History and Historical Geography.* New York/Kuala Lumpur: Oxford University Press.

Wang Gangwu, 1958, 'The Nanhai Trade: A Study of the Early History of Chinese Trade in the South China Sea'. *JMBRAS* 31:ii.

Wheatley, Paul. 1964. *Impressions of the Malay Peninsula in Ancient Times.* Singapore: Eastern Universities Press.

—— 1980. *The Kings of the Mountain: An Indian Contribution to Statecraft in South East Asia.* Second Sri Lanka Endowment Fund Lecture delivered at the University of Malaya, 16 July 1980, Kuala Lumpur: University of Malaya Press.

—— 1983. *Naga and Commandery: Origins of Southeast Asian Urban Tradition.* Chicago: Chicago University Press.

Abbreviations

BKI:	*Bijdragen tot Taal-, Land- en Volkenkunde van Neerlandsch Indie* Amsterdam)
JMBRAS:	*Journal of the Malaysian Branch of the Royal Asiatic Society* (Kuala Lumpur)
JSEAS:	*Journal of Southeast Asian Studies* (Singapore)
MAS:	*Modern Asian Studies* (Cambridge)
VBG:	*Verhandelingen van het Bataviaasch Genootschap van Kunsten en Wetenschappen* (Batavia)
VKI:	*Verhandelingen van het Koninklijk Instituut voor de Taal-, Land- en Volkenkunde van Nederlandsch-Indie* (The Hague)

Peter Boomgaard

Sacred Trees and Haunted Forests in Indonesia
Particularly Java, Nineteenth and Twentieth Centuries[1]

Destruction of forests is nowadays associated with tropical areas in South America, Central Africa and Southeast Asia. At the same time, however, many people seem to equate forest destruction with capitalism, a western (Christian) invention. These statements are not necessarily contradictory. Non-western people, so this argument runs, have always been much more careful with their environment than westerners, and the onslaught on tropical forests is a recent phenomenon, related to the penetration of capitalism. Forests are now being destroyed in areas where there is anything left to be destroyed, i.e. in tropical areas. The West has destroyed its own forests long ago (cf. White 1967).

This view is certainly not uncontested. Simmons, for example, argues that forest destruction has proceeded irrespective of creed or world-view (1989:7). 'The Maya, the Chinese and the people of the Near East were all capable of destroying their environment without the aid of Christianity', as Keith Thomas puts it (1984:24). Ponting similarly cites early examples of deforestation in North Africa, the Middle East, the Indus valley, China and Japan (1992:69–76).

At this high level of abstraction it will be almost impossible to solve the problem as to whether in practice, as opposed to theory, certain particular world-views are more damaging to the environment than others. Even when scholars are dealing with one particular area, the answers to this question can be widely divergent. Take, for example, two recent studies of deforestation in the Himalayas. Whereas Ramachandra Guha (1989) sees this as a post-1900 phenomenon brought about by British forest exploitation, Ives and Messerli describe deforestation as a long drawn-out process, accelerating in the eighteenth

---

[1] I would like to thank Freek Colombijn and Heather Sutherland for their comments on an earlier version of this article.

century under native rulers (1989:48–9).

One can, of course, try to solve this puzzle in a purely 'materialistic' way. High population densities and high levels of economic development (not necessarily capitalist development) are then the key to the question as to why certain civilizations are more prone to deforestation than others. Such an approach does not only explain early forest depletion in western Europe and the United States, but also, and often much earlier, in pre-capitalist civilizations such as that of the Mayas, the ancient Middle East, Greece and Rome, and pre-modern China and Japan.

Interestingly enough, however, explanations of differences in the exploitation of nature are often couched in religious terms. Christianity is usually regarded as the ecologically most destructive of the major world religions. Buddhism finds itself at the other end of the scale with its reputation of respect for all life-forms (Sponsel and Natadecha 1988).

Attitudes towards trees and forests do, indeed, vary between religions. Many pre-Christian religions in Europe regarded certain trees and forests as sacred. Examples can be found in Greece with its oaks of Dodona dedicated to Zeus but with an even older pedigree, and in Northwestern Europe with the holy oaks of Donar or Thor and its sacred forests (e.g. Ellis Davidson 1967:92–4). Christianity was much less inclined to attach special significance to trees or forests, and its early missionaries regarded the felling of 'heathen' trees as their Christian obligation. Tree worship in India was practised by Hinduists and Buddhists alike, but with the arrival of Islam, which did not recognize sacred trees and forests, this obstacle to deforestation became less effective (Sinha 1979; Simmons 1989:169).

In most of these and similar studies the influence of religious concepts is merely postulated. There has been no attempt to show how these concepts functioned in practice. It is, therefore, often impossible to establish clear links between beliefs and ecological change.[2]

In this article I have collected as many data as I could find on sacred trees, tree spirits and haunted or sacred forests in sources on nineteenth- and twentieth-century Java, with an occasional excursion to other Indonesian areas. Java is particularly interesting in this respect because of its syncretism. It was heavily influenced by Hinduism and

---

[2] For further critical comments on this approach see Worster (1988:303) and Morris-Suzuki (1990:81).

Buddhism before the arrival of Islam, but none of these major world religions has been able to erase Java's 'animistic' past entirely. This in itself is already a warning against attributing too much ecological influence to a dominant religion.

Another relevant feature of Java's ecological past is that it was already rather densely populated before European influence on its demographic development made itself felt (e.g. Cortesâo 1944:175). It is also evident that around 1500 Java had reached a high level of economic diversification and state-formation, two features which in any society impose heavy burdens on the natural environment (construction, ship-building, large-scale warfare) (Boomgaard 1989, 1991). Java, therefore, with its complicated beliefs and its pre-European tradition of forest exploitation, merits a more detailed investigation into the belief-environment nexus.

At the end of this introductory section a few words of caution are in order. In the first place, almost all data have been taken from writings by European observers. We depend, therefore, on their understanding of what they were told and on the accuracy with which they rendered their information. The possibility that not all of our observers meet these criteria cannot be excluded. Secondly, most of my data come from sources which were written between 1800 and 1950, and even for that period I cannot pretend to have seen all relevant material.

This article, therefore, has the status of an experiment. If it succeeds in getting people interested in the topics dealt with, encouraging their research, particularly of the pre-1800 and the post-1950 years, it will have served its purpose.

Forest exploitation and management

Before immersing ourselves in the Javanese spirit-world, a short section on the varying fortunes of the forests might be a good point of departure.[3]

Quantitative data on forest exploitation and timber-use by Javanese and Chinese carpenters and shipwrights for non-European customers during the period 1500–1700 are entirely lacking. We only know that indigenous ship-building was an important sector in this period. Around 1700, the Dutch East India Company (VOC) secured a firm hold on the

---

[3] Most data in this section have been taken from Boomgaard 1988 and 1994.

teak-forests of Java's northern coast for its own ship-building activities. In comparison to figures for the twentieth century, production data for the eighteenth century are not impressive. VOC production methods, however, were more harmful than those of the twentieth century, and conservation was largely restricted to the closing-off of exhausted forest tracts. Damage to the forests was therefore not proportional to production.

Nevertheless, it could have been worse, and it became so during the period of the so-called Cultivation System (1830–1870). Production increased considerably during these years and methods of production were not better than those of the VOC. The only redeeming feature of this period is the attempt at reafforestation in the teak areas. During the last quarter of the nineteenth century a professional and centralized government forest service was created that succeeded in stabilizing the proportion of forest cover after the turn of the century.

Around 1875, some 25 per cent of Java was still covered with forests. If we make creative use of a number of earlier figures, and if we do not shy away from heroic assumptions, it is possible to calculate this proportion for the early years of the Cultivation System and for the closing decades of the VOC period. For c. 1840 this would be some 40 per cent and for 1775 somewhat over 60 per cent. Although this is not a transition from an island entirely covered with 'pristine' forests to total deforestation (such as happened in seventeenth-century Barbados), the figures mentioned indicate a considerable loss of forest cover over a period of only one century.

This loss of forest cover can be partly ascribed to activities generated by the western sectors of the economy. Probably more important, however, was the influence of land clearing by a rapidly growing indigenous population. Between 1815 and 1880, the proportion of land in use by the peasantry increased from less than 15 per cent of Java's total surface area to over 30 per cent (Boomgaard and Van Zanden 1990:39). Although a high proportion of clearings was doubtlessly carried out on non-forested waste-land, it is equally clear that a land-hungry peasantry also made inroads into forest areas.

Tree-dwelling spirits

To many nineteenth- and twentieth-century Javanese, their surrounding world was, and continues to be, pervaded by all sorts of deities, spirits, ghosts, imps, nymphs and devils. Every animate and inanimate object can be the dwelling of a spiritual being, but spirits can also leave these objects and move around (Supatmo 1945:1–2). Some of these beings – or at least the labels attached to them – are recent arrivals: e.g. the *jinn* (spirit) and *setan* (devil) of Islam. Others are considerably older: e.g. the *dewa* (deity) and *widadari* (celestial nymph) of Hinduism. Predating the arrival of Hinduism in Java are the *hantu*, spirits or ghosts (Supatmo 1945:8, 12).

We are, of course, particularly interested in the *hantu alas*, the forest spirits, and the *hantu kayu*, spirits of trees or wood. Those who are inquisitive about the names of these beings can find many examples in Van Hien's classical compendium of spirits.[4] The tree or forest spirits most often mentioned in the literature are the male *Gendruwo* and his female counterpart, *Wewe*.[5]

In the Serat Centhini, an encyclopaedia of traditional Javanese culture written before 1800, we encounter the story of a group of people who are traversing the forest of Jembul, an abode of spirits, on their way to Gunungsari [Cirebon?]. Suddenly one of the women faints; she has the impression that she is having sexual intercourse with a Gendruwo (Pigeaud 1933:62–3).

The Gendruwo is tall, stout and hairy (Wiselius 1872:26). In 1891, the Gendruwo was even mentioned in an early tourist guidebook for West Java: the population of Sumedang [Priangan] believes that he dwells in the tallest trees and that he is wont to throw stones and spit *sirih* (betel) (Buys 1891:139). Van Hien, who calls him a *setan*, mentions the Gendruwo's ability to change his appearance. During the daytime he may appear as a beast of prey (tiger, serpent, crocodile, bird of prey). During the evening, however, he assumes the guise of a handsome young man who forces his attentions upon women walking alone.[6] He is not really dangerous, but a tease who throws stones and spits betel-juice. However, some people, and particularly children, can get so

---

[4] Hien 1933/4:214-6, 220-5, 251; the spirits mentioned on pages 214-6 and 251 are already present in the 1st [1894] edition, the others in the 1912 edition.

[5] Pigeaud 1933:62-3 [for the period before 1800]; Wiselius 1872:26; Buys 1891:139; Hien 1933/4:215-6 [1894]; Pigeaud 1938:171, 176; Supatmo 1945:11; Geertz 1960:18; Daszenies 1987:32-4.

[6] There is also a forest spirit who appears as a beautiful woman, bewitching men (Crawfurd 1820, II:231).

frightened from his appearance that they might fall ill (Hien 1933/4:215 [1894]). In Central Java, Gendruwo- and Wewe-mummers took part in folk-processions (Pigeaud 1938:171–6).

The Gendruwo can also be found in the postwar literature. Geertz (1960:18) – who does not call him a tree- or forest-spirit – mentions him as a being who is 'generally more playful than harmful and enjoy[s] playing practical jokes on people'. That is not all however: 'Sometimes the Gendruwos will take even more serious liberties. They will adopt the form of a woman's husband and sleep with her, she being none the wiser.'

In recent years his benign qualities seem to have become more pronounced. He is still a tease, and he might even abduct children temporarily, but he is also known to show people good places for fishing in exchange for cigarettes. He is a dweller of wooded areas but also of houses and their surroundings; the reference in Daszenies (1987:32) to wooded areas may have been taken from Wiselius (1872). He seems to have given up bothering women.

About the Wewe we have much less information; she looks like a witch with large, pendulous breasts, who steals children (Hien 1933/4: 216 [1894]). Daszenies (1987:33–4) mentions the same characteristics.

So what do we make of the Gendruwo? Between 1800 and 1987 he seems to have lost some of his more obnoxious characteristics, a process that may have started already at the end of the nineteenth century. He has also lost his exclusive association with trees and wooded areas. During the early nineteenth century he may have been a reason to avoid forests, nowadays he seems to be not much more than a bogeyman.

Around 1900, Kruyt could still write that forest spirits, as a rule, were able to make people ill or insane. This occurred not only when someone felled a tree in which a spirit had his abode, but also when people just walked through a forest (Kruyt 1906:504–7).

One wonders whether such a generalization could still be made to-day. One is tempted to speculate that the changes in the Gendruwo belief reflect the realities of the decreasing forest area. Far from keeping people from damaging forests, the Gendruwo seems to have shared their fate.

Sacred trees

Majestic trees, all over the world, have always impressed their beholders. Some of these gigantic trees, such as the *Ceiba pentandra* (cotton-tree), seem to be the object of veneration wherever they grow, in America, Africa and Asia. Small wonder, then, that according to the Indonesians such large trees are dwelling-places of spirits, which seems to apply particularly to many *Ficus* species. The Indonesians share their special regard for the *Ficus* family with the population of India, where the *Ficus religiosa* (pipal or bodhi tree) and the *Ficus benghalensis* (banyan tree) are held in high esteem (Marsden 1811:301; Kruyt 1906:504; Sinha 1979:27, 46–7; Mansberger 1988).

In Indonesia, particularly in Java, the *Ficus benjamina* or *waringin* is the most sacred tree, with its own legend of origin. The *waringin* can be found on most squares (*alun alun*) in front of a palace (*kraton*) or the house (*dalem*) of lower regional rulers (*bupati, wedana*). On the palace square of Yogyakarta and Surakarta, the most important indigenous royal capitals after 1755, there are always two *waringin*, surrounded by a square fence, the *waringin kurung*. The *waringin*, with its round top, overshadowing everything, represents the sky, and the square fence reflects the earth with its four corners. Or, alternatively, the *waringin* represents chaotic nature, whereas the fence is a representation of ordered human society or domesticated nature (Meijboom 1924:100–9; Pigeaud 1940:180; Lombard 1974:478; Schefold 1988:6).

Under the foliage of the *waringin* offerings were made, and it was also the place for all sorts of gatherings. In the village of Cimanuk, not far from Pandeglang [Banten], a gigantic *waringin* used to be the meeting place for rebellious Bantenese, until the Resident Buin had it cut down in 1847 or 1848 (Buddingh 1867, I:70).

To the Javanese, the cutting down of a *waringin* was, of course, an anathema. This applied also to other sacred trees or trees from sacred forests, unless such an action served a religious or ceremonial purpose. Such an exception was made for the construction of the palace of Yogyakarta, for which teak had been cut from the sacred forest of Karangasem in Gunung Kidul (Adam 1940:196).

Sacred trees were not a Javanese monopoly. The inhabitants of Sumba [Lesser Sunda Islands], for instance, would allegedly not cut their sandal-trees, although they did not forbid foreigners from doing so (Francis 1856, II:163). This version might be a slight distortion of the real feelings of the Sumbanese regarding the felling of sandalwood by foreigners, however. At least, that is implied by a somewhat different version of the same theme by another author. Roos (1872:37) reported that the Sumbanese were forbidden to cut the sandalwood trees, which they call *ai-nitu* or spirit wood, a restriction that also applied to foreigners, unless they were too powerful. The message seems to be clear: only the use of force could make the Sumbanese change their mind, unless one asumes that both stories are true, and that the attitude of the Sumbanese regarding sandalwood cutting really changed, perhaps due to increasing scarcity.

On the nearby island of Timor, sandalwood had been cut and exported for ages. It is generally assumed that the Indonesian sandalwood exported by Arab and Chinese traders between the tenth and fifteenth centuries came from Timor (Ferrand 1913, I:65, 83; Mills 1970:91). There are no indications that the Timorese objected to cutting the sandal tree, and in the nineteenth century it was one of their most important export products (Francis 1856:175).

Does that mean that we have to assume that beliefs regarding the sandal tree on two adjacent islands were entirely different? It is not impossible, but another explanation might be worth considering. Sandalwood was an important, or perhaps even the most important, part of the earnings of the Timorese nobility. Nine tenths of all sandalwood cut by the population went to the aristocracy (Francis 1856:184). Cutting sandalwood was, therefore, something of a corvée for the population. Thus, the responsibility for this activity rested squarely on aristocratic shoulders and not on those of the ordinary people. This phenomenon is also known from Java: if the overlord, either indigenous or foreign, gave an order, it was his responsibility when such an order implied a breach of some sort of taboo.

The sandalwood story might be a pointer to a more general tendency of export-led, state-formation-cum-taboo erosion. Foreign demand for a highly desired commodity stimulates the creation or growth of a group of *orang kaya* (merchants-cum-noblemen), the nuclei of a state, who tell their people what to grow, collect or cut. If such a commodity is subject to spiritual prohibitions, the population either gives in to increasing pressure from above or they shift the blame of the taboo infringement from themselves on to their betters. In the long run such a taboo might vanish entirely.

Finally, *il y a des accommodements avec le ciel*. As a rule, large trees are inhabited by spirits, and such a tree cannot be felled. If, however, one wants to fell a large tree, possibly the abode of a spirit, one propitiates the potential inhabitant of the tree with an offering before one goes on and cuts the tree anyway (Kruyt 1906:504). This mechanism may have played a role in the commercial expoitation of certain species as well. According to Nieuwenhuis (1911:14), the cutting of ironwood and camphor trees, both commercial species, had to be accompanied by offerings and incantations.

Haunted and sacred forests

Tree-dwelling spirits and sacred or spirit-inhabited trees should be approached with caution, but unless they constitute entire forests – as was the case with sandalwood – their environmental impact cannot be great. The Javanese acknowledged many such forests, for which the generic term is *angker*. An area which is *angker* cannot be inhabited or entered by humans; it is unapproachable. People who ignore this taboo disappear, become insane, or die. In West Java the term for such a 'possessed' forest was *sinapel*. The more general Malay word, used in many areas of the Indonesian archipelago, was and remains *pemali*.[7]

Areas could be *angker* for various reasons. Perhaps one of the most important reasons was the presence of tombs or antiquities (Hasskarl 1842:126–30; Roorda 1841/50, II:443; Boom 1863:130; Veth 1875/82, III:364; Tricht 1929:62.) As people tended to avoid these areas they became refuges of game of any description, including carnivore predators, which then reinforced the inclination to leave such a forest alone (Hasskarl 1842:130; Veth 1875/82, III:364). Sometimes these *angker* places were approached if one wanted to bring offerings to the tombs, which then attracted monkeys who ate the rice and bananas (Roorda 1841/50, II:443; Beauvoir 1873:243). Village graveyards were also *angker*; often the first inhabitants had left part of the original forest cover standing (Bergsma 1896:162; Jasper 1928:59).

In some cases the area which was regarded as *angker* was the 'land of the souls', where the spirits of the ancestors dwelt (Rigg 1850:122–32; Roos 1872:61; Tricht 1929:62). This is, of course, comparable to areas with tombs or graveyards. If a place had been inhabited by hermits or other holy men, it could also be taboo to enter or fell trees there

---

[7] Pigeaud 1933:63 [for the period before 1800]; Dissel 1870:274; Bergsma 1896;134, 142; Ham 1908:196; Nieuwenhuis 1911:25; Supatmo 1945:19.

(Teijsmann 1855:68–70).

The fear of entering some of these forests may have had a very real basis in the western sense of the word. In many cases forests were unhealthy, and people working in these forests would become ill (Cordes 1881:167; Bergsma 1896:142). To the Javanese mind, diseases were also caused by evil spirits, so there is no point in distinguishing between 'spirit' forests which were supposed to make people ill because they broke a taboo, or forests which were unhealthy owing to the presence of malarial mosquitos.

In 1908, Ham argued that without the influence of the Dutch, many forests would have been preserved, given the fact that so many places had been regarded as *angker* by the indigenous population. This was then no longer the case. He seems to imply that the notion of *angker* had disappeared or was about to disappear. He may have exaggerated slightly, but basically he was probably right.

One is left to speculate as to how this notion could have grown weaker. Part of the answer may be that government orders to cut down trees in hitherto forbidden forests had eroded the feeling that this was wrong. For another possible solution we have to go back in time a few centuries. In 1675, the Resident of Jepara reported to Batavia that the constantly rising price of timber might begin to drop, because he had started the felling of teak in a 'new' forest, where the superstitious Javanese had never worked before because it was haunted (Daghregister 1902:304). Seltmann (1987:46–7) suggests that this was possible because the VOC had employed so-called Kalang people, who were expert woodcutters, and who therefore knew the appropriate rituals for the exploitation of sacred forests. Thus, a combination of government orders and the use of specialists may have slowly eroded existing notions of forbidden forests.

Finally, it should be pointed out that haunted or sacred forests were not restricted to Java. I have seen references to similar areas in Bali, Bangka and Kalimantan, and I assume that they could be found in other regions as well. If the data on the postwar Tsembaga Maring in Papua New Guinea are anything to go by, we might even assume that large tracts of *pemali* forest are still to be found in less accessible and sparsely populated areas.[8]

---

[8] Nieuwenhuis 1911:27; Verslag 1917/9:26; Nieuwenkamp 1922:78; Verslag 1933/4: 90; Voogd and Slooten 1937:42/5; Adatrechtbundels 1937:287; Rappaport 1966:54.

Conclusions

Is it possible to formulate generalizations on the influence of – basically animistic – Javanese spirits beliefs on forest exploitation?

In the first place it must be assumed that some forested areas were saved from destruction because they were *angker*. If only very few trees were cut for the construction of palaces (Yogyakarta) or temples (Bali), a forest could survive as such through natural regeneration. The Sangeh forest, used for temples at Bali, did, indeed, survive in this way.

Secondly, there are indications that these beliefs, or at least their intensity, diminished along with the forests. Such developments doubtlessly varied as to time and place. It seems plausible to assume that people who witness the retreat of the forest from their immediate surroundings will be less inclined to cling to beliefs that are obviously no longer directly applicable. Through a 'positive' feedback mechanism, the forests will then disappear further. It may also have played a role that forests and trees were apparently cut down with impunity.

Thirdly, it is also evident that the state, western enterprises and the need of the peasantry for land were stronger than the fear of tree-spirits, sacred trees and haunted forests. The mechanisms that may have brought this about seem to have been the following:

- orders of government – indigenous and foreign alike – shifted the responsibility from the shoulders of the trespassers on to those of the rulers;

- experts with specialist ritual knowledge were employed in forests that were regarded as *angker*;

- there were always possibilities to appease individual spirits and ghosts with offerings.

Perhaps needless to say, not all forests were *angker* and not all trees were inhabited by spirits. Deforestation, therefore, could in those cases take place without 'spiritual' obstacles.

In the fourth place, Java was not entirely covered with virgin forests when the Dutch arrived, nor did they remove the whole forest cover. Forest clearing for agriculture and tree felling for construction and ship-building had been going on for ages. It is likely, though, that with the arrival of the Dutch, deforestation accelerated, until around

1900 an equilibrium had been reached.

We should distinguish between a direct and an indirect component of the impact of the Dutch presence. The Dutch influenced the proportion of the land-area under forest cover directly when trees were cut for commercial and governmental purposes. As the high rate of nineteenth-century indigenous population growth was largely, if not solely, the result of Dutch colonial policies, the effects of peasant clearings can be regarded as indirect results of the Dutch presence.

Between 1700 and 1900, therefore, the Dutch were clearly 'the bad guys'. As the case of Timor shows, however, the Indonesians did not need the Dutch to set the ecologically-speaking downward spiral of international commerce, state-formation and taboo-erosion in motion.

References

Adam, L. 1940. 'De pleinen, poorten en gebouwen van de kraton van Jogjakarta'. *Djawa* 20:185–205.

[Adatrechtbundels]. 1937. *Adatrechtsbundels XXXIX: Gemengd.* 's-Gravenhage: Nijhoff.

Beauvoir, le Comte de. 1873. *Voyage autour du monde. Australie, Java, Siam, Pékin, Yeddo, San Francisco.* Paris: Plon.

Bergsma, W.B. (ed.). 1896. *Eindresumé van het onderzoek naar de rechten van den inlander op den grond op Java & Madoera.* Vol. III. Batavia.

Boom, E.H. 1863. *Nederlandsch Oost-Indië.* Zutphen: Plantenga.

Boomgaard, P. 1988. 'Forests and forestry in colonial Java, 1677–1942'. In Dargavel, J., K. Dixon and N. Semple (eds), *Changing Tropical Forests. Historical Perspectives on Today's Challenges in Asia, Australasia and Oceania.* Canberra: ANU/CRES.

—— 1989. 'The Javanese rice economy, 800–1800'. In Hayami, A. and Y. Tsubouchi (eds), *Economic and Demographic Development in Rice Producing Societies. Some Aspects of East Asian Economic History, 1500–1900.* Tokyo: Keio University.

—— 1991. 'The non-agricultural side of an agricultural economy; Java, 1500–1900'. In Alexander, P., P. Boomgaard and B. White (eds), *In the Shadow of Agriculture. Non-Farm Activities in the Javanese Economy, Past and Present*. Amsterdam: Royal Tropical Institute.

—— 1994. 'Colonial forest policy in Java in transition, 1865–1916'. In R. Cribb (ed.), *State Without Citizens*. Leiden: KITLV.

Boomgaard, P. and J.L. van Zanden. 1990. *Food Crops and Arable Lands, Java 1815–1942*. (Changing Economy in Indonesia; a selection of statistical source material from the early 19th century up to 1940; edited by Boomgaard, P., Vol. 10) Amsterdam: Royal Tropical Institute.

Buddingh, S.A. 1867. *Neêrlands Oost-Indië. Reizen over Java, Madura (...) gedaan gedurende het tijdvak van 1852–1857*. III Vols. Amsterdam: Van Kesteren [1st ed. 1859].

Buys, M. 1891. *Batavia, Buitenzorg en de Preanger. Gids voor bezoekers en toeristen*. Batavia: Kolff.

Cordes, J.W.H. 1881. *De djati-bosschen op Java;hunne natuur, verspreiding, geschiedenis en exploitatie*. Batavia: Ogilvie.

Cortesão, A. (ed.). 1944. *The Suma Oriental of Tomé Pires. An Account of the East, from the Red Sea to Japan, Written in Malacca and India in 1512–1515*. London: Hakluyt Society.

Crawfurd, J. 1820. *History of the Indian Archipelago*. III Vols. Edinburgh

[Daghregister]. 1902. *Daghregister gehouden int Casteel Batavia vant passerende daer ter plaetse als over geheel Nederlandts India, 1675*. (Ed. by J.A. van der Chijs) Batavia/'s-Gravenhage: Nijhoff/Landsdrukkerij.

Daszenies, J. 1987. *Geistervorstellungen im javanischen Ueberzeugungssystem*. (Kölner Ethnologische Studien, Bd. 12) Berlin: Reimer.

Dissel, J.A. van. 1870. 'Eenige bijgeloovigheden en gewoonten der Javanen'. *Tijdschrift voor Neêrland's Indië*, 3rd series, 4(1):270–279.

Ellis Davidson, H.R. 1967. *Goden en mythen van Noord-Europa*. Antwerpen/ Utrecht: Aula [original English version 1964].

Ferrand, G. (ed.). 1913. *Relations de voyages et textes géographiques Arabes, Persans et Turks relatifs a l'Extrême-Orient du VIIIe au XVIIIe siècles*. Vol. I. Paris: Leroux.

Francis, E. 1856. *Herinneringen uit den levensloop van een' Indisch' ambtenaar van 1815 tot 1851*. III Vols. Batavia: Van Dorp.

Geertz, C. 1960. *The Religion of Java*. Chicago/London: University of Chicago Press.

Guha, R. 1989. *The Unquiet Woods. Ecological Change and Peasant Resistance in the Himalaya*. Delhi, etc.: Oxford University Press.

Ham, S.P. 1908. 'De grond-en boschpolitiek op Java'. *Tijdschrift voor het Binnenlandsch Bestuur* 35:109–273.

Hasskarl, J.K. 1842. 'Soemadang: op de grenzen van het district Lebak, in de Residentie Bantam'. *Tijdschrift voor Neêrland's Indië* 4(2):126–131.

Hien, H.A. van. c.1933/4. *De Javaansche geestenwereld*. Batavia: Kolff [6th edition; 1894 and 1912 editions also cited].

Ives, J.D. and B. Messerli. 1989. *The Himalayan Dilemma. Reconciling Development and Conservation*. London/New York: Routledge.

Jasper, J.E. [1928]. *Tengger en de Tenggereezen*. Weltevreden: Kolff [n.d.].

Kruijt, A.C. 1906. *Het animisme in den indischen archipel*. 's-Gravenhage: Nijhoff (for KITLV).

Lombard, D. 1974. 'La vision de la forêt à Java (Indonésie)'. *Etudes rurales* 53–56:473–485.

Mansberger, J.R. 1988. 'In search of the tree spirit: evolution of the sacred tree *Ficus religiosa*'. In Dargavel, J., K. Dixon and N. Semple (eds), *Changing Tropical Forests. Historical Perspectives on Today's Challenges in Asia, Australasia and Oceania*. Canberra: ANU/CRES.

Marsden, W. 1966. *The History of Sumatra*. Kuala Lumpur, etc.: Oxford University Press. [reprint of the third edition [1811] introduced by John Bastin].

Meijboom-Italiaander, J. 1924. *Javaansche sagen mythen en legenden*. Zutphen: Thieme.

Mills, J.V.G. (ed.). 1970. *Ma Huan: Ying-yai sheng-lan. 'The Overall Survey of the Ocean's Shores'* [1433]. Cambridge: Cambridge University Press (for the Hakluyt Society).

Morris-Suzuki, T. 1990. 'The environment in Japanese economic history'. *Asian Studies Review* 14(1):80–87.

Nieuwenhuis, A.W. 1911. *Animisme, Spiritisme en Feticisme onder de volken van den Nederlandsch-Indischen Archipel.* Baarn: Hollandia-Drukkerij.

Nieuwenkamp, W.O.J. 1922. *Zwerftochten op Bali.* Amsterdam: Elsevier [1st ed. 1910].

Pigeaud, Th. 1933. 'De Serat Tjabolang en de Serat Tjenthini; inhoudsopgaven, bewerkt door -'. *Verhandelingen Bataviaasch Genootschap* 72(2):1–89.

—— 1938. *Javaansche volksvertoningen; bijdrage tot de beschrijving van land en volk.* Batavia: Volkslectuur.

—— 1940. 'De noorder aloen-aloen te Jogjakarta'. *Djawa* 20:176–184.

Ponting, C. 1992. *A Green History of the World.* Harmondsworth: Penguin Books.

Rappaport, R.A. 1966. *Ritual in the Ecology of a New Guinea People: An Anthropological Study of the Tsembaga Maring.* [Ph.D. dissertation, Columbia University].

Rigg, J. 1850. 'Gunung Dangka or a paradise on earth; a tale of superstition'. *The Journal of the Indian Archipelago and Eastern Asia* 4:119–133.

Roorda, van Eysinga, P.P. 1841–1850. *Handboek der land- en volkenkunde, geschied- taal-, aardrijks- en staatkunde van Nederlandsch Indië.* III Vols. Amsterdam: van Bakkenes.

Roos, S. 1872. 'Bijdrage tot de kennis van taal, land en volk op het eiland Soemba'. *Verhandelingen Bataviaasch Genootschap* 36:1–160.

Schefold, R. 1988. 'De wildernis als cultuur van gene zijde; tribale concepten van "natuur" in Indonesië'. *Antropologische Verkenningen* 7(4):5–22.

Seltmann, F. 1987. *Die Kalang; eine Volksgruppe auf Java und ihre Stamm-Mythe.* Wiesbaden: Franz Steiner Verlag.

Simmons, I.G. 1989. *Changing the Face of the Earth; Culture, Environment, History.* Oxford: Basil Blackwell.

Sinha, B.C. 1979. *Tree Worship in Ancient India.* London/the Hague: East-West Publications.

Sponsel, L.E. and P. Natadecha. 1988. 'Buddhism, ecology and forests in Thailand: past, present and future'. In Dargavel, J., K. Dixon and N. Semple (eds), *Changing Tropical Forests: Historical Perspectives on Today's Challenges in Asia, Australasia and Oceania.* Canberra: ANU/CRES.

Supatmo [Raden]. c. 1945. 'Animistic beliefs and religious practices of the Javanese' (mimeograph, Columbia University, n.d.).

Teijsmann, J.E. 1855. *Uittreksel uit het dagverhaal eener reis door Midden-Java.* Batavia: Lange.

Thomas, K. 1984. *Man and the Natural World. Changing Attitudes in England 1500–1800.* Harmondsworth: Penguin Books.

Tricht, B. van. 1929. 'Levende antiquiteiten in West-Java; 1e gedeelte: de Badoejs'. *Djawa* 9:43–96.

[Verslag], various years. *Verslag Nederlandsch-Indische Vereeniging tot Natuurbescherming.* [11 issues, published for the years 1912–1938; issue 11 is also entitled *3 jaren Indisch natuurleven*] Batavia.

Veth, P.J. 1875–1882. *Java, geographisch, ethnologisch, historisch.* III Vols. Haarlem: Boon.

Voogd, C.N.A. de, and D.F. van Slooten. 1937. 'Het heilige bosch van Sangeh (Zuid-Bali)'. In Steenis, C.G.G.J. van (ed.), *Album van Natuurmonumenten in Nederlandsch-Indië.* n.p.: Nederlandsch-Indische Vereeniging tot Natuurbescherming.

White Jr., L. 1967. 'The historical roots of our ecological crisis'. *Science* 155 (10 March).

Wiselius, J.A.B. 1872. 'Iets over het geestendom en de geesten der Javaanen'. *Tijdschrift voor Neêrland's Indië*, new series, 1(2):23–33.

Worster, D. 1988. 'Appendix: Doing Environmental History'. In Worster D., (ed.), *The Ends of the Earth. Perspectives on Modern Environmental History.* London: Cambridge University Press.

Stephen Sparkes

Taming Nature – Controlling Fertility
Concepts of Nature and Gender among the Isan of Northeast Thailand

This article aims to explore the parallels between the taming of nature and the way in which men attempt to control women's reproductive powers. Among the Isan of Northeast Thailand, nature is anthropomorphized and gendered in the form of female and male nature spirits which represent idealized and simplified models of maleness and femaleness found in Buddhist texts and in the ideology of male authority.[1] At the same time, nature acts as a rich source for metaphors for human procreation and gender concepts. Both the process of anthropomorphization and the creation of metaphors from nature involve two asymmetric and interdependent relationships: nature vs. culture and female vs. male.

Nature, culture and gender

Ortner, in an early article entitled 'Is Female to Male as Nature is to Culture' (1974), discusses the universal submission of the female in terms of cultural ideology, roles of less prestige, symbolic devices, such as pollution, and exclusive social structures. She claims that in all cultures there is an underlying belief that culture is a means of asserting control over nature. Women are more closely identified with nature than men because of their ability to give birth and to breast-feed. According

---

[1] In Isan the common words for 'nature' are *chanit* (appearance) and *thaamachâat* or *thaamadaa* (according to the law of cause and effect). Although these words relate to the Buddhist concept of *dharma* (*thaama*) and the ephemeral quality of earthly existence, in daily speech they can be translated into English as 'natural' or 'usual'. Villagers rarely referred to other-worldly notions when discussing natural phenomena and their interaction with the environment.

to Ortner, this results in women being forced to accept a position of lower status in male ideological systems, a kind of 'middle-status' between culture and nature.

Many anthropologists have criticized this static distinction. Marilyn Strathern, in her study of the Hagen of Papua New Guinea (1980), states that the distinction between nature and culture is much more varied and complicated. She states that 'at one point culture is a creative, active force which produces form and structure out of passive, given nature. At another, culture is the end product of a process, tamed and refined, and dependent for energy upon resources outside itself' (1980:178). According to Strathern, it is not only a question of man's control over nature (order-imposing and taming) but a matter of complex, ambiguous and, at times, even inverted cultural categories: the terms of reference must be constantly shifted to maintain the dichotomy of culture vs. nature in relation to the dichotomy of male vs. female (ibid:183). There is a tendency in the West to see these two dichotomies as reinforcing each other when in fact neither dichotomy is consistent; Hastrup (1978) even goes so far as to state that there is merely a 'matrix of contrasts' which varies within each culture. Responding to Strathern and others, Ortner, writing with Whitehead, (1981) has modified her previous argument by stating that gender does not place the sexes in logical opposition but in gradations: inclusive-exclusive and hierarchical-complementary. Valeri (1983), investigating nature and culture concepts among the Huaulu of Seram, Indonesia, defends Ortner's dichotomy and hierarchy, and criticizes Strathern for ignoring the problem of why women's reproductive processes should represent a challenge to male authority and control.

This author acknowledges the importance child-bearing and lactation have for the formation of a concept of femaleness and the relation between women and natural processes as outlined by Ortner and Valeri. At the same time, however, Strathern's comments concerning the dynamism and cultural context of the dichotomies of both culture vs. nature and male vs. female is a key point. I would suggest that the primary dichotomy is one of gender concepts, and the alterations in the alignment of categories of nature and culture is to maintain gender categories, the most important of which is the hierarchical ordering of male over female. Among the Isan, this is most apparent when examining parallels between how gender categories are maintained during marriage ceremonies when the unity of female descent groups is temporarily destablized, and in rain-making ceremonies, when male nature spirits, representing the active forces of nature, are called into the village.

Ortner's (1974) universal categories of male as primarily 'cultural' and female as primarily 'natural' inadequately explain Isan cosmology and gender concepts. Nature is personified as both male and female in the form of nature spirits, and both men and women can represent 'culture' in different ritual circumstances. Male nature spirits embody the activating powers which fertilize Mother Earth, considered passive and female by villagers. Yet these same male spirits are invited into the village (standing for culture and female) under strictly controlled ritual circumstances. Menstrual blood is perceived as active and threatening the male-dominated ideology of Buddhism, representing in this case culture. Men aim to control the reproductive powers of women by means of various taboos on menstruation and restrictions on behaviour. Both the powers in nature and in female fertility are perceived as potentially disruptive and threatening to the social order and gender hierarchy but necessary for fertility and procreation. They must be controlled by means of ritual (culture) and by men (male authority) so that categories and boundaries might be maintained (cf. Douglas 1966).

The rituals referred to in this article were observed by the author in the Isan village of Naa Din Dam, twelve kilometres west of the provincial capital of Loei, in Loei province.[2] The Lao-speaking Isan of Northeast Thailand are lowland, wet rice cultivators. Over the centuries, they have expanded from what is now northern Laos to populate the Khorat Plateau and both banks of the Mekong River as far south as Kampuchea. Their kin system (female descent groups) and social organization (single self-sufficient households) allow for continual expansion and exploitation of new natural resources (cf. Hafner and Chantrasuwan 1985; Ng 1978; Mizuno 1968). The Isan consider themselves Buddhist but their cosmology is, in fact, a complex mixture of Buddhist doctrine, Hindu ritual practice and myth, and ancient Tai spirits and ancestors cults (cf. Sparkes 1993a; Kirsch 1977; Tambiah 1970). Nature spirits belong, for the most part, to the ancient Tai tradition and occupy the lowest levels of the all-encompassing, Buddhist, hierarchy. These spirits are what Leach (1968) calls 'practical religion', that is religion concerned with the material needs of villagers as opposed to Buddhist doctrine and spiritual salvation.

---

[2] Fieldwork (June 1991 till May 1992) was supported by the Norwegian Research Council for the Social Sciences in Oslo and the Nordic Institute of Asian Studies in Copenhagen.

Female nature spirits

Mother Earth, Mother Rice, Mother Water and the Lady of the Wood are the most important female nature spirits among the Isan. The image of the altruistic mother, constantly providing food, protection and shelter, is common to all these female spirits. Yet in order for these spirits to yield their bountiful harvest for mankind, they must first be acted upon by male nature spirits. Nature as personified by female spirits can thus be seen as passive, potential fertility.

Mother Earth (*mâe thorónii*) is the personification of the Earth, the source of all life. She is unlimited fertility and growth but dormant unless activated by the male sky spirit which is responsible for sending rain: a cosmic sexual union. Her powers must be re-activated each year by a series of rain-making festivals, and this assures mankind of food and all the material means necessary for survival. In addition, Mother Earth offers her services to mankind in return for only the simplest offerings or symbolic forms of payment. An example villagers often narrated concerned a lost buffalo in the forests: one would dangle a ball of glutinous rice at the end of a piece of thread and Mother Earth would reveal the direction of the lost animal. Each holy day (*wan phrá*) when water charged with merit is poured at the base of a tree in the monastery, she transports merit to the souls of deceased relatives who lie buried there. A well-known legend states that Mother Earth played an important role in protecting the Buddha from the demon Mara (Man) and his armies by unleashing a flood of water and drowning them (Terwiel 1976). Mother Earth's care for mankind and even for the Buddha, as if they were her children, is a metaphor for the idealized role of a mother in Isan society.

Similar to Mother Earth, is the benevolent Mother Rice (*mâe phõosòp*) who personifies the staple food of the Isan. Rice is commonly synonymous with food; *khão* means both rice and food. Her spirit resides in rice itself and wherever rice is found but predominantly in rice paddies and in the rice barns in each compound. Mother Rice receives small, token offerings of rice or bundles of leaves, candles and incense before and after a successful harvest. Rice is offered at every Isan ritual: it is given to monks in order to earn merit, to ancestors for protection and to various spirits for intervention and favours. Rice, therefore, is essential for the spiritual well-being of the Isan as well as being the staple food of the Isan diet. Mother Rice, however, needs to be activated by the male spirit of the sky and, in addition, protected by spirits of the rice fields, her male counterparts.

Mother Water (*mâe nám* or *mâe khong* from Gungga or Ganges) is associated with physical cleanliness and ritual purity. Water washes away sins and restores health and peace of mind in ritual baths. Although water in the form of rain is a sign of the male sky spirit and fertilizes Mother Earth, water in rivers and streams is personified as female.[3] The contrast between these two gendered aspects of water becomes apparent when one looks at the festival of Loi Krathong when banana-leaf boatlets with incense sticks, candles and food offerings are floated down rivers. There is often a prayer which accompanies these gestures, an apology to Mother Water for having soiled moving water by bathing, urinating or defecating in it (Textor 1960:482). This forgiving and passive nature of Mother Water is yet another characteristic of the idealized mother image, unlike the assertiveness of the male sky spirit.

Female tree spirits are referred to as 'ladies of the wood' (*naang mái*) and inhabit certain types of trees which are considered useful by the Isan; male tree spirits very often inhabit the Bodhi tree which is found in monasteries and associated with Buddhism.[4] Two of the most commonly mentioned trees where female spirits reside are the tamarind (*mái makhaam*), a fruit-bearing tree used in traditional medicine, and the red wood (*mái daeng*), the preferred building material. These trees may be utilized by man for his own purposes: they are ready resources to be exploited and are also symbolically associated with women or the female dominated household. Tamarind wood, for example, is used to make medicinal water for women who are recovering from childbirth so that they may gain strength and obtain a generous flow of mother's milk.

When a red wood tree is cut down, villagers believe that the creeking of the tree as it falls is evidence that the spirits are fleeing. They must be called back only when the tree is destined to become the

---

[3] Floods (*nám thawom*) were not a common phenomenon in the region of Loei. When villagers did comment on floods in other parts of the country no mention was made of attributing the cause to Mother Water. There is a complex relationship between the sky spirit which sends the rain, territorial spirits and perhaps Mother Water as to why floods occur but villagers expressed different opinions about this matter.

[4] The majority of the trees are neither classified as male nor female but are believed to be inhabited by inauspicious spirits of the forest. Male tree spirits are called *rúk thewadaa*, literally 'tree dwelling spirit', which are often the spirits of deceased monks (cf. Phithong 1989:655).

'spirit post' (*sāu khwān*) of a new house. When female tree spirits are called into the village, they are tamed with small offerings and thus domesticated. The 'spirit post' becomes the place where offerings to the ancestors of the female descent group are placed; the post linking the living with Mother Earth who transports the essences of food and drink to the ancestors. The spirit of the post performs this benevolent act and in addition protects the residents by forming the frame of the house. Stott (1978:16) claims that spirits of trees which are felled reveal a sense of self-interest and self-preservation which man should acknowledge and utilize properly or risk losing benevolent protection and inviting revenge. Villagers, however, have felled and continue to fell trees regardless of the risk of offending spirits. Only when the tree is to become the 'spirit post' of the house do they seek to be on good terms with this spirit by calling it back to occupy the post. The spirit then acquires attributes which are similar to the other female spirits mentioned above and becomes benevolent and protective. This ritual procedure illustrates the importance of the boundary between the forest, the abode of the untamed spirits (male and female), and the village, representing safety and sanctuary from the dangers of the forest.

Male nature spirits

Male nature spirits differ fundamentally in character from female nature spirits. They are aggressive, powerful and can threaten villagers when they do not receive regular offerings or tribute. In many ways these spirits metaphorically idealize the dominant position of men as household head within the kin system and male authority in politics. Powerful male nature spirits must be appeased and receive offerings or blood sacrifices in order that man may harness their energy, as in the case of the spirit of the sky and the Naga which provide rain, or coexist safely on the same territory and receive protection, as in the case of the spirit of the compound and spirit of the fields which 'own' the land.

Mother Earth's male opposite is the ancient Tai sky spirit (*phayaa thāen*) which causes the rain to fall, activating her fertile powers. Before the onset of the monsoon in May, a series of rituals are held in order to induce rain from the sky spirit by means of sympathetic magic, offerings of food and drink, and lengthy prayers, all culminating in the rocket festival which I shall describe below. If these rituals do not produce ample rain, further, more dramatic, measures are taken to satisfy the sky spirit, and this may include buffalo sacrifices.[5] The purpose of these sacrifices is to send the 'spirit' of the buffalo (*khwān khway*) to the sky spirit; it is unclear whether this is to make amends for previously neglected offerings or merely to satisfy this capricious and unpredictable spirit (Sparkes 1993b). In either case, villagers are totally dependent on rain and, therefore, the good will of the sky spirit. This spirit, which initiates the agricultural cycle, exemplifies the active male element in the cosmos.

There are several other spirits which have similar roles in the cosmology: the Naga, the Hindu snake demon (*nák*) which inhabits the earth or rivers and controls nature's fertile powers, the ancient Tai 'great spirit' (*phii luang*), which is the dominant spirit of a particular region and resides in the forests, and the swamp spirit (*uprákhrùt*), an amalgamation of a Buddhist saint, a son of a river spirit and the Buddha, and a local swamp spirit (Sparkes 1993b; Strong 1992). All of these spirits are associated with male behaviour or images, such as the Buddha, and with the forces of nature located outside the village, either in a river, swamp or forest. Similar to the sky spirit, the Naga has the power to activate the fertile powers which are latent in Mother Earth and in human beings; this is such a potent force that only in strictly controlled ritual circumstances is this power called upon and invited to enter the village proper.

Except for these rituals, the boundary between village and forest is maintained symbolically and reinforced by tales of dangerous animals, various forest spirits[6] and spirits of the dead which have not managed to reincarnate due to their bad karma (*phii prêt*). Nowadays, there are only a few areas covered by trees near the village of Naa Din Dam but these retain an important symbolic significance. Previously, villagers who died in accidents or women who died in childbirth (*phii phraay*) were buried in the forest, but they are now cremated in a small grove of trees to the west of the village. The spirits which threaten to create chaos or bring sickness to the village reside in the forest. This could be seen as a justification and motivation for clearing the land and ridding

---

[5] This is a rare ritual and, according to my informants, was only performed about once every ten years usually when there has been several years of consecutive drought. Tambiah (1970) mentions that in Ubon, a buffalo was sacrificed to a swamp spirit every three years, and Archaimbault (1975) records that buffalo were sacrificed to a spirit residing at Tàt Luong in Laos.

[6] Many forest spirits (*phii pàa*) have no specific gender.

mankind of a source of danger. However, these potentially dangerous forces of nature are necessary for fertility, so, despite deforestation, there are still some areas of forest remaining: tiny patches of contained but concentrated power.

These small woods near the village contain the house of the village spirit (*phii bâan*), which is the owner of the land on which the village lies, and various spirits of the rice fields (*phii naa*); collectively they shall be referred to as territorial spirits.[7] A constant flow of offerings of betel nut, incense and food (symbolic payments or tribute) ensures protection and the right to use the land. Although *phii* are often spirits of people who have died a long time ago,[8] they are associated primarily with having control over a particular territory. Although farmers possess land documents which give them the right to own and exploit the land, tribute must be given to the territorial spirits in order to ensure a successful harvest and protection against malevolent spirits of the forest. I would suggest that this relationship is similar to that of landlords to sharecroppers. When villagers fail to provide offerings, retribution can be swift and usually takes the form of sickness or accident. An example of how a disruptive spirit may wreck havoc in a family occured while I was residing in the village of Naa Din Dam. After suffering many mishaps, deaths and illnesses, the family called in a medium to establish the cause and alleviate the suffering. The medium claimed that a spirit of the rice fields had not received its proper offerings for many years and had become angry with the family who continued to use its land. The response was an elaborate series of offerings, including a pig's head, and the construction of a spirit house (Sparkes 1993a:98–102). The village spirit can also be revengeful if it is not properly informed of all the important decisions and festivals taking place in the village. These male nature spirits are demanding, and if not content with offerings, aggressive and threatening in contrast to the female nature spirits which provide food, shelter and protection with only occasional offerings of rice.

---

[7] Van Esterik (1982) states that in Central Thailand these *phii* were often fused with 'gods' (*thewadaa*) but in the Isan setting this was not the case.

[8] Many of these territorial spirits are the spirits of deceased local heroes and warriors. All are male but many communicate through female mediums; yet another example of the passive female role and the active male role and source of power (cf. Irvine 1984; Sparkes 1993a:98–103)

Taming nature and harnessing its energy

Agricultural fertility and material well-being can only be achieved when the female spirits are activated by or come into contact with male spirits, that is a cosmic sexual union. This is a potentially dangerous event since it requires the crossing of important symbolic boundaries: village vs. forest and nature vs. culture. Inviting the forces of nature into the village and harnessing the dangerous powers of nature can, therefore, only occur in strictly controlled ritual situations. In order to maintain the dichotomy of male vs. female, the village acquires a passive, female symbolic value in relation to the active, threatening male nature spirits. This seems to contradict Ortner's (1974) earlier claim that women are more closely associated with nature and men with culture since male spirits from the forest (untamed nature) invade the village, disturbing the normal social order and giving women a partial, temporary control.

The most spectacular festival of the Isan ritual calendar is a series of rain-making ceremonies (*bun phrá wêt* and *bun bang fai*) held in the spring before the planting season begins.[9] The Naga and the swamp spirit (*uprákhrùt*), both forest spirits associated with the powerful forces of nature, are evoked and invited into the village for two days. During this time, social norms which regulate interaction between the sexes are suspended resulting in a frenzy of drinking, eating of 'hot food', that is food which arouses the passions, dancing and flirting. Previously, there were also water fights and processions of men dressed as women or wearing cloth phalli. A tug-of-war contest is held in the monastery in which the men are pitted against women. The women must win (they always do) in order for the rain-making ceremony to be a success; a reversal of gender hierarchy in which women symbolically gain the upperhand in the village. To counter this atmosphere of abandonment and symbolic reversals, male ritual specialists invite the spirit of the village who acts as a 'policeman', and the monks, reminders of Buddhist moral order and symbolizing a separation and hierarchy of the sexes, perform sermons. On the final day of the festival, when the atmosphere reaches a crescendo, an orgy of dancing and wild behaviour, home-

---

[9] These rituals can be held at different times but are often combined as they were when I was conducting fieldwork in the village of Naa Din Dam in 1992. It is also reported that the festival of *bun phrá wêt* is a harvest festival (Tambiah 1970:153-178) but this was not the case in Loei province: the symbolism clearly indicates a rain-making ritual (Sparkes 1993b:13-14).

made rockets are fired into the sky, piercing the clouds, on their way to the sky spirit. This symbolic sexual act is, in fact, the reverse of what should follow: the rocket is fired from the Earth into the sky with the intention of initiating rainfall which fertilizes Mother Earth. The act completed, the village returns to 'normal', and the spirits are returned to the forest or swamp: the boundary between the village and untamed nature is re-established.

Other ritual unions of male and female nature spirits result in fertility but are on a lesser scale, often only involving one household. Before rice seedlings are planted, the spirit of the rice (*khwăn khâo*) is called forth and offerings of betel, tobacco and eight rice balls are laid out for the spirit of the field, representing payment for using the land and for protection against other spirits that might threaten the crop (Phinthong 1992:1050).[10] In order to obtain a good harvest of rice one requires the fertile powers of Mother Rice and the protection and permission of the male spirit who resides in the territory. Another example of the union of the spirits is the ritual performed when building a new house. Here the spirit of the Lady of the Wood is called to reside in the house post and is presented with gifts of food while permission is sought from the male spirit inhabiting the compound by offering money and alcohol. The raising of the post and planting it into the ground symbolize both an aggressive sexual act and man's domination of nature. Prayers to Mother Earth, the benevolent, female spirit of fertility, are chanted by the ritual specialist in order to ask for forgiveness for having 'wounded' her. Terwiel (1976), however, interprets this act as a stabbing of the Naga which represents the potentially dangerous and threatening forces of nature that must be tamed by man. Both interpretations are powerful symbols for man's exploitation and dominance of nature, expressed in terms of gender concepts.

The rituals above deal with the union of various male and female spirits, but it is important to remember that other rituals separate untamed nature, symbolized by forest spirits, from the village and the realm of mankind. The aim of curative rituals, for example, is to expel 'bad' forest spirits, which cause sickness and threaten life, from the

---

[10] Villagers used the expressions 'Mother Rice' (*măe phŏosòp*) or 'spirit of the rice' (*khwăn khāo*) interchangeably. The former refers to a personification of rice in the form of a goddess while the latter implies the spirit essence of rice itself. The calling forth the spirit of the rice involves invocations to Mother Rice and food offerings (cf. Rajadhon 1986:135-142).

house and village. The following are two examples of final verses from curative rituals: the first example calls on the gods to seek revenge on the evil spirits of the forest that have caused illness and suffering, and in the second example the priest is addressing the unwanted spirit directly:

> ...let us hope the gods will come and seek revenge.
> Take these things back into the forest!
> Take them away from the house!
>
> This house does not belong to you
> These paths do not belong to you.
> Do not tresspass, do not enter through the gaps in the floor boards.[11]

Only when the forces of nature are tamed and brought together in a controlled manner as in the rain-making rituals, can mankind harness nature's power and utilize it beneficially. We have seen how nature is anthropomorphized by gender concepts. Now let us examine how nature is a source of metaphor for gender concepts of maleness and femaleness.

Female reproductive powers

Gender concepts among the Isan are structured around the opposition between nature and culture. As Strathern (1980) points out in her article on the Hagen, the categories of nature and culture are related to the culturally perceived notions of maleness and femaleness and the roles of men and women in procreation. Nature spirits and the opposition between the village and the forest represent idealized gender values of male activity, authority and power, and female passivity and benevolence. The relationship between female reproductive powers and male authority in the village is more complex and ambiguous. According to Buddhist ideology, women are seen as belonging primarily to the material world and closer to 'nature' due to the role they have in bearing and raising children, in contrast to the role of the monkhood in

---

[11] Recorded by the author at *sà daue khraue* (avoiding the workings of fate) and *âap nám mun* (holy bath) rituals at the village of Naa Din Dam, Loei, in April 1992 (Sparkes 1993a:175-177).

which men transcend the world for the religious ideal. Keyes (1984) sums up the ambiguous position of women in Buddhist ideology when he states that the highest achievement possible is to bear sons who will later be ordained as monks: this acknowledges the importance of women but at the same time illustrates that men, alone, may enter the monastic order. In order to unravel female gender concepts, I shall examine the key symbol of menstrual blood.

Women's ability to bear children is analogous to Mother Earth's capacity to create all plant life. Unlike Mother Earth and other female nature spirits, whose power of fertility is a positive, hidden essence and only visible in their abundant produce, fertility in women is visible in the form of menstrual blood and has predominantly negative associations. Menstrual blood is not only evidence of the ability to procreate but also symbolically threatening to men and society as a whole if it is not carefully controlled and separated from the male sources of power, that is Buddhist texts. Menstrual blood combines the creative and the destructive powers of nature in the bodies of women.

Women are perceived of as passive since they do not control their own menstrual flow, and hence the powers of nature within them, as opposed to the ideal of controlled male sexuality, symbolized by the celibacy of the monkhood (Kabilsingh 1988:11; Smith 1986; Mougne 1984:3; Terwiel 1975:115). I would suggest that the power inherent in menstrual blood is similar to the potentially disruptive powers of male nature spirits of the forest which are only invited into the village during festivals strictly controlled by rituals; it is as if women, who are themselves not harmed by menstrual blood, contain the fertile powers associated with the forest within the confines of the village proper, constantly threatening order and gender hierarchy which are maintained by male authority and the ideology of Buddhism. As Mougne states: 'what men fear so violently...is women's inherent power of reproduction, over which men, ultimately, have no control' (1984:3). I propose that men attempt symbolically to control women and their powers of reproduction, and by implication nature, whence these powers arise.

Men avoid sexual contact with women who are menstruating, pregnant or during postpartum recovery. Villagers state that contact with menstrual blood or women's undergarments will weaken men, sap their physical and spiritual strength, and make them vulnerable to illness. This is why women's underwear and sarongs (a wrap-around garment used as a towel and thus possibly coming into contact with menstrual discharge) are always hung to dry on low clothes lines. If a man were to place his head, the seat of his 'life essence' (*khwãn*), below such items, it would be considered a scandal; a reversal of male authority, implying a subservience to female procreative powers. Similarly, women, according to male ritual specialists, should not attend Buddhist rituals or give rice to monks when menstruating. This apparently threatens the monk's store of merit and ruins the effectiveness of Buddhist prayers at rituals.

Further evidence of the power of menstrual blood is to be found in beliefs concerning pregnancy and postpartum recovery. Male villagers stated that intercourse with pregnant women or women who had just given birth was unthinkable. There was no mention of menstrual blood but villagers consider the blood discharged at birth and during the postpartum recovery to be even more dangerous than menstrual blood. This would infer that menstrual blood has accumulated in the womb and is released at birth in a more concentrated form. Women spend from ten days till one month resting by a fire (*yûu fai*), drinking medicinal water made from tamarind bark and refraining from work. Villagers explain that this is to 'dry out' the womb and to purify their 'blood' with the medicinal water. The fact that women are confined during this time could be interpreted as a symbolic, although temporary, boundary between a woman, who contains powerful procreative forces of nature, and the rest of the village, especially men and the monks whose power is threatened.

Although men and women express similar ideas about menstruation and women's role in reproduction, there is evidence that women are not as passive as the ideal role of Mother Earth implies. Textor reports that men fear that prostitutes regularly mix menstrual blood with water, called 'virginal water', and put it around the threshold of their rooms in order to weaken their clients and turn them into devoted slaves (1960:145–152). The fear that women could use this renewable power inherent in themselves, either unknowingly or on purpose, is a constant danger and threat to the position of men in society and to Buddhist hierarchy which upholds that position.

Male Authority

The source of male authority is the Pali Canon, holy texts concerning the life of the Buddha and his teachings which are the exclusive preserve of monks and male ritual specialists. Women have no direct access to the scriptures or their 'magical power' except through the medium of monks or other male members of the society since the essence of being female (bearing children and menstruating as outlined above) stands in opposition to the teaching of renunciation and spiritual salvation.[12] As in other Buddhist societies it is a popular belief that being born a woman is a sign of previous bad karma. Buddhist myths and legends are full of examples of negative images of women as sexually perverse, materialistic and cunning, and ideals of motherhood and submissive wives (Boonsue 1989; Bancroft 1986:86; Keyes 1984). The popular Vessantara Jataka sermon recited at one rain-making ceremony contrasts the demanding wife of a Brahman, who barters for sexual favours with the ideal wife of the king, *phrá wêt*, who obeys her husband always, even when she is given away to a gluttonous, lecherous Brahman (Keyes 1984:226–27).

These texts legitimize a series of rules restricting women and controlling their behaviour in the village. It is forbidden for women to enter the village temple, where the monks chant their morning and evening prayers, to climb the stairs to the upper floor of the abbot's residence and to touch statues of the Buddha. Terwiel states that girls are warned at a very early age not to come close to monks (1975:56). Since all men have been, or can become, monks, women are prohibited from touching the head of all adult men, even their husbands, since the top of the head contains the 'spiritual essence' with its store of male power derived from Buddhist texts.

The resultant hierarchical organization of gender places men, potential or previous monks, above women both symbolically and literally. During all Buddhist rituals, men sit closest to the monks and Buddha statues, the source of spiritual power. Women sit behind the men and must pass their offerings of food for the monks at the front via

---

[12] The sacred words of the Buddhist texts are chanted by monks and ritual specialists at all ritual events in order to charge objects or people with 'magical powers' of protection or enhance personal power. They function very much like magical spells and are often used in contexts which contradict their original meaning (cf. Terwiel 1982).

the men; this separates the sexes and at the same time devalues women's role in nurturing. Due to their lower status and lack of access to the monkhood, women's chief means of acquiring merit is by giving food to the monks on a daily basis (Keyes 1984). This can be seen as an extension of the mother's role as provider of food and is similar to the ideal roles of Mother Earth and Mother Rice. Men endeavour to control the distribution of food and gifts on holy days, making women, in effect, dependent on their services as mediators. Yet women play such an important role in sustaining the monkhood, that even the abbot of Naa Din Dam monastery acknowledged that without the women of the village, there would be no monkhood. This illustrates how men and monks are dependent on women and calls into question the notion of male dominance.

Another example of how men use Buddhist ideology to gain control over women is by making the male sex the determining one in procreation. Men claimed that they always lay on top of the women during coitus, implying that the women should be subordinate during this act. The word for sperm in Isan and Thai is *nám kaam*, literally 'karma water', that is water which determines the fate of the foetus. Yet the actions and attitudes of a pregnant woman influence the character and appearance of a new-born, seemingly contradicting the exclusive role of fate and its origins in the sperm. Women believed that handling sharp objects, especially knives and needles, could lead to a miscarriage, that stealing resulted in a child being born with an extra finger, and that arguing or fighting produced a choleric infant (cf. Rajadhon 1987:25–41). An elderly villager who had previously been a monk explained that at conception women contribute the liquid parts of the body (tears, mucus, spit, sweat, blood and bile) while the men contribute the solid parts (hair of the head, body hair, nails, teeth, skin, flesh and bones); what Lévi-Strauss (1969) calls a 'flesh and bone' society. After cremation, only the bones remain as evidence of the ancestor's presence, but the liquid parts, symbolizing the material and female, are totally consumed by the flames. However, the fact that female descent groups are the means by which society is spatially organized indicates, in my opinion, the importance of blood in procreation and, consequently, blood ties in social organization; both the bones and social ties represent continuity in the form of the ancestor and living relations.

Unlike gendered nature spirits, whose roles are idealized and dominated by male values, the world of men and women is more complex and ambiguous; the boundaries and hierarchy of gender being more unstable. Women's power of reproduction, symbolized by menstrual blood, is comparable to the powerful forces of nature embodied in the male nature spirits (potentially threatening to the social order) and is, at least, partially an active agent. Men must constantly exert their dominance over women by means of Buddhist ideology which considers women as materialistic and, at times, threatening to spiritual powers. Let us now examine the marriage ritual and the formation of a household in which male and female unite, paralleling the rain-making festivals joining male and female nature spirits.

Controlling the household and marriage

The creation of a new household through the marriage ceremony parallels the rain-making festivals discussed above in that male authority must be combined with female fertility. There are two complications here for male authority: women dominate the running of household and the incest taboo which involves a transfer of women between men (Lévi-Strauss 1963).

The division of labour and kinship among the Isan associates women more closely with the household and, at the same time, allows for men to retain ultimate authority over the household because of the hierarchy of gender. In order for a household to function practically, there must be at least one member of each sex: women are solely responsible for cooking food and the care of small children, that is the role of nurturer, and men deal with all contact outside the village and work in the fields, the role of provider and protector. This division is summed up in an Isan saying: 'a woman is big inside the house; a man is big outside the house' (*ying ben yâay nai bâan - chaay ben yâay nâuk bâan*). The Isan word for both household or family is *krâupkhruwa*, which literally means 'that which is covered by the kitchen'. This emphasizes the importance of commensuration and food which women alone cook. The kitchen hearth, moreover, is where some women give birth and where all women 'lie by the fire' (*yûu fai*) during postpartum recovery. Many women return to the kitchen of their mother or grandmother to 'lie by the fire', emphasizing the importance of continuity in the female descent group. Thus the kitchen is the most important room in the house for the women: a place for food to be prepared and for the birth of children.[13]

Today women spend a considerable amount of time working in the fields thoughout the year due to the introduction of cash crops, but previously they spent more time at home weaving, maintaining the household and looking after the children. The exception was the period of labour-intensive planting and harvesting of rice. Today, women are still responsible for cleaning the house, washing clothes and preparing all the food. Men, on the other hand, operate all agricultural machines, are responsible for constructing and repairing the house, and deal with the outside, that is with banks, government officials and agri-business companies.

Similarly, in rituals both sexes are necessary: women are responsible for preparing offerings, consisting mainly of food and decorations, and men alone sacrifice animals and act as ritual specialists. Rituals cannot be performed successfully for either the good of the household or the village as a whole without the participation of both men and women.

Before examining the process of the creation of a new household and the marriage ceremony, a few words concerning Isan kinship are necessary. I have chosen to decribe the structure of Isan kinship as 'female descent groups' (*phii chûa or phii diawkan*), similar to northern Thai kinship (cf. Keyes 1975; Wijeyewardene 1984). Descent is traced through the female members of an extended family group and men are incorporated through marriage.[14] This emphasizes again the attachment women have to their natal homes since daughters (primarily ultimogenitor) are responsible for looking after their parents in old age and build their homes within the same compound or at least in the same village. The majority of men, on the other hand, come from outside the village and are incorporated into the group. This process of incorporation is only completed when they acquire authority over their own household (if a single house) or a compound (upon the death of their father-in-law). Men are ranked according to the age of their wives, regardless of

---

[13] A little less than half the village women gave birth in their kitchens or their mothers' kitchens while I was residing in the village of Naa Din Dam. The rest gave birth at the district hospital but returned to 'lie by the fire' in their kitchens.

[14] The house of the eldest woman of the descent group is where the ancestor 'altar shelf' is located. Female descendents are responsible for feeding the ancestors on a regular basis, and it is through them alone that the ancestors communicate their needs, offer protection or mete out punishment.

their own ages, and they are under the authority of their fathers-in-law; the word for bridegroom implies the notion of 'slave' (*jâo bàaw*). Only when the man has sons-in-law of his own, by which time he should have established his own authority, is he addressed by a kin term and ranked within the descent group: thus son-in-law (*lûuk khei*) becomes maternal grandfather (*phâutaa*).

The female descent groups and the division of labour characterize the role women have as being strongly connected to the household or family compound and men as being associated with working in the fields and marrying into the group. This relationship is symbolized in the burying of the placenta: placentae of male children are buried in a mound in the rice fields (height symbolizing male authority) while placentae of female children are buried under the house (symbolizing continuity of the female descent group). This parallels the division of male and female nature spirits in which male spirits, such as the Naga, the swamp spirit and the sky spirit, inhabit the forest or areas outside the safety of the village while female spirits are connected to the home and its maintenance. Rain-making rituals bring powerful male spirits and fertile female spirits together in a controlled manner. Marriage achieves the same goal of union of male and female by incorporating men into female descent groups. Yet men, despite the fact they are originally from another descent group, obtain control over the group and especially over female fertility of the group, most importantly the reproductive powers of their wives and their daughters.[15]

Throughout the preparations for marriage, women assume a passive role and men an active role. Courtship (*pai thiaw*), for the most part,[16] still consists of eligible bachelors making numerous visits to the houses of the young women who are either chaperoned by family members or in groups together. When a young couple decide they would like to get married, it is up to the boy to inform his parents. His father then approaches the father of the bride and, if both families agree that the match is acceptable, negotiations for the bride-price (*khâa daung*)

---

[15] Women who become pregnant before marriage run the risk of being punished by the ancestors (*pit phii*). As a result of losing control over the sexuality of his daughter before marriage, the father loses financially as well since the bride price will become only a token payment (cf. Cohen 1984).

[16] The changing socio-economic conditions in Northeast Thailand make it more and more possible for couples to meet privately or while working in cities but parents are still consulted before marriage.

commence. Although the mother and other senior women are often consulted and have their say, they can only influence the negotiations in an indirect manner. The negotiations and presentation of the bride-price is the right of elderly men, the functioning heads of the descent groups. Arranged marriages are no longer practised although the daughter can be pressured into accepting the wishes of her parents especially since bride prices represent a considerable amount of money.[17]

Before the marriage ceremony, senior members of the descent group and the bride call forth the ancestors to inform them of the impending ritual and the initiation of the groom into the descent group. The authority of the ancestors resides in the 'maternal grandfather' (*taa*), the spirit of the last male head of the descent group to have passed away. His protection is also sought when daughters are pregnant so that the delivery may be problem-free.[18] The living and the ancestors are both under the authority of the men who have, or have had, the most important position in the descent group.

The actual marriage ceremony commences when the bridegroom's family and followers arrive at the house of the bride. At this point, the members of the female descent group prevent them from entering the compound, and a mock battle takes place, symbolizing, on one level, the reluctance of the male members of a descent group to lose control of a daughter's sexuality to a man from outside the group, and, on another level, the reluctance of a woman to lose her virginity and thus confirming her purity. Marriage can only successfully be achieved if the head of the female descent group establishes authority over the groom, thus gaining a member and reassuring the continuity of the group. The crossing of the descent group 'boundary' creates a temporary, unstable situation which is controlled by ritual acts; this parallels the entrance of the male nature spirit into the village (female) during the rain-making festival.

Once the groom and his family is finally let in and the bride price is formally accepted by the father of the bride, the couple and women from both parties sit around a pair of banana-leaf cones for the actual marriage ritual. A Brahman priest chants verses in both Pali and Lao

---

[17] I recorded no arranged marriages from 1980-91 but before 1950 the majority of marriages were arranged.

[18] This ritual is called *tau cha taa tien*, 'striking a deal with the maternal grandfather using candles'. I have explained this ritual in detail elsewhere (Sparkes 1993a:78-79).

and ties the wrists of the couple together with cotton cord, signifying union. Other cords tie together the garlands on the couple's heads and the cones. As was the case in the rain-making ritual, 'hot' food and alcohol which arouse the passions are force-fed to the couple in preparation for the night when the marriage is consummated. This ritual is an example of evoking sexual feelings but in a controlled ritual context. At the end of the ceremony, the couple are made to bow down in front of a bowl containing offerings of betel and tobacco for the ancestors of the female descent group, symbolizing that they are both under the authority of men in that descent group. The giving of offerings to the ancestors parallels the tribute offered to the various spirits and seeks the approval and protection from the male ancestors of the group. Although a father, and ultimately the ancestors, lose control of the sexuality of his daughter by giving her to another man, they rule over the son-in-law and ultimately his children. In an area, which was until very recently characterized by ample land and a shortage of labour, the acquisition of manpower is important to further one's quest for wealth and land as well as one's status and influence in the community (Ng 1978).

This struggle for control over female fertility between men operates on two levels: the sexual and the social. The father loses control over the sexuality of his daughter but gains control over his son-in-law who will be forced to work for and support the members of that particular female descent group and not his own. The son-in-law gains control over his wife, given the ideology of Buddhism mentioned above, but is on the lowest rung of authority within his wife's descent group.

As in the rain-making festival, the marriage ceremony also includes elements from Buddhism; although the monks are never present, Buddhist texts are chanted by the Brahman priest to consecrate the marriage. These texts are the highest possible form of 'magical power' available to the villagers and are normally recited by monks at Buddhist ceremonies and cremations. Given the goal of the marriage ceremony, that is sexual union, it is remarkable that texts which promote the ideals of renunciation of the material world and celibacy should be used.[19] Isan villagers make use of all means to ensure a successful outcome of the marriage and the continuity of the descent group. Thus

---

[19] The texts are in Pali and incomprehensible to the villagers but, at the same time, villagers associate them with Buddhist rituals and are familiar with the verses that the monks regularly chant on holy days.

the 'magical power' of Buddhist texts can be utilized to evoke female fertility with all its threatening and dangerous associations for men and monks alike. During pregnancy and during the postpartum recovery period of 'lying by the fire', Buddhist texts are also recited by Brahman priests and men who have previously been monks in order to strengthen the 'life essence' of the woman who is undergoing, what is considered, a traumatic experience. Before the introduction of modern medicine and trained midwives and nurses residing in the villages, many women died because of complications during delivery. At such a time a woman needs the protective 'magical power' of Buddhist texts to guarantee her safe recovery. The use of these texts when the woman is considered 'polluted' with bad blood (accumulated menstrual blood) in order to guard her against evil spirits, which are attracted to the smell of that blood, is an example of what Strathern calls 'inversion', a complete shift of reference of the dichotomy of culture vs. nature (1980:183).

Conclusion

The Isan anthropomorphize nature by giving it the characteristics of gender. In doing so maleness and femaleness are idealized as active and passive respectively. Male nature spirits are aggressive, initiate agricultural fertility and then protect it if given appropriate offerings by villagers. All of nature, however, whether male or female, is subordinate to culture in the form of Buddhist ideology. Nature can thus be exploited and at rain-making ceremonies is symbolically 'tamed' under strictly controlled ritual conditions. But nature can never be tamed completely, however, since it is the very powers in nature which create agricultural fertility. The same applies to controlling the fertile powers of women, symbolized by menstrual blood. Men, by means of Buddhist ideology and authority over the female descent groups, attempt to control women's fertility. Yet complete mastery is impossible because of the incest taboo which requires men to relinquish control of daughters and to initiate sons-in-law into the descent group. Just as the forces of nature invade the village at rain-making ceremonies, a crossing of the symbolic boundary between the forest and the village, the compound of the female descent group is invaded by another group (the groom's, an outside male's) temporarily shattering the solidarity of the group. The crossing of boundaries and linking of male and female spirits or descent groups assure agricultural fertilty and human procreation respectively.

Although there are clear dichotomies at work (female vs. male and nature vs. culture), they do not always correspond to Ortner's (1974) earlier notions of universal submission of the female, based on an association between agricultural fertility and female reproductive powers, and male control of the cultural ideology. There is also what Strathern (1980) calls inversion in order to maintain the primary dichotomy of male vs. female. Nature personifed as male spirits is threatening to the social order of the village. Yet the reverse is true when considering female reproductive powers in the form of menstrual blood: female 'nature' threatens the spiritual powers of men and monks, and by implication the social order of the village. This complicated inversion destroys neither the dichotomy of nature vs. culture nor the hierarchy of gender, it merely shifts the terms of reference of nature vs. culture in order to maintain the dichotomy of gender concepts.

References

Achaimbault, Charles. 1975. 'Le Sacrifice du Buffle à l'autel du T'at Luong (Wien Chan)'. *Ethos* 40:114–49.

Bancroft, Anne. 1986. 'Women in Buddhism'. In King, U. (ed.), *Women in the World's Religions, Past and Present*. New York: Paragon House.

Boonsue, Kornvipa. 1989. *Buddhism and Gender Bias: An Analysis of a Jataka Tale*. Women in Development Consortium in Thailand. Bangkok.

Cohen, Paul. (1984) 'Are the Spirit Cults of Northern Thailand Descent Groups?'. *Mankind* 14(4):293–99.

Diemberger, Hildegard. 1993. 'Blood, sperm, soul and the mountain'. In del Valle, T. (ed.), *Gendered Anthropology*. London: Routledge.

Douglas, Mary. 1966. *Purity and Danger*. London: Routledge.

Hafner, James A. and Samroeng Chantrasuwan. 1985. *Rural-Rural Migration to the Loei Uplands in the Northeast Region of Thailand*. Bangkok: Department of Social Science, Khon Kaen University.

Hastrup, Kirsten. 1993. 'The Semantics of Biology: Virginity'. In Ardener, S. (ed.), *Defining Females: The Nature of Women in Society*. Oxford: Berg Publishers.

Irvine, Walter. 1984. 'Decline of Village Spirit Cults and the Growth of Urban Spirit Mediumship: the Persistence of Spirit Beliefs, the Position of Women and Modernization'. *Mankind* 14(4):315–24.

Kabilsingh, Chatsumarn. 1988. 'Menstruation: Buddhist Perspective'. *Buddhist Perspective Newsletter on International Buddhist Women's Activities*, No.15, Bangkok.

Keyes, Charles. 1975. 'Kin Groups in a Thai-Lao Community'. In Skinner, W. and T. Kirsch (eds.), *Change and Persistence in Thai Society*. Ithaca, N.Y.: Cornell University Press.

—— 1984. 'Mother or Mistress but never a Monk: Buddhist Notions of Female Gender in Rural Thailand'. *American Ethnologist* 11:223–41.

Kirsch, A. Thomas. 1977. 'Complexity in the Thai Religious System'. *The Journal of Asian Studies* 36(2):241–66.

Leach, Edmund. 1968. 'Introduction'. In Leach, E. (ed.), *Dialectic of Practical Religion*. Cambridge: Cambridge University Press.

Lévi-Strauss, Claude. 1963. 'Structural Analysis in Linguistics and in Anthropology', in *Structural Anthropology* 1, Norwich: Penguin Books Ltd.

—— 1969. *The Elementary Structures of Kinship*. Boston: Beacon Press.

Mizumo, Koichi. 1968. 'Multihousehold Compounds in Northeast Thailand'. In *Asia Survey*. Institute of International Studies. University of California.

Mougne, Christine. 1984. 'Women, Fertility and Power in Northern Thailand'. In *Customs and Tradition: The Role of Thai Women*. Bangkok: Thai Study Program. Chulalongkorn University.

Ng R. 1979. 'Man and Land in Northeast Thailand'. In Stott, P.A. (ed.), *Nature and Man in South East Asia*. London: School of Oriental and African Studies.

Ortner, Sherry B. 1974. 'Is Female to Male as Nature is to Culture'. In Rosaldo, M. Z. and L. Lamphere (eds), *Woman, Culture and Society*. Stanford: Stanford University Press.

Ortner, Sherry B. and Harriet Whitehead. 1981. 'Introduction: Accounting for Sexual Meanings'. In Ortner, S.B. and H. Whitehead (eds), *Sexual Meanings*. Cambridge: Cambridge University Press.

Phinthong, Preecha. 1989. *Isan-Thai-English Dictionary*. Ubon: Sirithan Press.

Rajadhon, Phya Anuman. 1986. *Popular Buddhism in Siam and Other Essays on Thai Culture*. Bangkok: Suksit Siam.

—— 1987. *Some Traditions of the Thai*. Bangkok: Thai Inter-Religious Commission for Development and Sathirakoses Nagapradipa Foundation.

Smith, Kendra. 1986. 'Sex, Dependency, and Religion: Reflections from a Buddhist Perspecitive'. In King, U. (ed.), *Women in the World's Religions, Past and Present*. New York: Paragon House.

Sparkes, Stephen. 1993a. *Gender and Cosmology in an Isan Village in Northeast Thailand*. Social Anthropology Hovedfag thesis. University of Oslo, Norway.

—— 1993b. 'Buddhism and Rain-making Rituals in a Northeast Thai Village'. Paper presented at the 5th International Conference on Thai Studies. London: School of Oriental and African Studies.

Strong, John S. 1992. *The Legend and Cult of Upagupta: Sanskrit Buddhism in North India and Southeast Asia*. Princeton: Princeton University Press.

Stott, P. A. 1978. 'Nous avons mangé la forêt: Environmental perception and conservation in mainland South East Asia'. In Stott, P.A. (ed.) *Nature and Man in South East Asia*. London: School of Oriental and African Studies.

Strathern, Marilyn. 1980. 'No Culture, No Nature: the Hagen Case'. In MacCormack, C. and M. Strathern (eds), *Nature, Culture and Gender*. Cambridge: Cambridge University Press.

Tambiah, S.J. 1970. *Buddhism and Spirit Cults of North-east Thailand*. Cambridge: Cambridge University Press.

Terwiel, B.J. 'Leasing from the Gods'. *Anthropos* 71:254–74

—— 1979. *Monks and Magic: An Analysis of Religious Ceremonies in Central Thailand*. London: Curzon Press.

—— 1982. 'Buddhism: the Villagers' Perspective'. *South East Asian Review*. 7(1/2):87–96.

Textor, Robert. 1960. *An Inventory of Non-Buddhist Supernatural Objects in a Central Thai Village.* Ph.D. Thesis, Cornell University. Ann Arbor Microfilm, 1960.

Valeri, Valerio. 1983. 'Both Nature and Culture: Reflections on Menstrual and Parturitional Taboos in Huaulu (Seram)'. In Errington, S. and J. Atkinson (eds), *Power and Difference: Gender in Island Southeast Asia.* Stanford: Stanford University Press.

Van Esterik, Penny. 1982. 'Interpreting a Cosmology: Guardian Spirits in Thai Buddhism'. *Anthropos* 77(5/6):1–15.

Wijeyewardene, Gehan. 1984. 'Northern Thai Succession and the Search for Matriliny'. *Mankind* 14(4):286–92.

Graham E. Clarke

Thinking through Nature in Highland Nepal

This paper is an account of populist ways of thinking through images of nature in highland Nepal. By highland Nepal I am referring more particularly to the northern central Himalaya of Nepal, and the peoples of Sindhu Palchok and Dolakha districts.[1] The focus is not directly with people's perception of nature or the environment as a thing in itself, but with indigenous images and models of the natural environment as used in an understanding of other people, life and society. Though the Himalaya contains a great deal of patterned variation in social and cultural, as well as biological, features, such spatial and temporal variation is not a feature of this paper. On the contrary, it is the uniform experience of hierarchical linkages to the state, and their common cultural expression in Nepalese, the *lingua franca*, that form the key feature to the social context.

Though the examples come from these two districts alone, and as a sample may even be biased to the more remote parts of this region, I do not think that other such highland Himalayan areas of Nepal, whether traditionally Hindu or Buddhist, would be that different. There is also a general, but not an exclusive, sense in which the ideas presented are true throughout Nepal as a whole; and in that rural life in Nepal is similar to that in other rural Himalayan areas, and has close points of correspondence with that of people who live on the land in adjacent regions, the analysis may have a more general significance.

The account focuses on the indigenous understanding of plants and the use of land in agriculture as models for politics and society. The discussion uses examples, abstractions of images and metaphors from routine, daily comments and discussions of the local people, and

---

[1] I first carried out intensive fieldwork in a part of that area known as Yolmo or Helambu between 1974 and 1976, and worked subsequently more widely in the area in 1982, and in 1985, 1986 and 1987. Much of the ethnographic material used here is taken *verbatim* from conversations during campaigns for the local village and district elections in 1985 and 1986.

indicates how ideas of the natural environment are extended outwards and used as general models of life, of the reasons for success and failure.

Western anthropological and other cultural and historical analyses indicate how biological universals may be taken by societies as models, both for external nature and cultural domains. For example, the body may be used as a basic metaphor for bilateral symbolism, and in representing the division between 'right and left' may come to stand for other parallel divisions such as 'day and night', and for the abstract moral distinction between 'good and bad' (Needham 1973). In South Asian tradition the body can also represent a holistic model of the overall social hierarchy, that is in the Vedic or Hindu idea that the four-fold categories of caste (*varna*) originated from the primordial cosmic man, who was sacrificed at the beginning of creation: the mouth became the priest (*Brahmin*), the arms the warrior (*Kshatriya*), the thighs the merchant (*Vaishya*), and the feet the outcaste (*Sudra*).

In terms of a Durkheimean 'total classification' one would not expect a distinction between models of the environment and of other domains: in this sense there is only 'general theory' (Durkheim and Mauss 1963). The separation of knowledge into disciplines each with their own distinct bodies of theoretical knowledge is largely a western, post-Enlightenment development in the history of ideas. *A priori*, one would expect the more 'primitive' in the sense of historically prior features, such as the human body and relations to the world of nature, to form a symbolic model for the understanding of these other, subsequently elaborated, domains, such as the political and economic (Dumont 1977).

All the same, structural anthropological theory has taken the conceptual distinction between 'nature' and 'culture' as a more general feature of human modes of knowing (Levi-Strauss 1962). In South Asia the clearest representation of this contrast, if it exists in empirical form at all, is not to be found within the pre-literate world in itself, but in the distinction between populist, natural models and the codified literate worlds of the 'Great Religions', of Buddhism and Hinduism. Yet in practice such an opposition between, for example, the illiterate world of spirit-mediums controlling nature and spirits by magic and exorcism by night, and that of literate priests operating through ethics and the religious word by day, for all that it conveys a truth, is an over-simple and misleading dichotomy.

In accounts of symbolism in South Asian literature there has been a close concern with the relation of local ideas to these wider, overarching, Great Religions. Concern with the textual base of the Great

Religions has, quite correctly, acted as a corrective to over-simplified, non-historical, structuralist, analyses.[2] At the same time, in terms of overall balance, the concern may have obscured the full, contextual understanding of these indigenous schemata. Accounts of the natural world of the farmer extended outwards from his everyday life may be a relatively neglected area of ethnographic analysis.

In practice, in the social world of highland villages of Nepal, there are ceremonies that specifically link the worlds of nature and culture.[3] For example, in a highland Buddhist village of northern central Nepal dance ceremonies always led on smoothly from the recitation of textual religious precepts. Often, one of the first dances started with the following origin myth recited in song:

> If it were not for the sky and mountains there could be no clouds,
> If it were not for the clouds there could be no rain,
> If it were not for the rain there could be no streams,
> If it were not for the streams there could be no grass (crops),
> If it were not for the crops there could be no livestock (produce),
> If it were not for the produce there could be no village
> If it were not for the village then we, people, could not be here.

The dependency of the world of man on that of nature here is clear. In this example, however, the thought is stylised and prescribed, whereas our main concern here is on the use of the informal ideas of nature rather than any such fixed, collective, representations. The actual inter-relationships here are complex, and though in a historical (and possibly an empirical) sense these may be only part systems, such popular or vernacular cultural schemes are the ideas through which the mass of the population habitually thinks and have a direct psychological and social salience. Primarily, this is an account of the ways of explaining and arguing of people in this region who are Buddhist or Hindu, rather than the cultural representations of these Great Religions in themselves.

For reasons of presentation, these ideas are given in an idealised

---

[2] The historical link of northern Sindhu Palchok to the higher Buddhist tradition and state has been dealt with elsewhere (e.g., Clarke 1983, 1985, 1990, 1991).

[3] Healing rites and sacred journeys, for example, combine aspects of both worlds (Desjarlais 1992), and religious exorcisms specifically purify by combining ethics and action.

form, that is a system of logic that illustrates a unitary whole. In practice, of course, the empirical order is more fragmented and neither natural metaphors nor the literate ideologies of the Great Religions are the sole mode of thought available to individuals in these regions. There is also, of course, the ideology of economic modernity, with all the attendant rhetoric of development and progress. In that modernity implies culture contact and change, one key feature of modern ideology is that it embodies doubt and half-truths, rather than certainty and absolutism. Choice and individualism do not reinforce any such absolute perception, and the contrast between the traditional notion of change as distortion from the ideal or a heresy, and the modern notion of change as progress or development, is a striking change in perspective.

The dominant world-view presented here, then, though it touches on both, is not the collective world-view of economic progress and modernity, nor that of the traditional Great Religions of Asia. Rather it is a world, possibly much like our own routine, vernacular world, in which individuals think through their own daily experience using metaphor and allusions from popular culture.

Natural models of the political order

Conscious, popular thought and reflection in Nepal concerns not so much ideals or morality *per se*, as explanations of daily experience and activity, the variation in success and failure of various enterprises, individuals and groups. On a day-to-day basis, the principal such model available to farming peoples is that of biological, and in particular of agricultural processes, which are applied to individuals, politics and development as to many other domains.

One common example is the way in which people may be likened in characteristics to various types of animals, such as bears, foxes and monkeys. Another equally common idiom is the extension of biological terms beyond their literal sense, such as the use of 'to plant' as a common metaphor for to sow the seeds of a course of action. An illustration would be the farmer who, when asked who he was going to vote for in an election, replied as follows:

> When we plant seeds we may be sure that we will get some fruit; but will that fruit be sour or sweet? We have to wait and see.

Such 'folk wisdom' is deep in a number of ways. It embodies a modern virtue of empiricism, that is an open-mindedness, even a scepticism. We, too, use such terms metaphorically in speech, one difference being that we are not dominated by them. Given the wide variety of frameworks available in modern western thought, and the institutionalised and written basis to knowledge, their use for us does not have the same total salience or validity as in a non-literate society. When we use them it is as a momentary motif, one that may conjure up a rustic folk wisdom, be seen even as a conscious, contrived, archaism. Yet in Nepal, outside of the central towns, such ideas are more the norm and do not in themselves indicate a residual 'folk' imagery.

In rural Nepal today, such natural metaphors are commonly applied to economic, bureaucratic and political processes. In the above example the reply had such a directed goal: the context for the speaker was an election, and in electoral campaigns the cultural norm is for a promise of material assistance against promises of votes; the speaker was himself signalling openness to such an offer, and wished for a signal that this was indeed the context so that the transaction could proceed.

The context to such use of metaphor is implicit, and rarely signalled overtly in everyday speech,[4] and would be used by a speaker without him possessing any special skill in oral debate, or even literacy. Natural metaphors can be used in a highly sophisticated and creative manner by farmers. For example, one elaborate biological analogy for political activity came from a ward representative: he was non-literate, and not himself a candidate in that election, and was chatting over how local political activists came together to discuss things in asides at electoral time:

> If a tree can changes its leaves every year then why shouldn't we change a candidate once every five years? [The difference is that] leaves come down one after another, and fall at their right time from on high without making any noise; but when they [the old politicians] come down, there is a noise, because each is cursing the one following them, the large ones (of yesterday) say to the small buds (of today): today it is my turn, so I fall down, saying, "tomorrow it will be *your* turn": *that* is why there is all that whispering during an election.

---

[4] The rapid switches between directly literal and allusive use of language can render problems in comprehension, even for urban Nepalese.

This natural language has an implicit model of process, and provides a clear model of growth and decline. The idiom does not in itself specify any such transaction, but is the habitual model in terms of which any such exchange is thought through and legitimised. As such, it may direct habitual thought and predispose certain associations, as indicated in the following example:

> Those two have been exploiting and pressing-down on the people: it is all very well for those who have taken [literally eaten] thousands and thousands [of rupees], but how about for those who have not even received tuppence?

The term 'eaten', (*kannu*), has a wide application in Nepalese and can be used for the consumption of almost any material.[5] Material success here is seen in terms of feeding and growth to the extent that the term can sometimes be best translated as 'to consume' or 'to use up' rather than to eat; the extension to other domains is so normal that it has no necessary association to foodstuffs. Yet the underlying model is still biological and cyclical: as a baby suckles milk at the breast of its mother to grow, so to grow in political stature a candidate also has to eat.

'Milking the system' is one such expression that we still use in the West, but in highland Nepal the notion of milking of all processes is commonplace and has no negative moral connotation: that which in the West connotes corruption and immorality would here be seen as normal and natural. Moreover, this metaphor of milking and imbibing as a natural path for growth is extended to mechanical areas, where in an industrial society it may appear not so much immoral as technically inappropriate and dangerous. For example, a helicopter stopped regularly in one village. One day the pilot allowed the members of the household where he was taking tea to take kerosene from the fuel tank. This was done by pressing the fuel-dumping stopcock on the 'belly' of the helicopter, and the villagers later referred to this as 'milking the bird'. When next the helicopter came, the villagers gave him tea, and many households sent a member down to 'milk the bird'. The idea that a 'bird' might need to 'eat' all its own 'milk' to fly home did not enter such a pattern of thought, and the course of action nearly led to the

---

[5] 'To eat' (*kannu*) cannot, however, be used for the sonsumption of alcohol.

emptying of the fuel tank, and so possibly to disaster.[6]

Such biological images of production carry over to success in secular activity. A region that has received assistance for economic development may be referred to in pastoral images of abundance such as an area 'flowing with milk and honey'. To us the idiom appears merely as biblical, but to the farmer the idea of a reciprocal or direct return of the produce to the cultivator is almost a reflex of thought. Overall, politicians redirect and redistribute the wealth, or 'fruit', to those who are their supporters. The dominant model of statecraft here is not the disinterested technocrat, allocating goods and factors of production according to Benthamite utilitarian procedures to where they will produce the greatest good for the greatest number; rather it is a natural model of growth through feeding, with redistribution of fruit through processes like 'milking', conducted on the basis of personal relations.

The model also provides an explanation for failure and the lack of material fortune. As has been commented a number of times in the general anthropological literature, notions of impersonal or abstract forces or statistical chance are rarely seen as a sufficient explanation for individual events, and those close by, in particular outsiders who are present or those from one's own community, are likely to be seen as causal agents (Evans-Pritchard 1937). An explanation of good or bad fortune may take an abstract or supernatural form, as in magic and witchcraft; here it is viewed more prosaically as an immoral capturing or redirection of natural processes, as a personal agency responsible for the absence of the conditions for germination and growth.

For example, the following are comments from discussions on why no development assistance had come to a village:

> And why are we oppressed in this way today? We are pressed down, aren't we? And what is that has pressed us down? Is it the earth? Is it the sky? Or is it people who have pressed us down? Let us have a look at this too!

> Some say "just wait, and I will do something for you". Yes, some of our friends and brothers are like that; but later they say, "Oh, brother, I can't do it now". And in the future, this same person may take a knife to us,

---

[6] This idea of 'milking the bird' had combined with a village notion of equity and reciprocal exchange in hospitality; the draining of the tank was halted only by the pilot running out screaming and waving his arms to disperse the crowd, who then regarded him as unstable or slightly mad.

throw rocks at us, or knock our house down. The types who speak like that are our friends and brothers too!

The terms 'press-down' and 'oppression' appear to us as a colourful and extreme idiom. Though an etymological link between the English concepts 'to press down' and 'oppression' is obvious enough, this association is not at the forefront of modern English usage in which the normal idiom would be one of having been 'held-back'. Again, the Nepalese expression derives from the habitual associations of the idiom of thought, based on agricultural conditions of growth in which a plant that has been planted or pressed down too far will not germinate, will not rise up and grow, will not flower or bear fruit.

There is a contrast and complementarity here, and explanations of success and failure circle around stories of who has 'risen up' and of who has 'pressed one down'.[7] 'To rise-up' (*utnu*) is the opposite of 'to force down' (*thicnu*), and has a complex of senses as in 'to wake-up', 'to be alert', 'to germinate', 'to come alive', 'to rise in position', and 'to stand-up' both literally and 'to stand' for office in an election. The term is also used in the sense of to 'wake-up':[8] to say that someone has 'woken-up' is to liken them to a seed that has germinated and is growing; by contrast, a person who is 'pressed down' is the opposite, like a seed that is dormant and does not germinate.

This particular pair of 'rise-up' and 'press down' illustrates the way in which vernacular speech follows such complementary ideas. Such pairing and complementarity is normal, and other relevant pairs here are 'up and down', 'big and small', 'give and take', 'to eat and dry-out'.[9] In most cases, the one term corresponds to high rank and status and forms the positive, dominant, term of a contrast, and there is an inferior complement; meaning coming from the contrast between the two.

---

[7] To press down, *dabāunu* or *thicnu*.

[8] Wake-up has the same sense as used in the US political slogan 'Wake-up America'.

[9] In southern Tibetan and a Tibeto-Burman language of the locality (Kagāte), abstract concepts may be formed through the pairing of such contrasting concrete terms: for example, 'height' may derive from the conjunct 'up-down'. For a wider discussion of the social meaning of the pairs 'up and down' and 'high and low', see Clarke 1985.

In these ideas, it is natural for a politician on the way up in his career to be fed, that is to receive material gain and the rewards that allow him to acquire more power and grow further, to 'give and take'[10] and become a 'big man'. This is a cyclical and finite process. One is fed, one swells up, rises and grows and bears fruit; but in this virtuous cycle, ultimately, as in the example of the leaf above, one declines.

There is a converse pathway to this virtuous, natural, cycle of growth that comes from being fed and eating, namely one of decay and desiccation from the beginning, that is of being 'dried out' (*sukeko*), rather than bearing fruit. Here the terms to 'dry-out' and 'pressed-down' are associated. For example, crops that have not been watered are termed *sukeko*, and a child who is stunted in growth is termed *sukeko*.

There is also a close association between *sukeko* and the term for non-irrigated or 'dry' land, *pakho*. *Pakho* has the multiple senses of land left at the side, land on a hill-side, and land which is barren, which all usually are linked characteristics of marginal land in highland Nepal; *pakho* contrasts to the rich, irrigated, flatter land at the valley-floor (*khet* or *bari*) which bears abundant crops. Most significantly, the term *pakho* is also used for *the people* who live on such dry land on the side: hence the sense of simple and rough, and backward and undeveloped, that attaches to people from poor, dried-out, hill-land, who can be known simply as *pakhey*. A gloss as 'hillbilly' conveys some of these associations, but not the idea of stunted natural development.

It is not only that those who have germinated and who are growing can be contrasted to those who have failed to grow and have dried out. As the language of kin, neighbour and community suggests, the functional link between the two can also be understood in terms of natural processes. This is especially the case if the two are physically close to each other. A large tree will have an extensive root system that draws off all the water from below, and a full canopy that prevents sunlight reaching down from above, and so keep other plants and especially those of the same kind dry and cold, so that they do not grow. In the same way, the rise into power of one relative, neighbour or an adjacent community is thought to explain why others close by do not develop.

To this way of thinking, the proximity of one's own kind can be a bad thing, can be a precondition for damage. Hence the commonplace in rural Nepal of the assertion that those close by, such as brothers,

---

[10] 'Give and take', or literally 'take and give' (*linu-dinu*).

neighbours, have kept one 'pressed down', have taken that which one needs. As it is with individuals and households, so it is with communities, and here a failure to receive material benefits from the state will often be seen as the result of the success of a community close by.

For a person or community to be so dried out and 'exploited' (that is *sosak samanthe*), is the complement and opposite to another enjoying him or themselves with material pleasures, 'imbibing goods', (that is *moj garnu*). There is an opposition, a complementarity, in the linkage between neighbours in this model of biological development, which forms an implicit, concrete model, both of structure and of the processes of a progressive social differentiation.

Religion and power

Many complaints about development assistance are couched in this manner, namely that one group has 'eaten everything', from the moral standpoint of 'equality' and fairness. There is an emphasis on the importance of equality and redistribution in social relations that cannot easily be stated in images of nature, that is of a cultural corrective to this natural tendency to inequality.[11] This is contained in the domains of religion, of the 'proper order', that is of *dharma*. Ideally, here, the state should follow the model of the good farmer, and should not leave any areas of land barren, and un-watered on the side, any peoples unassisted and undeveloped in the hills.

As a whole, the biological model may be seen to contrast to such a religious model which presents an 'other-worldly' alternative.[12] Other-worldliness is linked to ascetic ideas which, though obviously not part of the daily routine of a householder, are readily accessible in Nepalese and South Asian culture as an institutional whole.[13] In the popular understanding such power comes from a denial or a renunciation of consumption, with images of self-mortification, pilgrimage, and Buddha

---

[11] Communities with a cultural focus on hierarchy, such as Hindu villages, may have a notion of justness other than that of strict equality.

[12] This also contrasts strongly with some technical western notions of economic development, in which a critical mass of assistance to one single location may be seen as a precondition to change.

[13] Power from retreat and isolation, that is the power of the world-renouncer, is an important concept equally for the Buddhist virtuoso and the Saivite ascetic.

fasting to enlightenment under a tree. The term 'self-development' is used here quite literally, and though there is a double-meaning now, in the primary sense this is seen to come through abstinence. This stands outside the life-cycle of rise and decline and the power here comes not from consumption and growth but from the reverse. Even so, in popular rendition this strength is often perceived through natural metaphor, and may be likened to the walnut, the shell of which is wrinkled and dried out but tough and strong.

In a simplified sense, in exchange and civil action, the prime idea is that of the disinterested or pure gift, a prestation made without thought of return (*dhan*).[14] The authority to act and intervene publicly itself comes from a collective recognition of moral purity and selflessness of the individual, rather than from worldly office. The power of religious purity, like that of the forest monk, comes from a divestment of the material possessions of this world, of formal office or the holding of goods. Such use engenders a contradiction, as 'this-worldly' power comes from an 'other-worldly' attitude; once the worldly-path is returned to there is a necessary decline, as some 'contamination' with this world, decay, and hence reduction of purity and power to act, must necessarily follow. To become engaged is to enter a cycle that ultimately results in mortal decline. Overall, the notion of purity and sacred power contrasts to that of secular or worldly power, the one as transcendent and timeless, the other as a mortal cycle of life and death.[15]

Development itself (*bikās*), is often seen as a gift from above, an expression of support through personal and state patronage, rather than as the result of one's own efforts.[16] There may be a public ideology of purity and disinterested action, that is of assistance in what we can term the public service model of Gandhi, which derives directly from Asian models of abstinence and renunciation. But in practice there is usually an underlying idea of direct return by at least one of the parties to any

---

[14] These ideas of renunciation (*tapas*), pure thoughts (*swaccha bhāvanā*), the disinterested gift (*yogdhan*) and assistance and help (*sahayog*) are part of the same complex.

[15] This albeit stereotypical contrast helps explain one other focus in popular political discourse, at the time of elections, which can give greater significance than is empirically reasonable to reports of death and killing, with the idiom of 'to eat bullets'.

[16] 'Development (*bikās*) in Nepal: Mana from Heaven', manuscript under preparation.

such transaction, that is a 'biological' model of investment, even if the minimal expectation is of the exchange of material for continued political support in the civil arena. Notions of purity of intent and selfless conduct appear more prescriptive in bureaucratic areas, when there is no link to resource allocation.

The idea of disinterested action rarely applies directly at a local level in practices that affect natural resources and farming. This is reasonable enough: one farms to obtain returns for oneself rather than just casts seeds into the wind. Even in community forestry programmes, better results are achieved through providing seedlings from a nursery for planting on private land, and in helping to provide clear private rights to land, than in trying to encourage planting on purely public land.

All the same, there are certain models that occasionally come to the fore, especially among Buddhist communities, that imply that respect for life is a public value. The popular Buddhist soteriology in which killing is proscribed is used to back up the decision not to use pesticides on apple trees; but this should not be thought to exclude a 'rational choice'/material self-interest explanation at the same time. The same Buddhist people are not averse to eating meat, only to killing animals, and it is routine to maintain a milk herd of yak crossbreeds by keeping young male calves away from the mother, so that they die 'naturally'. As with ourselves, there are many legalistic ways through moral dilemmas, and one must be careful not to take single-dimensional, ideological statements as sufficient explanations of cultural practices.

At the same time, the 'line' of decisions shifts culturally. For example, I recall men who customarily left leeches on their feet, to have their fill of blood, before dropping-off 'naturally'. Our cultural classifications, such as in extending the terms 'pest', 'vermin' and 'weed' to plants and animals we do not like, objectify, as do our more abstract concepts such as 'labour', to our humanity itself. The cultural classifications and soteriology of popular Buddhism tend to extend sentience outwards into the animal world, and people can have the same moral dilemmas over insects and leeches as do we over foxes and deer.

Further conclusions

In popular thought, ideas of consumption and growth taken from nature and agriculture, as well as ideas of power from religious renunciation, are used to explain politics and development. Ideas of religious power through purity depend for their popular efficacy on the contrast to the prior natural modes of thought of the householder. In the wider arena, in Nepalese thought, both these two, commonly available models may combine in complex ways.

The codes of Great Religions, like all ideologies, do not in themselves specify habitual modes of thought, or even the customary ways of thinking of the members of a hereditary priesthood away from certain public or ceremonial occasions. However, they are accessible in the cultural complex as a whole, and, standing in contrast to natural images, help to define them. In their *praxis*, these ideologies are transformed and contained by local modes of thought; they in their turn provide over-arching codified systems, often linked to state institutions, that re-interpret, and so contain and reduce parochial local beliefs against their more elaborate standards.

Certainly, the Great Religions are one pole to life that consists of a redefinition of nature, a traditional encompassing 'culture' that could be opposed at some level of analysis to a more 'primitive' pole of 'nature'. Yet one equally salient and primary fact is the ethnographic context, the social context of routine, which contains and can transform the sense of these literate cultures in manifold ways. It is not that these two ways of perceiving exist alongside each other on separate tracks, or that the one subsumes the other. Popular patterns of thought interact with, contrast to and also incorporate in a transformed manner, parts of these traditional ideologies that in context and implication they overlap with. They also do the same to modern economic ideology.[17]

The main account given here has been one of populist perceptions, the everyday logic among farming communities, the ways of thinking and arguing of people who are Buddhist or Hindu, in their everyday lives. Here a natural, developmental cycle of growth through feeding, of the production of fruit, that is reproduction, and of natural aging and decline, that is decay, has been outlined. In describing these perceptions as 'natural' no simple dichotomy with 'culture' has been intended. If anything, the populist model of nature on which we have focused is the reverse, a form in which nature itself is taken as the model for culture, which is viewed as an aspect of nature. Yet that people should habitually perceive and argue from what they know on a daily basis,

---

[17] This is the sense in which the terms 'Little Tradition' and 'Great Tradition' were proposed by Redfield (1955).

that is the natural processes that link land, animals and people, to more abstract ideas of society, including the state and economic activity, is not in itself surprising.

This position is distinct to that of western phenomenology, or a High Buddhist theology in which all is an aspect of 'mind' or 'nothingness', as it is from a medium-level Buddhist theology or western Judaeo-Christian thought, both of which separate the worlds of the animate from the inanimate. In the same way as the Darwinist evolutionary theory of western, educated, scientific circles in the nineteenth century extended the world of nature backwards to incorporate the world of man, this popular model views the human and social worlds as an extension of the same processes and cycles as those of the natural worlds, and hence itself as 'natural'.[18]

References

Allen, N. J. 1981. 'Towards a Compararative Mythology of the Bodic Speakers'. In Aris, M. and A.S.S. Kyi (eds), *Tibetan Studies in Honour of Hugh Richardson*. Warminster: Aris and Philips.

Clarke, Graham E. 1983. 'The Great and Little Traditions in the Study of Yolmo, Nepal'. In Steinkellner, E. and H. Tauscher (eds), 'Contributions on Tibetan Language, History & Culture'. (The Proceedings of the Csoma de Körös Symposium held at Velm-Vienna, Austria, 1981), Vienna: *Wiener Studien zur Tibetologie und Buddhismuskunde*, Heft 10.

—— 1985. 'Equality and Hierarchy Among a Buddhist People of Nepal'. In Barnes, R. and D. de Coppet (eds), *Context and Levels: Anthropological Essays on Hierarchy*. Oxford: JASO.

—— 1990. 'Ideas of Merit (*bsod-nams*), virtue (*dge-ba*), blessing (*byin-rlabs*) and material prosperity (*rten-'brel*) in Highland Nepal'. *Journal of the Anthropological Society of Oxford* 21(2):165–84.

---

[18] Of course, one further epistemological position common to western and eastern philosophy is that any such 'natural' perception in itself necessarily embodies a prior conceptualisation of the natural process, that is the pre-existence of 'culture' or 'mind'.

—— 1991. 'Nara (*na-rag*) in Yolmo: A Social History of Hell in Helambu'. In Steinkellner, E. (ed.) 'Tibetan History and Language' (Studies dedicated to Uray Géza). Vienna: *Wiener Studien zur Tibetologie und Buddhismuskunde*, Heft 26.

—— 1993. 'Development in Nepal: Mana from Heaven'. In Karmay, S.G. and P. Sagant (eds), *Festschrift pour Alexander W. MacDonald*. Paris: laboratoire d'ethnologie et de sociologie comparative, Université de Paris-X, Nanterre.

—— 1994. (forthcoming) *Collected Essays of Yolmo*. Kathmandu: Bibliotheca Himalayica. Ratna, Pustak and Bhandar.

Desjarlais, R.R. 1992. *Body and Emotion*. Philadelphia: University Press.

Dumont, L. 1977. *From Mandeville to Marx: The Genesis and Triumph of Economic Ideology*. Chicago: University Press.

Durkheim, Emile and Marcel Mauss. 1963. *Primitive Classification*. London: Cohen and West. (Transl. R. Needham.)

Evans-Pritchard, E. E. 1937. *Witchcraft, Oracles and Magic among the Azande*. Oxford: University Press.

Levi-Strauss, Claude. 1962. *La Pensée Sauvage*. Paris: Librairie Plon.

Needham, Rodney (ed). 1973. *Right and Left: Essays on Dual Symbolic Classification*. Chicago: University Press.

Redfield, R. 1955. 'The Social Organisation of Tradition'. *Far Eastern Quarterly* 15(1):13–21.

Are Knudsen

State Intervention and Community Protest
Nature Conservation in Hunza, North Pakistan

There has recently been a growing interest in common property regimes and systems of local resource management (Berkes 1989; Bromley 1991, 1992; McCay and Acheson 1987; Ostrom 1990). This paper is particularly concerned with situations where property rights are contested and the implications of this for a legitimate change in property regime. Specifically, can natural resource management be sustainable in a situation where there are contesting claims to ownership and dispute over legitimacy?

To highlight such management problems in the Greater Himalaya, three case studies from Pakistan's Hunza valley are compared (Map 1). They show varied community responses to the state's appropriation and exploitation of wildlife and forest resources from 1974 onward. It is argued that the state has failed to ensure an equitable exploitation of natural resources, a fact that has been aggravated by a legitimacy problem *vis-à-vis* the local communities. The state has neither been able to manage Hunza's resources, nor to establish an institutional framework that could bridge the gap the change from private to state property regimes represented (Bromley and Cernea 1989:11ff.). Hence, this paper argues for an empowerment of local communities through granting informal property rights comparable legal status as formal rights vested with the state (Pinkerton 1987).[1] Complementing a study of perceptions of 'Nature', the paper proposes a theoretical focus on ownership to natural resources, which is critical to understanding local resource management and responses to state intervention.

---

[1] She defines 'informal property rights' as 'the ability or power of communities to exercise their collective will in resource management, an ability unrecognized by law' (Pinkerton 1987:345).

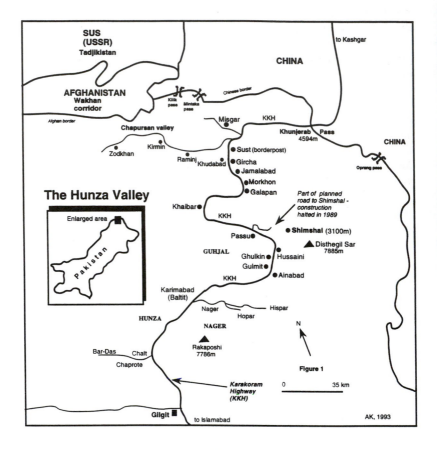

Map 1: The Location of Hunza Valley

Historical setting

The Hunza valley is a beautiful place. In the summer when the tall poplar trees and green fields are set against majestic mountains and brilliant white snow, Hunza gives the impression of being a Shangri-La. It is understandable that the first travellers believed that this was an appropriate setting for good health, vigour and longevity (Rovillè 1988:159). Since the turn of the century and until today, a stream of travel literature offers such a romantic, even 'Orientalist' (Said 1979; Street 1990) view of Hunza.[2] The Hunza valley, as well as the region itself, is characterized by a profound ethnic, linguistic and religious variation. Four different ethnic groups – Burusho, Shin, Wakhi and Dom and two Shia sects, Ismaili and Twelver Shia – contribute to Hunza's striking plurality (Ali 1983:14).

Under Hunza's unblemished facade, there are dark images of a long and troubled past. The Hunza peasant was at the bottom of a rigidly stratified feudal system. The king (*Mir, Tham*) and princely lineages were sustained through the extraction of surplus production as tax (*ilban*) and the conscription of corvée labour (*rajaaki*), causing recurrent spring famine among the commoners (Allan 1990).

Cutting through the Western Karakoram into Chinese Turkestan (now Xinjiang province), the Hunza valley was strategically important to the British who competed with Tsarist Russia for hegemony in inner Asia in the so-called 'Great Game' (Hopkirk 1990). In 1891 a short conflict between the British Garrison in Gilgit forced the two Mirs to accept British suzerainty. When British rule ended in 1947, the Mir of Hunza acceded to Pakistan. Little changed until 1972, when the Mir of Hunza's feudal estate was nationalized. Two years later, in 1974, the Hunza kingdom was formally abolished by the then Prime Minister Zulfiqar Ali Bhutto. At the same time, the 'Gilgit Agency' as the area was called under British rule, became the Northern Areas (NA).[3] After his removal, Mir Mohammad Jamal Khan, the last Mir of Hunza, was given state pension until he died in 1976. The much less popular Mir of Nagar, Mir Shaukat Ali Khan, across the river from Hunza, had been shaken by a popular uprising in 1971 and was unseated in 1972 (Dani 1988). As we shall see later, however, the feudal structures have reasserted themselves to a considerable degree.

Until 1974 nature exploitation was regulated by the Mir, and animals such as the Himalayan brown bear and the snow leopard were shot only by the Mir and his family (Dani 1988:258). The people of Hunza were only allowed to cut firewood for their own use. To cut logs for house construction, a special permission from the Mir was needed.

---

[2] Scholarly contributions include works by geographers (Kreutzmann 1989; Paffen *et al.* 1956; Visser and Visser-Hoft 1935-40), anthropologists (Ali 1983; Dani 1988), colonial agents (Biddulph 1880; Durand 1899) and travellers (Shipton 1990; Staley 1969).

[3] A list of all abbreviations used is found at the end of the paper.

With the abolition of the Hunza and Nagar kingdoms, an effective, though repressive, control of forest and wildlife resources vanished as well. The power vacuum following the integration with Pakistan meant that for some years natural resources lacked clear ownership, leading to uncontrolled exploitation.

Contemporary Hunza

Since the late 1940s, a dirt road crossing the notorius Babusar Pass linked the NA with Pakistani Punjab. In 1959, it was replaced by the Indus Valley Road (Kreutzmann 1991). The modern age, however, first dawned on the NA with the joint Pakistan-China road project, the Karakoram Friendship Highway, better known as the Karakoram Highway (KKH). Completed through Hunza in 1978, the construction damaged much of the local forest, since wood was needed to heat the tar (Dani et al. 1987). The KKH was formally opened for civil traffic in 1982 and finally also for foreigners in 1986, which led to a rapid expansion of tourist facilities (Allan 1989).

In 1982 the non-governmental organization, the Aga Khan Rural Support Programme (AKRSP), started its rural development programmes in Hunza. The AKRSP offered cheap loans and credit arrangements for rural development projects (cf. The World Bank 1990). Moreover, the AKRSP introduced elected Village Organizations (VOs) in villages that were involved with the AKRSP's programmes. The VOs replaced the feudal consensus assemblies (*oyoko*), which had served as links between the Mir and the individual villages. More important, the VOs developed into fora for community action and reassertion of ownership of local resources.

The Northern Areas' importance in national politics is determined by their role as a stumbling block in India-Pakistan relations (Lamb 1964, 1991; Rais 1991:381). Recognized as a hardship area, legislation exempts most from paying taxes and important foodstuffs are subsidized. Despite this, state funds have primarily gone to Army installations and to developing infrastructure like the huge Karakoram Highway, serving to bolster Pakistan's claim to the region. A result of the unresolved border dispute between India and Pakistan is that the NA are not a self-governed province, but under federal administration by the Ministry for Northern Areas and Kashmir Affairs in Islamabad. Locally, the NA are governed by a centrally appointed Administrator and an elected council, The Northern Areas Council, which is the region's highest authority. The Northern Areas are divided into districts and sub-divisions (*tehsil*), where each subdivision is governed by a locally elected Councillor. People can vote for their choice of a local Councillor, but cannot vote in national elections.

With an annual precipitation of less than 150 millimeters, Hunza is a high altitude desert (cf. Miller 1984). Agriculture is based on gravity fed irrigation of glacial meltwater, with average landholdings of about 1.1 hectare.[4] The agro-pastoral systems found in Hunza are a combination of lowland agriculture and extensive seasonal movement of animals from lowland winter, to alpine summer pastures. The traditional pattern of moving sheep, goats and yaks to mountain pastures has changed since new work options opened up, first with the jeep road through Hunza in the 1960s and especially after the completion of the KKH. The most significant change is the very high migration of men to downcountry jobs. From the villages along the KKH, few bring their animals up on the alpine pastures any longer, which causes localized overgrazing (Allan 1989:135; Kreutzmann 1993:33; Klötzli et al. 1988).[5]

The Khunjerab National Park

Mountain villages tend to be remote by their very nature, and therefore to some degree outside the immediate control of central authorities. Compared to the lowland villages, they show a more recent incorporation into the nation state. Unlike pastoralists who have been intercepted by emerging nation states (Shahrani 1978, 1979), mountain agro-pastoralists are, with their much shorter migrations, more resistant to state intervention and forced sedentarization. The Wakhis in upper Hunza (Ghujal) have traditionally specialized in animal husbandry of sheep, goats and yaks. Since 1975 the state and the Wakhi communities have been locked in a protracted battle over the Khunjerab National Park (KNP).[6]

---

[4] For a discussion on irrigation systems and agriculture in central Hunza, see Kreutzmann 1988, 1989 and Whiteman 1988.

[5] For an overview of range management in Pakistan, see Mohammad 1989.

[6] Detailed information on the concrete effects of the park are found in Ahmad 1991; Butz 1989; Knudsen 1991 and Mock 1990.

The KNP was set up primarily to protect the endangered Marco Polo sheep (*Ovis ammon polii*) whose habitat straddles the border between Pakistan and China. The idea of the park came from the noted field zoologist Dr. George B. Schaller. Schaller, who had pioneered the protection of large Asian mammals, single-handedly drew up the park's borders after a short field survey in 1974. Schaller surveyed only a fraction of the total park area and hardly spent any time in the shared grazing areas of the Wakhi villages in the Khunjerab. In Schaller's own words, he:

> felt that northeastern Hunza would make a perfect national park. .... This mountain block, 877 square miles in size, is scenically spectacular, biologically complex, and contains some rare wildlife. Aside from snow leopard, brown bear, and Marco Polo sheep, it harbours the country's only population of bharal and is visited by kiang or Tibetan wild ass. The Karakoram Highway provides access, but there are no permanent villages within the proposed area. The fact that people from several communities graze their livestock for about three months each summer at Khunjerab, Shimshal, and other uplands poses some problems, for by definition a national park should be free of such disturbances.. [but].. such details could be resolved later (Schaller 1980:98ff.).

Based on Schaller's recommendation, the park was formally gazetted on April 29, 1975 by the then Prime Minister Zulfiqar Ali Bhutto who declared that: 'It must become the world's famous Park. ... This is an iron directive' (Bhutto, quoted in Bell 1992:15). To be recognized as a national park, a park must comply with international standards laid down by the International Union for Conservation of Nature (IUCN). Since the beginning, the KNP had been planned as a 'category two' national park. In a 'category two' national park, wildlife gets the highest possible protection and human activity is banned (cf. IUCN 1990). The park did, however, lack clear management objectives, and in the following years it was little more than dotted lines on a map. The lack of adequate staffing and inability to enforce park regulations meant that the KNP was ignored by the affected villages, and despite the ban, the villages continued their now 'illegal' grazing inside the Khunjerab, the plateau close to the Chinese border that gave the park its name. This was a particular eyesore to the government, which felt that the Wakhi villagers blatantly breached park regulations.

Acknowledging the many shortcomings of the way the KNP had been managed, the IUCN commissioned, in 1988, the Norwegian wildlife biologist Dr. Per Wegge to do a rapid wildlife survey of the KNP, the first since Schaller in 1974. One of Wegge's most important research findings was that there was no scientific basis for the alleged competition between wildlife and domestic animals (Wegge 1988), and hence no need for a strictly defined 'category two' national park. Based on his field survey, Wegge proposed reclassifying the KNP into a multi-purpose park, which made room for domestic grazing and a commercial hunting programme with profits siphoned off to the Wahki villages (ibid.). He further acknowledged that most of the illegal hunting of the Marco Polo sheep was not done by local people but by high ranking Pakistani civil and military officials.

In the summer of 1989 the Pakistani governmental organization, the National Council for Conservation of Wildlife (NCCW), convened a workshop in Gilgit to draft a new management plan (Bell 1992). The participants overlooked Wegge's proposal and instead declared that their mandate was exclusively to draft a management plan for the original 'category two' national park. The delegates that were present at the workshop did not support Wegge's plan, probably because this would strain relations with the government, as well as implicitly endorse downgrading the KNP from a national park to a biosphere reserve. This would involve changing the current legislation[7] and mean that further work with the KNP would be delayed. The World Wide Fund for Nature (alias World Wildlife Fund, WWF), which represented the wildlife interests, was vehemently opposed to a revision of the KNP's status. In the words of WWF-Pakistan's Regional Director (ibid.:47): 'All factors antagonistic to the general principles of the National Park should be eliminated.' A minority of the participants asked the government to settle the compensation issue before continuing with the park planning (ibid.:137). The majority, however, reiterated the claim that all grazing inside the park should be phased out, or if possible, stopped immediately (ibid.:22). Wegge has since been a harsh critic of the Gilgit workshop and the government's approach to the KNP (Wegge 1989, 1990). He argued that the insistence on a national park was based on financial considerations – it would benefit tourism and create more revenue than any other protection category – rather than finding the best management solution for the area and its people. Conceding to

---

[7] The Northern Areas Wildlife Preservation Act of 1975.

much of Wegge's criticism, the IUCN has in the years since the Gilgit workshop distanced itself from the KNP problem altogether (cf. Slavin 1991:52).

The preparations for the new management plan heralded a period of new research activity, which increased the tension in the affected Wakhi villages. Especially, there was concern over the compensation of lost grazing. Due to the controversy over pasture rights and monetary compensation, three men representing the villages which shared grazing rights in the Khunjerab plateau filed a case against the state (cf. *Civil Case File No. 64,* 1990). This was especially linked to the twelve-square-kilometer area of core habitat for the Marco Polo sheep where the ban on hunting and grazing had been enforced since 1975. The villagers claimed ownership of the Khunjerab on the grounds that:

> the Nala Khunjerab is the exclusive property of the plaintiffs since their forefathers' time. .... Upon oral agreement with defendants No. 6 [Forest Department NAs, Gilgit] the suit pasture was given on certain conditions, to provide alternative pasture as well as an annual share of income from the National Park revenue as royalty as per household of the plaintiffs at the rate 5,000/- per year. Despite a lapse of about eighteen years the defendants have failed to fulfil the conditions. So the plaintiffs are entitled to cancel the oral agreement (ibid.).

In other words: the Wakhi villages claimed ownership of the Khunjerab, based on customary rights (de facto). Since the state had failed to fulfil the conditions for the transfer of such rights, the villages no longer felt bound by the oral agreement. The state, through its Forest Department, naturally took a different view of the ownership:

> Defendants No. 6 [Forest Dept.] challenged the contention and said that the suit pasture is crown land, and the Govt. has declared through its notification as Khunjerab National Park an area of 877 square miles, and so the plaintiffs are not entitled to have the suit pasture (ibid.).

Since the Khunjerab, according to the state is 'crown land', that is the *de jure* property of the state, the condition for allocating compensation did not exist.[8] The state also claimed that there had never been an oral agreement on compensation.

The preliminary ruling was announced on October 15, 1990 and asked both parties to keep the status quo. Until a final agreement on compensation could be found, the court allowed the Wakhi communities to continue grazing their animals elsewhere in the Khunjerab, but not in the twelve-square-kilometer zone where domestic animals had been banned since 1975. Shortly after, Wakhi villagers, in a show of defiance, entered the twelve-square-kilometer zone. They stayed there until May 1991, when they were forcibly evicted by armed men from the paramilitary Khunjerab Scout Force. A checkpoint was erected at the border to prevent animals and herdsmen from drifting in again. The incident caused spontaneous demonstrations in the affected villages where people took to the streets, blocked the traffic on the KKH and shouted slogans criticising the government (Slavin 1991).

Why did the state initiate this action exactly at this point and on the basis of the preliminary ruling of October 15, 1990? It is likely that the authorities wanted to use this as a show of strength *vis-à-vis* the defiant Wakhi villages, rather than being motivated by a sudden wish to protect the Marco Polo sheep – the original pretext for setting up the park. By any standard, the protection of the Marco Polo had failed – poaching had reduced the number of Marco Polo sheep from an estimated three hundred in 1975, to about one hundred in 1980. The last reliable confirmation was in 1986, when twenty-eight Marco Polo sheep were spotted (Wegge 1988:5; Mock 1990:2).

For the people of upper Hunza very much is at stake. They see their entire lifestyle, income base and livelihood threatened by the plans. Living in the single-crop zone makes them more dependent on pastoral animal husbandry than the villages in central and lower Hunza. The fact that pastures are central to household viability, is supported by the current dispute over pasture rights shared by villages (Abidi 1987). Even if these pastures are less used now, there is a need to defend rights to pastures in order to secure the villages' subsistence capabilities.

The KNP is especially threatening to Shimshal, the most isolated village, which stands to lose most of its precious grazing land. At the moment the Shimshalis perceive their life as encapsulated by the state.

---

[8] Compensation on the grounds of customary rights is not unknown in Pakistan. In the Chitral Gol National Park, the government agreed to compensate loss of grazing privileges (cf. Malik 1985:105).

Not only is there a concern with the viability of households but with the viability of the community itself. Should they be forced by the government to accept the plans for the park, it would eradicate their pastoral economy. As one Shimshali man said: 'If they make it a national park, Shimshal will be a tomb' (Knudsen 1992). Another quote underlines the seriousness of the situation: 'First they can kill us, then they can come and make a national park' (Slavin 1991:49).

The Chaprote forest

Pakistan as a whole has only a 4.9 per cent forest cover, and consequently forest is a prized commodity (IUCN 1986:40ff.). Most of the forest is found in the valleys in Northern Pakistan. Four main types of rights to forest exist: private individual property, private community property (*shamilaat*), community forest managed by the state (*guzara*),[9] and state-owned forest managed by the state through its Forest Department (cf. Husain 1992:7ff; PNCS 1992:105, 170). With their economic importance, rights to forest are contested and form a source of conflict and dispute between the state and the local communities.[10]

Chaprote, a secluded valley in lower Hunza, had a very good stand of pine, deodar and juniper forests. The Chaprote forest was originally the *de jure* property of the Mir of Nagar, filling the need for firewood and building materials of the six surrounding villages. With the abolition of the Mir of Nagar's feudal estate in 1972, the local forest came under the jurisdiction of the Northern Areas Forest Department. In the Forest Act of 1927, the villages were granted rights to forest for their own use, but commercial felling was the prerogative of the Forest Department (Dani 1989). Legally, it was now a state owned forest and the Department issued felling permits to private contractors. Felling should be done on a sustainable basis and quotas reflect a controlled outtake of timber. Instead, officials in the Department issued permits for logging, against bribes or profit sharing. The result was a net felling five

---

[9] The communities are granted from 60 to 80 per cent shares in the proceeds of the sales of timber.

[10] For an account of the spread of organized vengeance and its links with commercial logging in a Kohistani community, cf. Keiser 1986, 1991:69ff. The link between politics and forestry has also been discussed in Ahmed 1986:115 and Dove and Rao 1990:6.

times the official estimate, which made a mockery out of the system's original intention (Dani 1989; Hunzai 1987; Mumtaz and Durr-e-Nayab 1991). The local people responded to this by increasing their now illegal logging in order to get their share before it was too late.

Alarmed by the uncontrolled felling of their forest, and angered by the corrupt system for allocating felling permits, the Village Organizations of the surrounding villages formed their own forest committee in March 1986.[11] They decided to put up a checkpost next to the Forest Department's own checkpost. Manned by local guards round the clock, this naturally challenged and embarrassed the Forest Department and could, as the Department saw it, set a dangerous precedent for other communities. After two years of tug of war with accusations and counter-accusations, the surprising outcome was that the Administrator of the Northern Areas, as well the Conservator of Forest in Islamabad, relinquished their control and implicitly agreed to a co-management of the Chaprote forest. The local, Northern Areas Forest Department has been less cooperative, seeing the result as a loss of prestige.[12]

It is now impossible for contractors to get felling permits, and the communities' own Committee forwards requests to the Department on behalf of the villagers for felling. In a way, the forest is now co-managed by the community and the Forest Department, and the *awami* ('people's') barrier is manned day and night by locals who are paid for their work. Under the new system, the communities have agreed to a self-imposed ban on lopping branches off living trees for firewood. Only dead trees can be felled. Flaking off the bark or setting a tree on fire to kill it, is now outlawed and breaches fined.

Protection of wildlife in Bar-Das

Because the feudal ruler in the old Nagar kingdom feared for his position and the changes the KKH could bring to his isolated kingdom, he managed to have the KKH constructed outside the areas under his

---

[11] 'Islahi Committee Baraye Tahaffuz-e-Junglaat' (Reform Committee for the Conservation of Forest).

[12] Since Village Organizations were involved, the Forest Department accused the AKRSP of meddling in the case (Slavin 1991:53). An effect of this has been that the AKRSP has refrained from taking sides in the ongoing dispute over the Khunjerab National Park.

rule (Allan 1989; Dani 1988). The KKH therefore crosses the Hunza river to avoid areas belonging to the former Nagar kingdom, now administered as the Nagar subdivision. This part of the valley is dominated by Shina speaking people (Shins), who are predominantly Twelver Shia (Ali 1983:14). The communities were kept under strict feudal rule and, by the ruler's diversion of the KKH, they were prevented from taking part in the economic boom caused by the construction of the KKH.[13] Shia communities have up till now lagged behind in development, having been sidelined in central Hunza by Ismaili communities which have taken the lion's share of the tourist traffic. At the same time as there is a tendency towards Islamic orthodoxy, there is a growing concern over economic backwardness.

Some kilometers' distance from Chaprote, a cluster of Shia villages known as Bar-Das approached the IUCN, the WWF-Pakistan and the AKRSP in 1990 with plans to stop all hunting of wild animals, especially ibex, snow leopard and Himalayan brown bear. To ban hunting, a preliminary two-year deal was negotiated between the state and the villages, with an annual budget of Pakistani Rs. 240,000 (Ahmad 1990).[14] The major part of the money was provided by the District Council in Gilgit and the rest collected in montly instalments. In addition to compensate for loss of hunting privileges, the money was used to pay for game wardens, recruited from the villages. By the end of the two-year period, the plan involved relaxing the ban on hunting and initiate a program of trophy hunting. In late October 1990, the agreement was signed and the villagers agreed to stop all hunting. Months later, however, nothing had happened and no money had arrived.

Some interpreted this as the government's way of hitting back for the problems caused in nearby Chaprote. The official version was that the government felt that there was no trustworthy system that could check whether the villagers really had stopped hunting as they pledged. As of July 1991 no solution had surfaced. The villagers had grown impatient and had by then lost many goats and sheep in the period they had heeded the ban. It is important to note, however, that in this agreement there was no mention of restricting grazing rights. The

---

[13] For a more detailed discussion on resource management, gender issues and pre-Islamic beliefs in Shia villages, see Butz 1987; Buzdar 1988; Dani 1988; Hewitt 1989; and Knudsen 1994.

[14] The equivalent of about USD 10,000 (1990).

people in Bar-Das were aware of the conflict over the KNP, but why did they initiate the protection-for-money deal with the IUCN, the WWF, the AKRSP and the Northern Areas administration? The plan was the work of a liberal political activist, who as a Syeed and prominent Shia scholar, was able to overcome cleavages in the villages due to politics – Mir versus Syeed factions – and clan rivalry (*shin, yeshkun*). As a respected political leader, with close contact with key AKRSP personnel, this man played an important role as a mediator, and convinced the villagers that protection was advantageous, and could in particular be used to promote tourism. Making the villagers agree to this plan was an innovation on his part. It was also a breach with the traditional scepticism about tourism which some feel compromises their religion and threatens female chastity. This village cluster got its link road to the KKH in 1986, and this made work migration more common and mountain pastures and wildlife roaming there less valuable. New work options, both locally in the Pakistani Army and in the larger cities in Punjab and Sind, have changed the villages' income base. There has been a reversal from a situation where rangelands and wildlife were the most valuable assets of the villages, to a situation where wildlife as a commodity can help to sustain and bridge the transition towards intensified agriculture, work migration and tourism.

Politicization and community action

What formal political channels are open to Hunza communities? The Northern Areas' administration is military rather than democratic. Hence there is a lack of political channels. The people of Hunza have limited access to political arenas and fora where decisions affecting them are made. The particular form the integration of the Hunza and Nagar kingdoms took, marked the beginning of a growing politicization in Hunza. The abolition of the feudal kingdoms was the work of late Prime Minister Zulfiqar Ali Bhutto, who led the Pakistan People's Party (PPP). This move led to a strong support of the PPP in Hunza. However, it did also reaffirm the feudal structures. Those who lost their feudal privileges continued to support the Mir (Mir faction) (cf. Kreutzmann 1989:177).[15]

---

[15] Rather than being a political party, it signals political allegiance to the Mir. Both the 'PPP', 'Mir' and 'Syeed' are better understood as idioms of local political conflict, rather than as genuine political statements.

Both Mir Ghazanfar Ali Khan, son of the last Mir of Hunza, and Mir Shaukat Ali Khan, former Mir of Nagar, have contested elections to the Northern Areas Council and are presently Councillors for their respective subdivisions, Hunza and Nagar. In central Hunza the split between the Mir versus the PPP allegiance came to include whole villages, depending on a preferential treatment from the Mir during the feudal era. An example of such preferential treatment could be privileged access to water or pastures (cf. Dani 1988:252ff.). In the Wakhi villages, however, the line of cleavage more often ran through the single village. In the affected Wakhi villages there are supporters both of the Mir as well as the PPP (Knudsen 1992). This aspect of Wakhi social organization has, in combination with the local political structure, limited the options for community protest through formal channels.

In Wakhi areas, rights to pasture are vested with the villages (*dior*). This makes it possible to unite villagers as a corporate group, resulting in collective opposition to the park and informal ad hoc actions and protest aimed at affronting the state. The Wakhi villages have, however, been unable to overcome divisive political loyalties. The formal way of making a petition to the government is through the Councillor's office, which will bring the case before the Northern Areas Council. If the Wakhi villages had wanted to petition against the KNP plans, they should have brought the case before Mir Ghazanfar Ali Khan. The reason, I propose, why a formal petition through the Councillor's office has not taken place, is connected with the problem of getting a consensus on this among the PPP and Mir factions in the Wakhi villages. Mir Ghazanfar Ali Khan represents a direct link to the feudal period through his father, Mir Jamal Khan, the last Mir of Hunza. Moreover, he is also a member of the board of the WWF-Pakistan (Mock 1990). This has, I believe, precluded a consensus in the affected villages to put their case before the Councillor. Instead, they have pursued the case through the local judiciary in Gilgit. When their case was not heard, they lacked other formal channels where they could voice their concern and were therefore left with civil disobedience as their only means, ultimately leading to the present open defiance of central government and its implementing agencies, the NCCW and the IUCN.

There is, however, a further possible cleavage here between the Wakhi villages. Shimshalis do not under any circumstances agree to a compensation package, although it is this that the other affected Wakhi villages are pressing for. The other villages are either situated along the Karakoram Highway or are very close to it, and they are less dependent on the pastures in the Khunjerab (cf. Kreutzmann 1986). Compensation for lost grazing can be acceptable to them but cannot satisfy the Shimshalis. It is therefore possible that the state will be able to strike a deal with the other villages, leaving Shimshalis alone in their opposition to the park.[16]

How can we explain that the state, through its Forest Department, implicitly agreed to a co-management of the Chaprote forest? That the villagers were able to initiate such a deal, is a tacit recognition by the government that the villagers have legitimate de facto rights and that state management has failed. The successful campaign for local resource management launched by the Chalt-Chaprote villages is connected with the presence of the AKRSP VOs, which have developed into fora for community action. The present co-management of the Chalt-Chaprote forest was made possible by uniting the villages and launching a protest which exposed the state's damaging forest management. The new system of 'dual enforcement' (Dani 1989) is perhaps the best possible way of safeguarding local resources.

The Bar-Das pilot project was a novelty since, from the outset, it was based on giving compensation to villagers. This is all the more astonishing since the deal was sponsored by the WWF, the same agency which opposed compensation in the KNP case. Unlike the Wakhi villages, and Shimshal especially, the Bar-Das communities are freely giving up their rights to hunt in return for financial compensation. The Bar-Das case is also connected with the politicization in Hunza. The former Mir of Nagar, and the present Councillor, Mir Shaukat Ali:

> survives ... as a political faction leader with the support of his former subject villages. ... Villages are entirely with or entirely opposed to the *mir* (Dani 1988:254).

The Bar-Das pilot project was largely the work of a mullah-cum-politician. He is the leading liberal politician with his own following, heading the populist anti-Mir lobby (Syeed faction). He has still been able to round up support for the plan through partly bridging political allegiances (Syeed versus Mir factions), and partly by relying on his own power base in the Bar-Das villages. The rapid socio-economic

---

[16] In fact, this was exactly what happened. In January 1992, the WWF-Pakistan reached an agreement with all the Wakhi villages which shared grazing rights in the Khunjerab. The one exception was Shimshal (cf. Agreement 1992).

ascendancy among the neighbouring Ismaili communities has made the Twelver Shias eager to regain lost ground in economic development. New roads and better accessibility (Allan 1986) have made the distant pastures and wildlife less valuable as sources of income. Under such circumstances, villagers are willing to exchange wildlife for money. If the problem of monitoring the hunting ban can be found, the Bar-Das pilot project will have achieved its aims.

Conclusion

Helped by the PPP government, the people of Hunza had shed a repressive feudal autarchy in 1974. This marked the beginning of a strong politicization and the emergence of opposing feudal and populist lobbies. Moreover, the discontinuity caused by the abolition of the Hunza and Nagar Mirdoms resulted in a situation where land claims were contested. The village organizations and political lobbies have become fora for 'grassroots' movements and outlets for protest, aiding in reasserting communal property rights. By contrast, political cleavages inside the Wakhi villages have limited their options for protest through formal channels.

More than earlier, the state is now directly concerned with resource management at the village level. This has lead to a confrontation between state interests and local communities' wish to remain in control of natural resources. Instead of bowing to the pressure and relinquishing their control, the communities have challenged the legitimacy of the state's quest for control of forest and rangeland.

The nature conservation conflicts in Hunza suggest that the change from private property (the Mir's feudal estate) to state property regimes (belonging to the state of Pakistan) left a legitimacy problem on the part of the state and infringed informal property rights. The government's view was that following nationalization, the ownership of the feudal fiefdoms was transferred to the state (*de jure*). The local communities, however, claim ownership reverted to them based on customary use (de facto) (Figure 1).

Who should manage Hunza's resources? I have argued that local communities have legitimate de facto rights to natural resources and are entitled to participate in their management. To empower local communities, informal property rights should be granted comparable legal status as formal rights vested with the state. The still unresolved

Khunjerab National Park issue will be a test case as to whether this principle can win over the considerable prestige that is at stake here. The co-management of the Chaprote forest could, hopefully, serve as a model for resolving the resource management conflicts in Hunza.

Figure 1. Ownership of forest and rangelands in Hunza

Legal Status	Pre-1974		Post-1974
Formal/legislative *de jure*	Mir	transfer -->?	State
Informal/customary de facto	Mir	transfer -->?	Community

Collectively, these case studies may offer some insights into how contested claims to ownership and dispute over legitimacy may lead to serious environmental degradation. The implication following these case studies from Hunza is a theoretical focus on transfer of rights as a crucial aspect of resource management and central to understanding how local communities respond to state intervention.

Abbreviations

AKRSP	Aga Khan Rural Support Programme
IUCN	International Union for Conservation of Nature
KKH	Karakoram Highway
KNP	The Khunjerab National Park
NA	Northern Areas
NCCW	National Council for Conservation of Wildlife
PPP	Pakistan People's Party
VO	Village Organization
WWF	World Wide Fund for Nature

References

Abidi, S. Mehjabeen. 1987. 'Pastures and Livestock Development in Gojal'. AKRSP Report, No. 5, mimeo.

Agreement, 1992. 'Text of Agreement between the Graziers of Khunjerab and the Local Administration'. January 5, mimeo.

Ahmad, Ashiq. 1990. 'The Feasibility of Wildlife Protection and Wise Use through Local Communities in the Bar Valley of Nagar Sub-Division (Northern Areas)'. Report prepared for the AKRSP, IUCN, WWF-Pakistan and Forest Department, Northern Areas. Peshawar: Pakistan Forest Institute.

—— 1991. 'The Feasibility and Application of Different Management Options to Resolve the Problems of Khunjerab National Park (Northern Areas)'. Peshawar: Pakistan Forest Institute, mimeo.

Ahmed, Akbar S. 1986. *Pakistan Society: Islam, Ethnicity and Leadership in South Asia*. Karachi: Oxford University Press.

Ali, Tahir. 1983. *The Burusho of Hunza: Social Structure and Household Viability in a Mountain Desert Kingdom*. Unpublished Ph.D. Diss., University of Rochester, N.Y.

Allan, Nigel J.R. 1986. 'Accessibility and Altitudinal Zonation of Mountains'. *Mountain Research and Development* 6(3):185-194.

—— 1989. 'Kashgar to Islamabad: The Impact of the Karakorum Highway on Mountain Society and Habitat. *Scottish Geographical Magazine* 105(3):130-141.

—— 1990. 'Household Food Supply in Hunza Valley, Pakistan.' *Geographical Review* 80(4):399-415.

Bell, Barbara Goodman (ed.). 1992. *International Workshop on the Management Planning of Khunjerab National Park June 7-16, 1989*. Proceedings. United States National Park Service, The Government of Pakistan, National Council for Conservation of Wildlife and The World Conservation Union.

Berkes, Fikret (ed.). 1989. *Common Property Resources: Ecology and Community-Based Sustainable Development*. London: Belhaven Press.

Biddulph, J. 1880. *Tribes of the Hindoo Koosh*. Calcutta [Reprint, Graz 1971].

Bromley, Daniel W. 1991. *Environment and Economy. Property Rights and Public Policy.* Oxford: Blackwell.

Bromley, Daniel W. (ed.). 1992. *Making the Commons Work. Theory, Practice and Policy.* San Francisco: ICS Press.

Bromley, Daniel W. and Michael M. Cernea. 1989. *The Management of Common Property Natural Resources. Some Conceptual and Operational Fallacies.* Washington D.C.: World Bank Discussion Papers, No 57.

Butz, David A. O. 1987. *Irrigation Agriculture in High Mountain Communities: The Example of Hopar Villages.* Unpublished MA thesis, Department of Geography, Waterloo, Ontario: Wilfred Laurier University.

—— 1989. 'Pastures and Pastoralism in Shimshal'. Preliminary Report to AKRSP, Gilgit, mimeo.

Buzdar, Nek. 1988. *Property Rights, Social Organization and Resource Management in Northern Pakistan.* Working Paper No. 5, Environment and Policy Institute, East-West Center, Honolulu, Hawaii.

Civil Case File No. 64. 1990. 'Suit for Declaration and Consequential Relief.' In the Court of Civil Judge Ist Class No. I, Gilgit. Announced October 15, 1990.

Dani, Anis A. 1988. *Peripheral Societies in a Nation-State. A Comparative Analysis of Mediating Structures in Development Process.* Unpublished Ph.D. Dissertation, University of Pennsylvania.

—— 1989. 'Chaprote: Where the Forest Lives Again'. Gilgit: AKRSP Village Case Study No. 19, mimeo. (Also published in *Newsline*, December 1989).

Dani, Anis A., Cristopher J.N. Gibbs and Daniel W. Bromley (eds). 1987. *Institutional Development for Local Management of Rural Resources.* Honolulu: East-West Environment and Policy Institute, Workshop Report No. 2.

Dove, Michael Roger and Abdul Latif Rao. 1990. *Common Resource Management in Pakistan: Garrett Hardin in the Junglat.* East-West Center, Environment and Policy Institute, Working Paper No. 23.

Durand, Algernon. 1974. *The Making of a Frontier.* Akademische Druck und Verlagsanstalt, [Reprint of the original 1899 edition]

Hewitt, Farida. 1989. 'Woman's Work, Woman's Place: The Gendered Life-World of a High Mountain Community in Northern Pakistan.' *Mountain Research and Development* 9(4):335-352.

Hopkirk, Peter. 1990. *The Great Game. On Secret Service in High Asia*. London: John Murray.

Hunzai, Azhar Ali. 1987. 'The Political Economy of Forestry: The New Management System of Forest in Chalt-Chaprote'. Gilgit: AKRSP Village Case Study No. 10, mimeo.

Husain, Tariq. 1992. *Community Participation: The First Principle*. Karachi: Government of Pakistan and the IUCN – The World Conservation Union.

IUCN. 1986. *The Nature of Pakistan*. A Guide to Conservation and Development Issues, No. 1. Gland: Conservation for Development Centre.

—— 1990. *United Nations List of National Parks and Protected Areas*. Gland: The International Union for Conservation of Nature.

Keiser, Lincoln. 1986. 'Death Enmity in Thull: Organized Vengeance and Social Change in a Kohistani Community.' *American Ethnologist* 13:489-505.

—— 1991. *Friend by Day, Enemy by Night. Organized Vengeance in a Kohistani Community*. New York: Holt, Rinehart and Winston, Inc.

Klötzli, Frank, R. Schaffner and A. Bosshard. 1989. 'Pasture Development and Its Implications in the Hunza Valley – High Pasture Mission'. Aga Khan Rural Support Programme and International Union for Conservation of Nature and Nature Resources, mimeo.

Knudsen Are J. 1991. 'Traditional User Rights Versus Conservation. A Management Problem in the Khunjerab National Park'. Report to IUCN-Pakistan, mimeo.

—— 1992. 'Household Viability and Adaptability in a North Pakistan Mountain Village in Transition´. Unpublished MA thesis. Department of Social Anthropology, University of Bergen, Norway.

—— 1994. 'Cows, Fairies and Diviners: Resource Management and Cosmology in a Shi'i Community, N-Pakistan'. Paper presented to the NFU conference on 'Knowledge and Development', Tromsø, May 27-29.

Kreutzmann, Hermann. 1986. 'A Note on Yak-Keeping in Hunza, Northern Areas of Pakistan.' *Production pastorale et société* 19(Autumn):99-106.

—— 1988. 'Oases of the Karakoram. Evolution of Irrigation and Social Organization in Hunza, North Pakistan.' In Nigel J.R. Allan, G.W. Knapp and C. Stadel (eds), *Human Impact on Mountains*. Rowman & Littlefield.

—— 1989. *Hunza – Landliche Entwiklung im Karakorum*. Berlin: Abhandlungen Anthropogeographie, No.44, Dietrich Reimer Verlag.

—— 1991. 'The Karakoram Highway: The Impact of Road Construction on Mountain Societies'. *Modern Asian Studies* 25(4):711-736.

—— 1993. 'Challenge and Response in the Karakoram: Socioeconomic Transformation in Hunza, Northern Areas, Pakistan.' *Mountain Research and Development* 13(1):19-39.

Lamb, Alastair. 1964. 'The Sino-Pakistan Boundary Agreement of 2 March 1963.' *Australian Outlook* 18:299-313.

—— 1991. *Kashmir. A Disputed Legacy 1846-1990*. Hertingfordbury: Roxford Books.

Malik, Mohammad Mumtaz. 1985. 'Management of Chitral Gol National Park, Pakistan.' In McNeely, J. A., J.W. Thorsell and S.R. Chalise (eds), *People and Protected Areas in the Hindu Kush Himalaya*. Kathmandu: King Mahendra Trust for Nature Conservation and ICIMOD.

McCay, Bonnie J. and James M. Acheson (eds). 1987. *The Question of the Commons. The Culture and Ecology of Communal Resources*. Tucson: The University of Arizona Press.

Miller, K. J. (ed.). 1984. *International Karakoram Project*. [Two Volumes]. Cambridge: Cambridge University Press.

Mock, John. 1990. 'Field trip report and discussion paper on conservation and management of the Khunjerab National Park'. Consultancy report to World Wide Fund for Nature, Pakistan, mimeo.

Mohammad, Noor. 1989. *Rangelands Management in Pakistan*. Kathmandu: ICIMOD Senior Fellowship Series No. 1. Nepal.

Mumtaz, Sofia and Durr-e-Nayab. 1991. 'Management Arrangements of the Chaprote Forest and their Implications for Sustainable Development'. *The Pakistan Development Review* 3(4):1075-1086.

Ostrom, Elinor. 1990. *Governing the Commons. The Evolution of Institutions for Collective Action*. Cambridge: Cambridge University Press.

Paffen, K.H., W. Pillewizer and H.J. Schneider. 1956. 'Forschungen im Hunza-Karakorum'. *Erdkunde* X(1):1-33.

Pinkerton, Evelyn. 1987. 'Intercepting the State. Dramatic Processes in the Assertion of Local Comanagement Rights'. In McCay, Bonnie J. and James M. Acheson (eds), 1987. *The Question of the Commons. The Culture and Ecology of Communal Resources*. Tucson: The University of Arizona Press.

PNCS. 1992. *The Pakistan National Conservation Strategy (PNCS)*. Karachi: Government of Pakistan, Environment and Urban Division in Collaboration with the IUCN – The World Conservation Union.

Rais, Rasul B. 1991. 'Pakistan in the Regional and Global Power Structure'. *Asian Survey* XXXI(4):378-392.

Rovillè, G. 1988. 'Ethnic Minorities and the Development of Tourism in the Valleys of North Pakistan. In Rossel, P. (ed.), *Tourism: Manufacturing the Exotic*. IWGIA Document No. 61.

Said, Edward. 1979. *Orientalism*. New York: Vintage Books.

Schaller, George B. 1980. *Stones of Silence. Journeys in the Himalaya*. London: Andre Deutsch Ltd.

Shahrani, M. Nazif Mohib. 1978. 'The Rentention of Pastoralism among the Kirghiz of the Afghan Pamirs'. In Fisher, James F. (ed.), *Himalayan Anthropology: The Indo-Tibetan Interface*. The Hague and Paris: Mouton Publishers.

—— 1979. *The Kirghiz and Wakhi of Afghanistan. Adaptation to Closed Frontiers*. Seattle and London: University of Washington Press.

Shipton, Eric. 1990. 'Blank on the Map'. In *Eric Shipton – The Six Mountain-Travel Books*. London and Seattle: Diadem Books Ltd. and The Mountaineers.

Slavin, Terry. 1991. 'Survival in a Vertical Desert'. *Tomorrow – The Global Environmental Magazine* 1(2):42-53.

Staley, John. 1969. *Words for My Brother: Travels Between the Hindu Kush and the Himalayas*. Karachi: Oxford University Press.

Street, Brian. 1990. 'Orientalist Discourses in the Anthropology of Iran, Afghanistan and Pakistan'. In Fardon, Richard (ed.), *Localizing Strategies: Regional Traditions in Ethnographic Writing*. Edinburgh and Washington: Scottish Academic Press and Smithsonian Institution Press.

Visser, P. C. and J. Visser-Hooft, (eds). 1935-40. *Wissenschaftliche Ergebnisse der Niederländischen Expedition in den Karakorum und die angrenzenden Gebiete in den Jahren 1922, 1925, 1929/30.*
Vol. 1: Geographie, Ethnographie, Zoologie. Leipzig, 1935
Vol. 2: Glaziologie. Leiden, 1938
Vol. 3: Geologie, Paläontologie und Petrographie. Leiden, 1940.

Wegge, Per. 1988. 'Assessment of Khunjerab National Park and Environs, Pakistan'. Report submitted to IUCN - Pakistan, mimeo.

—— 1989. 'Khunjerab National Park in Pakistan: A Case Study of Constraints to Proper Conservation Management'. In Wegge, P. and J. Thornback (eds), Proceedings of: *Conservation of mammals in developing countries.* Workshop, Fifth Theriological Congress, Rome.

—— 1990. 'A Khunjerab Workshop Gone Awry'. *HIMAL,* Sept-Oct. 1990:33-34.

Whiteman, Peter T.S. 1988. 'Mountain Agronomy in Ethiopia, Nepal and Pakistan'. In Allan, Nigel J.R., G.W. Knapp and C. Stadel (eds), *Human Impact on Mountains.* Totowa: Rowman and Littlefield.

The World Bank. 1990. *The Aga Khan Rural Support Program in Pakistan. Second Interim Evaluation.* Washington D.C.: A World Bank Operations Evaluation Study.

Birgitte Glavind Sperber

Nature in the Kalasha Perception of Life

> – We call this world beneath Bareloi, which means underneath.
> All the way around Bareloi there is a very long snake – down in
> the earth around the entire world. This snake binds the world
> together. If the snake was not there, the world would fall apart.
> ... To carry this world, to hold it above the world underneath,
> there is a gigantic bull named Melbara. The bull carries a pillar
> on his head and this supports this world so that it doesn't fall
> down. Several hundreds of people tend to this bull feeding him
> all the time because he must not move. If they don't feed him
> for just one minute, he moves. That is earthquake, *bonjao*
> (Khrosh Nawaz 1983).

It is commonly asserted that spiritual matters are one thing and material concerns another.[1] Perceptions and descriptions of nature, however, are often subject to 'conflicting categories' depending on the observer's background – on his or her position in time, space and society.

In Europe, after the Renaissance when natural sciences gained importance after shedding the yoke of the church, a mechanistic perception of nature gradually took over considering nature a source for exploitation. Moreover, natural sciences became more important than religion and magic when natural phenomena were explained. During the nineteenth century a romantic perception of nature (sometimes semi-religious) appeared and, through art and literature, spread among bourgeois people not living directly from nature. These two ways of perceiving nature still co-exist, often in open conflict.

Industrialization has caused a global environmental crisis which during the last decades has been regarded by many people as a failure of the mechanistic view of nature. Hence, our trust in technology has

---

[1] I am most grateful to Arne Kalland for an inspiring dialogue, for his valuable suggestions and co-operation during the writing of this work.

been shaken. A growing ecological awareness and quest for alternative explanations and solutions have made 'holistic' views popular. Combined mythical-scientific explanations, like for instance the Gaia hypothesis (Lovelock 1977), have a strong appeal to secularized westerners.

In the postmodern search for identity there is a renewed interest in our own traditional myths and legends that folklorists have 'salvaged' from disappearing into oblivion. They give another dimension to our appreciation of nature than does a set of scientific explanations.

Science, religion and magic have often been seen as alternative ways to explain the world (e.g. Malinowski 1925). A scientific worldview has also been used as one of the ways to separate 'us' (the developed) from 'them' (in need of development). Many disillusioned westerners, though, nowadays turn to 'them' in search for better man–nature relationships, strongly attracted by 'their' views on nature.

In this paper we shall take a look at nature and the man–nature relationship from the perspective of the Kalasha people for whom myths and legends have always played important roles. Not every Kalasha knows all the mythical explanations but there are elders who serve as a kind of communal reference library, like Khrosh Nawaz who told the myth which opened this essay. To most Kalasha, though, the basis of the myths is true. To them God, spirits, fairies and demons exist and their existence has a great impact on their lives, not least as the rightful owners of natural resources. From the very beginning until the present, supernatural beings have told the Kalasha how to behave by sending messages through shamans (*dehârs*) who are brought into a trance mostly through the aromatic smell of purifying juniper smoke.

Basic to the Kalasha world view are the concepts of 'purity' (*onjesta*) and 'impurity' (*pragata*), concepts that appear frequently in myths and legends as well as in daily conversations. They structure the world spatially, temporally and socially. They form a central pair in a set of binary oppositions providing metaphors for man and woman, mountain and valley, goat and cow, pasture and field, summer and winter, and so on. Natural disasters – e.g. earthquakes, floods and epidemics – and, as we shall see towards the end of the paper, man-made environmental degradation, are interpreted in terms of purity and impurity, or by greed.

Nature as framework – a geographical view

The three Kalasha valleys – Rumbour, Bomburet and Birir – are western tributaries to the Chitral Valley, which is situated in northwestern Pakistan between the Karakoram Mountains and the high peaks of Hindukush forming the border between Pakistan and Afghanistan. Passage from Chitral towards the north is blocked by Tirich Mir (7,706 meters), so the traveller is compelled to turn eastwards via Shandur Pass (3,720 meters). In the south, the road via Lowari Pass (3,118 meters) is difficult, and at times even impossible, to use during the snowy months.

Chitral lies in the rainshadow of the Lowari Range, which is why the area is arid and agriculture is totally dependent on irrigation. However, the Chitral River is too fluctuating and wild to allow drainage through irrigation canals. Thus, the human settlements (like Chitral at an altitude of 1,480 meters) and the fields are situated on old, fluvioglacial terraces or alluvial fans irrigated by water from the tributary rivers coming out from the side valleys.

The average temperature in Chitral ranges from 4°C in January to 28°C in July, lower in the higher situated Kalasha valleys. The precipitation varies considerably from year to year but falls mainly during winter when depressions pass that far from the Mediterranean regions. Occasionally the monsoon crosses the Lowari Pass or local depressions may result in showers but the summer is generally dry. The mean annual precipitation in Chitral is about 450 millimeters but more in higher altitudes. It is estimated that the glacier regions above the snow line receive about four times as much precipitation as Chitral. The snow subsequently melts into the numerous streams that water the fields and settlements in the form of an elaborate system of irrigation canals.

The natural vegetation is divided into zones up the mountainside (see Figure 2 on p. 141) but the altitude of a given vegetation zone varies with the orientation and steepness of the slope. The lowest parts are covered with arid steppe, with willows and poplars along the streams. Higher up, a zone of evergreen holly oak forest takes over. Still higher the relative humidity increases due to the altitude, so that clouds and dew-drops allow a coniferous forest to grow. In the Kalasha valleys the holly oak forest begins at an altitude of between 1,300 and 1,800 meters and the coniferous forest at 1,900–2,400 meters. A narrow zone of birch ends the forest zone at an altitude of about 3,300–3,400 meters.[2]

---

[2] There are areas which are so poor in rain that there are no forest zones at all.

A zone of alpine vegetation of scrub and meadows, which takes over when temperature and humidity become too low for forests, gives way to a zone of subnival pioneer vegetation at an altitude of about 3,800 meters. The snow line is between 4,700 and 4,900 meters (Haserodt 1990).

The environment of the Chitral Region is harsh and is often hit by devastating natural disasters such as floods and earthquakes (like the major earthquakes on 30 December 1983 and 1 February 1991). The Indian tectonic plate is pressed under the Asian plate by strong geological forces causing tensions and folding of steep mountains. The Kalasha valleys debouch into Chitral Valley through narrow gorges but at higher altitudes the valleys are wider with green, cultivated valley floors. However, arable land is scarce as it is found only where the ground is sufficiently level for irrigation and where canals can provide water. Only 1.2 per cent of the total area of the Chitral region can be used for agriculture but of this 95 per cent is irrigated and 40 per cent allows more than one crop a year (Haserodt 1990). The small area of agricultural land has a population density of more than 350 per km^2 and the densely populated villages are placed above the arable land – with the houses typically constructed step-wise above each other.

In the Kalasha valleys two crops are harvested in the village zone; wheat as a winter crop and maize, beans and vegetables as summer crops, while at the higher 'summer places' only one crop is harvested.[3] Barley and millet used to be important but seem to be vanishing nowadays. A wide range of fruit trees – walnut, mulberry, apricot, apple, pear and *jujube* (*Zizuphus jujuba*) – provide food and give shade.[4] These trees are also irrigated and grow in the villages, along the roads and in orchards. Old vines cling to the holly oak trees and provide the grapes for production of wine that only non-Muslim minorities like the Kalasha are permitted to produce and drink in the Muslim state of Pakistan.

---

[3] During the summer, women and children move their cows and oxen to more dispersed settlements, 'summer places' (*guru*), surrounded by fields. Both the village and the summer places are located within the holly-oak zone. The men and male youth move in May to the lower pastures located in the upper regions of the conifer belt and continue to the higher pastures the following month. With the first snowfalls, they retreat to the lower pastures and down to the village in October.

[4] The bark of the *jujube* (*sitjin*) also excretes a sap (*sitjin'non*) which the women use as a combined shampoo and hair jelly.

Bread baked on an open fire is the dominant food. Dried fruits are an important addition to the diet in the winter. The men do the hard field labour: they remove the stones that have been brought down by floods or earthquakes, construct and maintain the canals, plough with oxen and harrow and sow. Then the women take over the strenuous weeding and irrigation work but the men may help them with the harvest. The fields need to be irrigated at three to five day intervals when water from the canals is led from plant to plant along grooves made by the feet and a stick. This is also women's work and the area a family can irrigate depends therefore on the number of women in the household.

Subsistence is only possible because in May the Kalasha move to summer places where the women stay and take care of the fields and the few cows. Most of the men take their big herds of goats and a few sheep to the summer pastures where they stay until October, thus exploiting pastures ranging from the lower ridges in the forest region to the highest pastures at 3,500 meters or more.

The pasture vegetation is transformed into meat, dairy products and manure, which is brought down to the village. The forests provide timber for houses, canals and tools as well as firewood. Meat is only eaten after sacrifices or feasts – billy-goats are eaten only by men.[5] The meat is always distributed throughout the community. The goat cheese produced during the lactation period in the summer is an essential protein source, though most of the cheese is eaten by the men. The forest and alpine zones are also used for hunting.

In October the goats and sheep are taken down the valley. During the winter season they stay in the goat houses (*gosht*) situated at the edge of the village and field zone.[6] The goats are daily taken up the slopes to browse on the evergreen holly oak trees, while sheep and cows are fed on dried weeds and hay from the summer places. The goats' droppings are used as manure in the fields during the spring. French agricultural experts suggest that the fields give a very high yield (G. Lefeuve pers. comm.) and it is possible for even large households to subsist on a single acre of cultivated land (Parkes 1987).

---

[5] However, women may eat the meat from billy-goats if these are slaughtered in the Muslim way during funerals or other big feasts (Parkes, pers. comm.)

[6] The goat houses are large, elaborate structures accomodating up to 3-400 goats in addition to cows and sheep. There are sleeping quarters – as most men sleep here during periods of sexual abstinence – and a place to cook food. The goat house is also the place where men and boys assemble for recreation.

Nature in use – a Kalasha view

> We have a word for 'Nature'. It is 'Talibana'. It is everything,
> which is not cultivated. It is all *onjesta* – above and below the
> community (Saifullah Jan, Oct. 1991).

When the Kalasha tell about the agricultural year, it is obvious that
more than just ecological conditions decide their strategies for survival.
They believe that communities, animals and crops are safeguarded by
fairies, spirits and Khrodaij/God with whom people have to be reconciled and who are celebrated on particular occasions during the farming
year. The three major festivals – *Joshi, Utjao* and *Chaomos* – are all related
to the agricultural calendar and thus structure the Kalasha year.

Joshi, in May, celebrates the coming of spring and the fairies who
come down from the high mountains. The entire valley is purified with
goats' milk and by people waving walnut branches. In the Bomburet
Valley also people are purified by being sprinkled with milk. *Utjao*, in
August, is a celebration of the harvest. On the festival day a large, finely
decorated cheese prepared by shepherds is brought down from each of
the high pastures to the shrine of *Sajigor* – the major spirit of Rumbour
Valley. The shrine is located in a holly oak grove and is the most sacred
place in the valley. Here all the cheese is shared among representatives
from the households of the valley.

Chaomos, in December, is the most important of the festivals and
involves a number of elements, such as transition rites for small
children, rites for the ancestors, sending symbolic gifts to all clan
daughters married into other clans and sacrifices inside the houses to
the female spirit Jestak. In this way new houses constructed during the
year are also initiated for habitation. The valley, houses, women and
men are all purified prior to the arrival of the male spirit *Balumain* from
Tsiam (the Kalasha's mythical country of origin). Prayers addressed to
him asking for fertility among humans, animals and fields mark the
culmination of *Chaomos*. After the purification rites for women and men
have been performed there is a period of seven days during which lovemaking, braiding the women's hair and eating of chicken, maize and
cow's products are taboo. Most of the men sleep in the 'pure' goat
houses for these seven days.

The agricultural year is also marked by a series of minor festivals.
Just before the full moon in February, for example, *Basun-marat* ('spring

sacrifice') signals that the work in the fields can begin. During this festival a bull and two goats are sacrificed at the altar of *Sajigor* with prayers asking for fertility. Ploughing can begin after *Kish-saras* ('the ploughing offering'), which is celebrated on the day before the full moon in March when people gather below *Sajigor* for a communal meal after which praying men sprinkle cows' milk upon the ploughing bulls. And in June and July night dances *Ratnat* safeguard the growth of maize.

Purification rites are important elements in the Kalasha life strategies, whether they are performed during the festivals related to the farming cycle or in case of occurring disasters like earthquake, flood or serious diseases. It is therefore necessary to take a closer look at the pure–impure dualism in the Kalasha worldview.

The concepts of *onjesta* (pure) and *pragata* (impure) permeate the life of the Kalasha. In the valleys the words *onjesta* and *pragata* are frequently mentioned in connection with locations, persons, objects and time. *Onjesta* and *pragata* are not absolute categories but relative and complementary and thereby define each other.

Space – the houses and the valleys – is divided according to the principle of purity. The family house is placed with its most *onjesta* part towards the mountain slope and with the entrance facing the valley. Fire is *onjesta* as well as the shelf on the back wall representing the female family spirit, Jestak. Thus, the house is divided into zones with the fireplace and the area behind it being defined as *onjesta*. Women are not permitted to enter this *onjesta* area but only to reach with the arms and the top of the body into it. The loom is *pragata* and is placed near the door – weaving is always done outside.[7] The inside of a family house is more *onjesta* than the outside, and so the goats may die if adultery is committed inside the house. This progression from the outside to the inside is also expressed during funerals when the widow(er) first sleeps outside the house, then inside close to the entrance before finally moving upwards to sleep upon the bed.

Whereas purity is related to the inside and impurity to the outside of dwellings, purity is associated with 'up' and impurity with 'down' when it comes to valleys (see Figure 1). A movement up the valley towards the shrines, the goat houses and into the high mountains where the fairies dwell is a movement towards increasing purity. The high

---

[7] According to Khrosh Nawaz, the loom is *pragata* because the first loom was made by a man who became *pragata* when he broke the strict rule of extra-clan marriage.

Figure 1: The Kalasha world view

(The 'degree' of purity increases from the left to the right.)

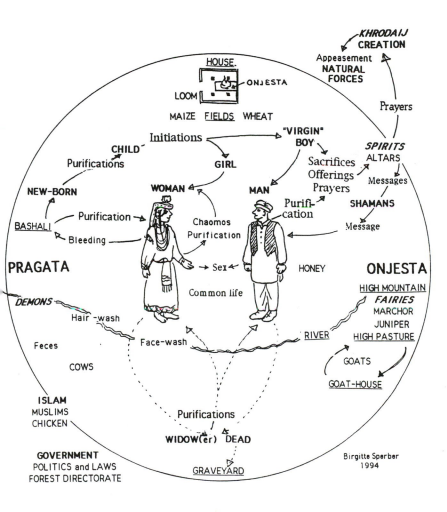

KHRODAIJ
CREATION
Appeasement
NATURAL
FORCES

Prayers

HOUSE
ONJESTA
LOOM
MAIZE FIELDS WHEAT

Initiations
CHILD
Purifications
GIRL
"VIRGIN" BOY
Sacrifices
Offerings
Prayers
SPIRITS
ALTARS
Messages

NEW-BORN
WOMAN
MAN
SHAMANS

BASHALI
Purification
Chaomos
Purification
Purifi-cation
Message

Bleeding

PRAGATA
Sex
Common life
HONEY
ONJESTA

DEMONS
Hair-wash
HIGH MOUNTAIN
FAIRIES
MARCHOR
JUNIPER
HIGH PASTURE

Feces
Face-wash
RIVER

COWS
GOATS
GOAT-HOUSE

ISLAM
MUSLIMS
CHICKEN

Purifications

WIDOW(er) DEAD

GOVERNMENT
POLITICS and LAWS
FOREST DIRECTORATE

GRAVEYARD

Birgitte Sperber
1994

pastures are pure because they belong to the pure fairies. In the men's mind this world is associated with harmony. On the other hand, as women and fields are the main reasons for conflict, the areas with women – the valley bottom, the fields, the paths and the villages – are in the men's minds associated with disharmony (Parkes 1987).

Although a woman may wash her hands wherever she goes, she can only wash her face and clothes down in the valley at a certain distance from the shrines there. She has to wash her body and braid her five plaits further below. The very *pragata* menstruation and parturition house (*bashali*),[8] where she spends the five days of menstruation, gives birth and stays with her baby for twenty days after the delivery, is located even further down the valley in an area where only women are permitted access.

In relation to the outside world, the Kalasha consider themselves *onjesta* while the Muslims around them are *pragata*. However, within the Kalasha world, men are regarded as *onjesta* whereas women during their menstruating stage of life are *pragata*.[9] This affects the movement of Kalasha women who are more restricted in their movements than men. Women must never enter the *onjesta* shrines and during the menstruating stage of life they may not visit the *onjesta* goat houses. During the periods of menstruation and deliveries they are confined to the area around the parturition house (or to a Muslim house). For three months after a delivery lovemaking is taboo and the woman is not permitted to go above the village to the fields (which gives her the time to recover before returning to the strenuous field work). Women are not allowed to go to the high pastures except in rare cases when they may stay only for one night lest it might invite lovemaking which is polluting to the high pastures. When the Kalasha have returned to the villages from the

---

[8] Peter Parkes has gathered evidence that the reason why the *Bashali* is *pragata* is that the *pragata* demons are attracted by the female blood (Parkes, pers.comm.).

[9] That women are *pragata* should not lead the reader to the erroneous conclusion that women are looked down upon in Kalasha culture. They are considered the common pride of the valley and the men proudly talk about 'our women' meaning all women from the valley or from the clan. The women have selfdetermination in all matters of love affairs, and within the strict exogamic rules and periods of abstention a woman alone decides whom to marry and when and with whom to make love. If a man is not good to his wife – for instance if he talks rudely to her or pulls her by her plaits – she normally leaves the house. She might herself take a lover and nobody can force her back again. Women's elopements are the main reason for conflicts (Parkes 1983, 1987), followed by disputes over fields.

summer places and the high pastures, the valley is purified above the upper village and the women are not permitted beyond this point. This means that the women's freedom of movement is further limited during the winter.[10]

Men's activities are regarded as more *onjesta* than women's and this is expressed in their attitude towards work and domesticated animals. The shrine, high pastures, goat houses and (during winter) the holly oak forests on the lower slopes are the world of men and goats whereas the valley bottom and the fields are more closely associated with women and cows.

To the Kalasha the goats are sacred (i.e. *onjesta*); they are taken to the high pastures and are looked after by men who also prepare their dairy products as well as spin and weave their wool. The women spin and weave the wool of sheep, however. Meat of billy-goat and goat cheese brought to an altar during the *Utjao* festival are regarded as *onjesta* and cannot be eaten by women. The *Stumsaras* festival in April is, moreover, specially dedicated to *Goshedoi* (one of the two guardian spirits for goats, this spirit being replaced by *Surizan* at the beginning of *Chaomos*). During this festival the goat houses are covered with flowers, and offerings of small pieces of bread are thrown among the goats as offerings to the ancestor spirits present there. The same is done at the *Kalas-saras* ritual, performed ten days prior to *Joshi*. On the ancestors' day during *Chaomos* the men go to the graveyard and invite the spirits of the ancestors to the clan temples by throwing miniature bread into the area.

The few cows and oxen, on the other hand, are taken care of by women during the summer and stay in the village and at the summer-places. The cows are to a certain extent considered *pragata* – although they are kept in the pure goat houses – and their products should not be eaten during the pure period at *Chaomos*. Chickens are regarded as

---

[10] The women appreciate this as it means the men have to fetch the heavy firewood during the coldest season. Generally the women perceive the mountains as threatening and feel safe and protected where they have to stay. The Kalasha women therefore do not consider themselves restricted but rather free. (See, for example, the film *Kalasha Rites of Spring* by Parkes, P. and J. Shepherd [Granada Television Disappearing World Film, Granada Television of England 1990]). Their standard of reference is the Muslim women, who cover their faces behind veils and whose movements are even more restricted. The Muslims, on the other hand, pity the Kalasha women for having to work in the fields and consider their uncovered faces a sign of being less virtuous. (This attracts a lot of young male Pakistani tourists resulting in a great nuisance to the Kalasha women due to this misunderstanding.)

even more *pragata*, as they symbolize Islam, and all chickens must be removed from the village prior to the purification of the village at *Chaomos*.[11] Although most men would like to eat eggs and chicken except during religious festivals, shamans, dream seers and other very pious men, who are all considered more *onjesta* than the average male Kalasha, do not touch such food at all.

The division into spheres of *onjesta* and *pragata* is also a matter of time. These concepts structure the year. The summer can be interpreted as *onjesta* and the winter as *pragata*. This is expressed through the metaphors of 'up' and 'down' by people moving up towards the highland pastures during the summers and down to the lowlands during the winter. At the same time the *onjesta* sphere expands down into the valley imposing, as already mentioned, further restrictions on women's freedom of movement during the winter.

Like the seasons, people's lives, which are closely related to religion, oscilliate between *onjesta* and *pragata*. Purifications are essential elements in life: of people, places or objects if these have been in contact with the *pragata*; of women after menstruation and parturition; of people before approaching the even more *onjesta* spheres of the divine and fairies and so on.[12] Purification rites also mark the stages of life.

Children are born in the very impure parturition house and amidst female blood which is also considered polluting. However, they are gradually incorporated into the society through a series of purification rituals. After the first ritual, which takes place five or six days after birth, the baby's face can be shown to others. A second purification rite is performed twenty days after birth when the mother and child leave the parturition house. A ritual also has to be held in spring before the child can be taken up the valley to the fields. At the age of between four and six years the child receives the traditional dress during *Chaomos*, and thereafter the child is considered a true Kalasha, which means that

---

[11] According to a myth, the first chicken appeared before a female shaman in a trance at the time when forcible conversion to Islam started some hundred years ago. Today, people keep chicken for their eggs and meat which are used as food as well as a source of income.

[12] Purification can be done in several ways, for example by sprinkling blood from a sacrificed animal on a person (as done during the male purification ceremony at *Chaomos*); by throwing iron objects into a polluted area; or by circling fire and smoke from burning juniper or holly oak over a place, person or group of persons (as done during the female purification ceremony at *Chaomos*). Green walnut branches, water from rivers and springs, goat milk and pure wheat bread are all purifying agents.

a big funeral must be held if the child happens to die. For a boy there are two *Chaomos* ceremonies at two-year intervals and after the second ceremony he becomes a member of the men's society. This marks the beginning of the most *onjesta* period of his life, a period which comes to an end when he starts having sexual relations with girls. During this pure period boys have special religious functions to perform as, for example, the milking of goats near the shrine of Mahandeo and purifying the valley with the milk during *Joshi*. In this way the Kalasha can be said to emphasize male 'virginity' whereas nobody cares whether a girl is a virgin or not.

Both men and women pass through periods of *pragata* and *onjesta*. Whereas males become relatively more *pragata* when they become sexually active, females become more *pragata* with the onset of menstruation. After menopause they again become purer. The attitude towards death is, on the other hand, ambivalent. The ancestors are associated with the *onjesta* goats and are buried at high grounds. Although most Kalasha today deny that death is defiling, death is nevertheless followed by a number of what, to an outsider, seems to be purification rites and pollution taboos.[13] In the Birir Valley the dead body is sometimes purified with water. As the slightly isolated Birir Valley has preserved certain cultural traits which elsewhere are extinct – for example the ancient type of women's headdress, *kupas* (Sperber 1990) – this might indicate that death has been associated with pollution. It is with this in mind that the widow(er)'s progressive movement of the sleeping place from the outside of the house to its inner parts might be interpreted as a process from *pragata* towards *onjesta* after death.

---

[13] A mourning period lasting until the next major festival – or to the following festival if the person dies less than twenty days prior to the first festival – is respected by all clan members. During this period the widow(er) eats from a special cup. Moreover, the widow takes off all her necklaces and removes all decorations but the cowries from the big headdress (*kupas*) which she and the female clan-sisters of the deceased wear during the mourning period without using the smaller headdress (*shushut*). The bed of the deceased is placed in the river for some days and after the funeral all the male clan members shave their heads and then do not shave again until the day prior to the next festival. On returning from the graveyard, people wash their hands. The Kalasha themselves explain these observations not in terms of pollution but in terms of the need to break the very strong ties that exist between husband and wife.

The world of fairies and demons

> Up valley the mountain sides are *onjesta* because of the fairies.
> The fairies and the angels are at the highest places and paths.
> We only go there in the summer. We go out at day time and the
> fairies at night. When we go down the fairies perform
> purification rites after us, and then they can stay there again.
> They live on all the highest mountains (Khrosh Nawaz 1984).

Onjesta and *pragata* are important concepts in the Kalasha attitudes to
nature. In their view 'Nature' belongs to the fairies, demons and spirits,
and people can only use nature after they have asked them for
permission through sacrifices, purifications and prayers. For example,
when the shepherds give offerings to the fairies on the high pastures
every seven days and on the day before the full moon in January there
is a special ceremony (*dewaka*) for the fairy woman who permits the men
to hunt in the high mountains. The big marchor goat which is regarded
as the most prized game among the Kalasha, is extremely rare and,
moreover, is believed to be the cattle of the fairies and during *Choamos*
goat figurines are made to safeguard a good marchor hunt. The hunters
can only shoot the animals which 'the fairies have already eaten –
animals that are only "apparently alive"' (Lièvre and Loude 1990:66).

The doings of fairies and demons are of great relevance to the
Kalasha. Natural features are associated with them, with fairies tending
to live in the highlands, both highlands and fairies being regarded as
onjesta. In the forest zone, fairies are believed to reside in cedar trees and
a logger must be cautious and give offerings every year (Lièvre and
Loude 1990:86).[14] Fairies may dwell in lakes, too. 'The lakes are situated
at high altitudes – the most *onjesta* zone, closest to the divine. They fill
the humans with awe. Nobody dares to go there alone or to disturb the
lake by throwing stones into it' (Lièvre and Loude 1990:80). Unlike
mountain fairies which accept human presence during the summer, lake
fairies seem to be more hostile to people. In a lake on the way to
Nuristan, for example, fairies are believed to inflict immediate death on
anybody who approaches the lake.

Although fairies are generally benevolent towards people, they can
turn malicious if treated badly. On the other hand, the demons are

---

[14] According to Saifullah Jan (see note 15, p.144), sacrifices to trees were only
given if they were used as grave monuments (*gandauw*).

mostly regarded as evil although one demon is believed to have given the water-mill to the Kalasha. Demons tend to live at lower altitudes where they, according to Lièvre and Loude (1990:131), are associated with cow dung and barren leaves and may steal the harvest. Demons are, in other words, closely associated with cultivated fields but they are also believed to reside in mysterious springs. At times a demon looks like a human with an animal's head, at other times it looks 'like a Muslim' (Mirzadana 1987, pers. comm.).

Whereas fairies are generally benevolent, live at high altitudes and are regarded as *onjesta*, demons are clearly associated with evil and lower altitudes and are *pragata*. This can be expressed in the following set of binary oppositions:

fairy	:	demon
good	:	evil
onjesta	:	*pragata*
up	:	down
mountain	:	valley

We have earlier seen that men and their particular activities are regarded as *onjesta* while menstruation and childbirth are classified as *pragata*. This scheme is also extended to domesticated animals. Moreover, we have seen that women and fields are the most frequent sources of conflict in Kalasha society, and both women and fields tend to be regarded as *pragata*. Finally, in relation to outsiders the Kalasha are *onjesta* while the Muslims are *pragata*. We can then extend our scheme of binary oppositions thus:

men	:	women
goat	:	cow
pasture	:	field
nature	:	cultivated
harmony	:	conflict
Kalasha	:	Muslim

In conclusion, it can be said that the Kalasha perception of nature and the entire Kalasha way of life are closely related to the concept of purity imbedded in the Kalasha worldview in a dynamic interaction between nature and worldview. Relations between the Kalasha and the Muslims, between man and woman and between young and old are all expressed through the idoms of purity and impurity where the degree of purity increases as one passes up the valley, as shown in Figure 2.

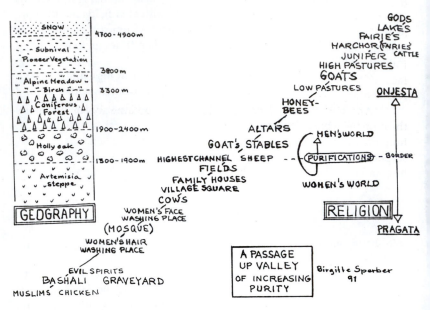

Figure 2: The relationship between altitude and purity

(Inspired by Peter Parkes' model of Kalasha animal values and relative altitude 1987:648).

Myths, gender and resource management

> In the beginning – a long time ago – it snowed with cheese and everybody picked it up and ate it. Then there was a woman who did not show the snow respect; she washed her baby's bottom with it. So the fairies got very angry. They had tried to help the humans by letting the cheese fall down from the sky, you know. Then they changed the cheese into the snow we have now, and the winters became cold (Khrosh Nawaz 1983).

Kalasha legends and myths are rich in explanations for both natural and social phenomena. The above myth, which is typical of the genre, is important for several reasons. It takes us back to a blissful, mythical past before snow and cold winter forced the Kalasha to retreat from the *onjesta* mountains to the *pragata* valleys. The myth is a Kalasha version of the eviction from the Garden of Eden, but whereas Eve's misdeed was disobedience – and thus a sin – toward the almighty God, the Kalasha woman broke a purity taboo by bringing together food and faeces. Again, we see the importance of the concept of purity in the Kalasha worldview.

Another myth explains how the women became *pragata* and why the humans were expelled from Heaven. According to this myth the first humans lived in Heaven where they did not eat until Sheitan fooled the serpent guarding the entrance to Heaven in order to sneak into the human body. Inside Heaven he met Bibi, gave her a letter and said:

> 'This is a letter from your husband. It tells you to eat a grain of wheat from the wheat tree above your head'.
>
> She ate it and at once began to defecate. There was nowhere to hide it, so she tried to hide it here (under the arms) and here (between the legs) and where she hid it hair started to grow.
>
> She asked for help from the wine tree, from the pumpkin tree and from the fig tree. They gave her leaves, but it was impossible to hide it. Then Khrodaij – the world creator – asked the four angels to expel the humans from Heaven. He sent the man towards the west and the woman towards the east, so that they could never see each other (Khrosh Nawaz 1984).

It is also because of a woman's wrongdoing that women are not allowed to eat the meat from *onjesta* male goats. At his own 'live funeral' Sumuluk – a man who had saved a fairy girl from being eaten by a snake – invited people from far and near to a huge feast:

> When it was all over and people came from the funeral carrying the rest of the food, the shaman sat on a pot in the middle of the path. He asked everybody – Kalasha, Muslims, everybody: 'How was Sumuluk, did he give you much or little?
>
> They all answered: 'Oh, he gave us a lot.'
>
> At last a Kalasha woman came walking along the path. The shaman asked her: 'How was it? Did you get meat and every-

thing? Did you get enough at Sumuluk's funeral?'
She complained and said: 'I didn't see anything. The funeral was bad – I got nothing'. In the very moment she said so she stumbled. A lot of meat poured out from the bundle she carried.

Then the shaman ordered that from then onwards the Kalasha women are not allowed to eat the meat from male goats. If they do so, we'll lose our animals. That is why the women don't eat the meat from the male goats (Khrosh Nawaz 1983).

Among the Kalasha there is a strong tradition for the sharing of pastoral and agricultural products which contributes towards an optimal use of resources and if someone accumulates too much higher powers might force him to share. For example, in one legend a farmer turns mad after a bumper harvest of wheat – until he invites people to a big feast and sacrifices to the deities (Sperber 1992:125–126).

In another legend four boys were turned into honeybees because they had been too greedy in their hunt:

> [Nuristanis had killed an entire village in the Bomburet Valley and only seven boys and seven girls escaped, as they had been away making love. The girls were then eaten one by one by a dragon residing in the spring where they fetched water. The boys were frightened, ran away and hid in a big cave where they settled down.]
>
> The four of them went out hunting every day. The fifth went to catch firewood, the sixth went for water and the seventh cooked the food. Once they were all in the cave, a man appeared. He asked them: 'What are you doing?'
>
> Then the first one said: 'I'm fetching water.' The second said: 'I'm fetching firewood.' The third said: 'I'm cooking.' And the four other boys said: 'We go hunting.'
>
> Then the man took out the first three boys with him and closed the cave with the four others inside it. They started to scream. Then he took his spear, pierced the rock and made a little hole and he said: 'Become honeybees and come out through this little hole!' The boys had hunted so many marchors that there were hardly any left, and this was their punishment.
>
> Since then we have the honeybees. Still on that place we can see that honeybees come out from a little hole in the cave (Khrosh Nawaz 1983).

Greed in hunting may cause revenge from the owners of the game, as in the above myth. According to other myths, greed may cause ecological disasters and it might therefore be tempting to ask whether such legends and myths are ways of storing local knowledge about ecosystems and thus protecting the environment. It is impossible to know whether myths about disasters caused by greed and rewards received after sharing were created to encourage people to conserve their natural resources or whether they were originally created for some other purpose. Whatever the case might be, these myths seem to encourage the Kalasha to conserve their natural resources. The idea that natural resources belong to spirits makes the Kalasha use these resources with care.

Nature and a new Kalasha identity

The Kalasha culture is today experiencing a revitalization and there are several reasons for this. Firstly,

> '... in 1975, a livestock epidemic devastated their goat herds. Kalasha responded with an upsurge of ritual observances, where the epidemic was widely interpreted as an attack by evil spirits (*aphāt bala*) that had invaded the valleys as a result of ritual negligence. A shaman of Rumbour rose to sudden prominence after years of obscurity. Together with a new factional leader of the valley, he demanded more stringent respect for traditional rules of ritual "purity" and "impurity", whose breach he diagnosed as responsible for the misfortunes' (Parkes 1990).

Secondly, the political work of Saifullah Jan came as a response to the growing outside pressure on the Kalasha valleys.[15] The Muslim culture

---

[15] Saifullah Jan was born in Rumbour in 1957 and was the first Kalasha to graduate from high school without conversion to Islam. He studied law for a period but devoted himself to political work – in the surrounding world fighting for the rights of his people, inside the community as a settler of disputes and as a mediator between individuals and the public system. For many years the government chose him to represent the Kalasha. In December 1987 he was elected Kalasha representative to the District Council, Chitral. His work for researchers as interpreter of his culture has been a cross-cultural exchange which, combined with his personal qualities, has increased his religio-cultural consciousness and ecological awareness – attitudes he wants to strengthen in his people.

has gained a foothold in the valleys through settlements and conversions. During the later years, though, this has increased the religious and cultural awareness among the Kalasha themselves. Moreover, the Pakistani authorities strongly want to promote tourism in the valleys and see a big potential in this for which reason the culture has to be protected (or even petrified into an open-air museum). Tourism is adding to the pressures on the Kalasha culture and their environment. On the other hand, the Kalasha by observing the foreigners' enthusiasm realize the value of their own culture.

The Kalasha valleys are among the scarcely forested areas in Pakistan but the exploitation of the valleys' own population seems to have been sustainable. However, in Pakistan there is an increasing demand for timber to construct houses for a rapidly growing population. Moreover, in most places in the north firewood is the only source of fuel for domestic use. A heavy influx of Afghan refugees to the north of Pakistan, including to the Chitral area, has also resulted in a considerable increase in the consumption of wood for house building, fuel and small-scale industries. Hence, deforestation goes on with increasing speed – also in the side valleys to Chitral, including the Kalasha valleys, with hardly any reafforestation programmes being carried out. The soil easily gets slippery even after only light rainfall because the slopes are steep and the rocks are mostly from mica slate or silt full of small mica pieces. Without trees to hold back the soil, erosion is rampant.

The number of floods seems to be on the increase the more the forests disappear but not all Kalasha are aware of the wide-ranging consequences of logging. Moreover, poverty has forced some Kalasha men to take employment as loggers for the Directorate of Forestry. A few individuals broke the norm and started to sell timber. This was soon stopped, though, by the elected Kalasha leader. He argued in traditional terms:

> 'I made the people aware of ...'s selling timber. They realized his greed and stopped him. They do not understand that the cutting of forest is responsible for the floods. They just believe that God made it happen due do some wrongdoings. So I tell them the forsts are needed to keep them warm in the winter, and without the forests we will die. In that way I make the people understand ... ' (Saifullah Jan, July 1993)

Greed is today seen as a major threat to sustainable use of resources and accusation of being greedy is a powerful means of keeping the Kalasha to the old values of sharing.

Disputes with outsiders are also interpreted in terms of moral conduct. A case in point is the dispute over logging rights. The forests are under the Forest Directorate which sells permits for logging. According to the law, the inhabitants of the area are entitled to royalties but the people of the Rumbour Valley have never received any. For about ten years they have been battling in courts for influence over management and royalties. It is a major concern for everybody in the valley and is used by the elders to make the people live according to the religious norms. In a speech given to Kalasha men in May 1990 Kata Sing thus said:[16]

> 'When God faced us with a dispute with the Muslims he was testing our faith. He will return your rights to you. This is our hope from God. For God's sake ... we must achieve agreement as one community. We are a poor, ragged people and we are very backward but we are equal to all men. ... Maybe we are just from Rumbour but God is on our side. ... On behalf of the elders I am asking you: Keep your faith and God will give us honour. Justice will be done.'

Maybe not all the Kalasha understand the wide-ranging consequences of logging. However, all are aware of the necessity of having sufficient resources for sustaining the life for a growing population. All Kalasha are desperate when seeing the floods washing fields and houses away.

Development programmes are implemented. A few individuals (the same ones who are interested in selling timber for money) are interested in profitable contractorships for whatever project might arise. However, the vast majority of the Kalasha agree with Saifullah Jan in his work to convince the authorities that development programmes (beside health and educational programmes, of course) first of all have to deal with the protection and enlargement of the ecological resources. They

---

[16] Kata Sing is one of the important elders of Rumbour, former representative in the District Council and one of the important partners to Saifullah Jan in the struggle for Kalasha legal rights. The quotation is from the film *Kalasha Rites of Spring* (Parkes, P. and J. Shepherd, Granada Television Disappearing World Film, Granada Television of England 1990).

want reafforestation programmes, protection walls against floods and more irrigation canals to gain more fields.

The majority of the Kalasha stick to the rules of the culture and think that greed is harmful to the community. They are interested in keeping alive the culture they are proud of, but this is threatened in its ecological basis by the economic greed and materialistic view of nature prevailing in the surrounding world.

References

Cacopardo Alberto and Augusto Cacopardo. 1985. 'The Kalasha (Pakistan) Winter Solstice Festival'. *Ethnology* 28(4):317–329.

Darling, Elisabeth G. 1979. 'Merit Feasting among the Kalash Kafirs of Northwestern Pakistan'. University of Vancouver (unpublished ms.)

Edelberg, Lennart and Schuyler Jones. 1979. *Nuristan*. Graz: Akademische Druck- und Verlagsanstalt.

Haserodt, K. 1990. 'The Geographical Feature and Problems of Chitral'. Paper from the Second International Hindukush Cultural Conference in Chitral.

Jettmar, Karl. 1975. *Die Religionen des Hindukusch*. Stuttgart: W. Kohlhammer.

Jettmar, Karl and Lennart Edelberg (eds). 1974. *Cultures of the Hindukush*. Wiesbaden: Franz Steiner Verlag.

Lièvre, Viviane and Jean-Yves Loude. 1990. *Le Chamanisme des Kalash du Pakistan*. Lyon: Presses Universitaires de Lyon.

Loude, Jean-Yves and Viviane Lièvre. 1980. *Kalash. Les derniers 'infidèles' de l'Hindu-Kush*. Paris: Berger-Levrault.

—— 1984. *Solstice païen*. Paris: Presses de la Renaissance.

Malinowski, Bronislaw. 1925. 'Magic, Science and Religion'. In Needham, J. (ed.) *Science, Religion and Reality*. London: Macmillan Company.

Parkes, Peter. 1983. *Alliance and Elopement. Economy, Social Order and Sexual Antagonism among the Kalasha ('Kalash Kafirs') of Chitral*. Doctoral thesis,

Oxford University.

—— 1987. 'Livestock Symbolism and Pastoral Ideology among the Kafirs of the Hindukush'. *Man* (N.S.) 22:637–660.

—— 1990. 'Kalasha rites of spring. Backstage of a ˌDisappearing World, film'. *Anthropology Today* Vol.6(5).

—— 1990. 'The Kalasha Rites of Spring'. Disappearing World, Granada Television of England.

—— 1991. 'Temple of Imra, Temple of Mahandeo: A Kafir Sanctuary in Kalasha Cosmology'. *Bulletin of the School of Oriental and African Studies, University of London*, Vol.LIV, Part 1.

Robertson, G. Scott. 1896 (Reprint 1985). *The Kafirs of the Hindu-Kush*. Oxford: Oxford University Press.

Saifullah Jan. 1990. 'Development and History of the Kalasha People'. Paper from the Second International Hindukush Cultural Conference, Chitral.

Sperber, Birgitte G. 1990. 'Kalasha dresses, body decorations and textile techniques'. Paper presented at the 2nd International Hindukush Cultural Conference, Chitral. (To be published in Bashir, E. [ed.] *Proceedings from the IInd International Hindukush Cultural Conference, Chitral 1990*. Karachi: Oxford University Press.)

—— 1992. 'Nature in the Kalasha Perception of Life and Ecological Problems'. In Bruun, O. and A. Kalland (eds), *Asian Perceptions of Nature*. Copenhagen: Nordic Institute of Asian Studies.

—— 1993. 'Kalasha Development Problems'. Paper presented at the International Conference for Kalasha Researchers, Moesgård, Denmark.

Klas Sandell

Nature as the Virgin Forest
Farmers' Perspectives on Nature and Sustainability in Low-Resource Agriculture in the Dry Zone of Sri Lanka[1]

> ...Question: 'Was fertilizer applied in the past?'
> Farmer: 'Chi [an expression of negation]! No fertilizer was applied. No plant was used as fertilizer and no chemicals were applied.'
> Q: 'Was the fertility, *pohora gatiya*, of the soil good?'
> F: 'The level of fertility was very good. Fertility in the soil was very good. But after the new fertilizers were applied, unless you apply them again, the fertility is not good.'
> Q: 'What could be the reason for that?'
> F: '[Laughter] I don't know, why there is taste, *rasaya*, in the soil. If there is taste in this great earth which allows things to grow, the villagers were fools, *moda wuna*, when they listened to the government. They were addicted to fertilizers. They accepted what they [the government officers] said, for example "that much is usually harvested and this much will be harvested" [by applying chemical fertilizers]...' (interview with an old Sri Lankan farmer).

In this article the farmers´ perspectives on nature, agriculture and sustainability are brought into focus. They are an often under-utilized resource of knowledge and experience in the search for a more sustainable development. Even though it is important not to accept every

[1] This article incorporates excerpts from the author's dissertation monograph (Sandell 1988), in which further discussions and references to relevant literature can be found (available at: Water and Environmental Studies, Linköping University, S-581 83 Linköping, Sweden). For their generous financial support, I am indebted to the Swedish Agency for Research Cooperation with Developing Countries and to the Nordic Institute of Asian Studies.

aspect of the farmers' perspectives in an uncritical manner there are many elements of what could be labelled an 'ecological long-term perspective' to be found in the villages studied. At the same time there is an increasing interest in sustainability as an important aspect of development among various authorities and international agencies dealing with Third World agriculture. Therefore, a crucial question is how these two perspectives of 'ecological awareness', from below and from above, are interrelated.

With the help of technological improvements and exchange with other regions, it is possible to raise the carrying capacity of an area (supporting more people and/or supplying more goods per person). How sustainable this level of carrying capacity will be depends partly on the ability of social systems (politics, economics, engineering) to maintain necessary physical structures. Discussing sustainability therefore involves a judgement concerning the dynamics between the human possibility of raising the carrying capacity of an area and the fact that, at least on a global level, the resources available are limited.

With regard to agricultural technology, there is a large amount of evidence of unsustainability in the practices presently in use in the industrialized countries. Some of the major indications of this are that short-term returns of inputs to the agricultural system are optimized, and aspects such as depletion of non-renewable resources (for example fossil fuel) and pollution of the environment are neglected. Concerning further development of low-resource agriculture in the Third World, these non-desirable side effects have to be minimized, and to this end the approaches offered by the green revolution are not always feasible. Or as expressed by Myers (1985:60): 'The Green Revolution has only given us a breathing space'.

As a part of a multidisciplinary research project dealing with sustainability aspects of low-resource agriculture (mainly with regard to nutrient supply in lowland paddy rice cultivation) in the dry zone of Sri Lanka, a study of farmers' perspectives on water, nutrients and sustainability was carried out. The study focused on five villages. Information concerning, for example, current population, land areas, number of cattle, and agricultural practices was collected by conducting one primary and two supplementary surveys that included all the 262 households. Also statistics, publications, and maps were used as sources of information. The ethno-perspective of the farmers, in relation to soil fertility, different sources of nutrients and water for agriculture, was investigated by using some 75 semi-structured interviews in addition to the surveys. The possibility of exchange of information within the multidisciplinary research team was an important prerequisite for the design of the study.[2]

After some human-ecological notes concerning the villages studied, this article will discuss the farmers' views of nature and sustainability. First a brief 'ethnosemantic' study will be presented and thereafter follows a discussion of seven common themes among the farmers as deduced by the author from the empirical findings. The study was gradually focusing on water and nutrients as inputs in agriculture and the focus on the farmers, especially the heads of households (mainly adult men), was linked to this objective. As with all generalizations, it will be difficult to find one single person embodying all aspects of every theme. There will, however, be very few who do not relate to the substance of most of them. The article will finish with a discussion of the farmers' perspectives using the conceptual framework of three general 'ecostrategies' and thereafter present a critical discussion of sustainability perspectives 'from above or from below'.

Some physical and cultural features of the case-study area

Due to the monsoon climate there are two growing seasons a year in most parts of Sri Lanka. In the Anuradhapura district, where the case-study villages are located, the annual precipitation is around 1,400 mm, half of which is received during the main growing season. For successful cultivation of paddy rice under erratic precipitation conditions, rainwater is stored in irrigation tanks (reservoirs). Although rice is the staple food in Sri Lanka, 'under British rule the economy of the island was developed almost exclusively for the export of plantation crops to the neglect of the peasant paddy rice producing sector' (Johnson and Scrivenor 1981:51). Nevertheless, the development is impressive and the degree of self-sufficiency (in terms of domestic production compared with import plus domestic production) has increased from between fifty to sixty per cent in the 1950s to almost a

---

[2] The research project was entitled 'Irrigated Agriculture and Eco-development' and was carried out during the 1980s as a joint work involving Swedish and Sri Lankan researchers of both Natural and Social Sciences (primarily biology and geography). See, e.g.: Daléus 1988; Daléus et al. 1988; Karunanayake 1983; Madduma Bandara 1987; Palm 1988; Palm and Sandell 1989; Tilakasiri 1984.

hundred per cent in the 1980s (Sandell 1988:29). The increased yields are largely a result of the so-called 'green revolution' involving high yielding varieties (HYV), chemical fertilizers and so on, and the extension of areas under cultivation is mainly a result of large-scale gravity irrigation schemes.

All five villages have irrigation tanks, rice fields, houses with gardens, and *chena* cultivation (slash-and-burn) in the surrounding forests. This agricultural system is well-integrated in the ecosystem of the area, having existed for at least two thousand years. The populations of the five villages, which have roughly doubled during the last twenty years, varied from about 50 to 530 inhabitants (with a total of about 1,250 in all five villages). Almost all the villagers are Buddhists and belong to the Kandyan Sinhalese group.

A major change concerning agricultural management was brought about through the introduction of the 'green revolution'. It includes a package of techniques, knowledge and concepts. The farmers often talk of the 'old methods', *purana kramaya* (for example, traditional paddy rice varieties, methods for getting rid of crop diseases, and the use of buffaloes) as opposed to the 'new methods', *aluth kramaya* (for example, HYVs, chemical fertilizers, chemical pesticides/herbicides and tractors).

According to survey figures in the largest (and somewhat more remote) village, about one third of the farmers who owned paddy rice land (including lease from the government; a total of 63 out of 106 households) used chemical fertilizers, and almost sixty per cent of the same 63 farmers used pesticides and herbicides for the rice. Tractors (mainly two-wheelers) were used by about one third, and slightly more farmers used buffaloes for land preparation. The corresponding figures for the other four villages were further in favour of the 'green revolution package', with about half to three quarters of the farmers using chemical fertilizers. Farmers who used chemical fertilizers commonly used about half of the recommended doses. These figures are in line with official statistics for the area. The active usage of biofertilizers, like green manure and dung manure, was almost negligible.

Due to the pressure of the increasing population on the available arable land, it is doubtful today whether the threefold agricultural system in the study area is sustainable. For example, circulation time for *chena* cultivation has decreased from about ten to fifteen years to about three to six years. From the 1930s to the 1980s the surface area of the irrigation reservoirs in these villages is roughly unchanged but the population and areas under paddy rice cultivation have increased (by about three to four times and twice, respectively). During the same period the cattle population per area under paddy rice cultivation, as well as *chena* land per capita, decreased (by about two to five times and three to four times, respectively). In these comparisions climate factors were considered as stable and the use of HYVs and chemical fertilizers was not taken into consideration (Sandell 1988:97-101). This comparison illustrates the common theme of a downward fertility situation, as claimed by the farmers.

Ethnosemantics

Some initial research was carried out concerning the general man-nature perspective of the villagers. For this part of the study a method called 'ethnosemantics' was used. The material was analyzed together with a linguist familiar with the method and the results are a product of our joint work.[3]

Words are seldom simple in their meanings. They are vague and often ambigiuous and 'nature' is no exception. A question was included in a survey among 106 adult members of all households in the largest village asking for explanations or examples with regard to six Sinhalese words corresponding to the English word 'nature' (*swabhawaya, swabhavadharmaya, laksanaya, lokaye pavatina swabhawaya, sahaja gathiya* and *wargaya*).[4] The suggested definitions or perceptions of the first word, *swabhawaya*, could be summarized under six headings: ontological, emotive, deontological, aesthetical, cognitive and religious.[5] This word, *swabhawaya*, seemed to be the most general term with *swabhavadharmaya* as a close synonym. The other terms appeared to refer to specific dimensions in the conceptual field but not to the conceptual field as a

---

[3] Concerning the method see e.g., Allwood 1980; Ericsson n.d.; Hirsch 1980a, 1980b. Concerning this case study, see: Hirsch and Sandell n.d..

[4] All the key forms of the six selected words are late derivations from Sanskrit and have a more technical connotation and denote nature more as a physical feature than do the more genuine Sinhalese cognates (P.B. Meegaskumbura, pers. comm. 1985). But, since Sanskrit forms are often used to denote technical connotations in Sinhalese, and the framework of this study was agricultural technology, it served the purpose. Diacritical marks of the six words are found in Sandell 1988:184.

[5] It should be noted that here 'religious' is used in quite a strict sense to indicate the practical aspects of, for example, worshipping.

whole. The question remained whether the meaning of *swabhawaya* could be generally characterized in a way that would relate all these apparently divergent meanings, or, in other words, if there is a common core to the conceptual field.

From the joint analysis with Richard Hirsch the following, abstract, common core was formulated: 'that which comes of itself'. From this common core the various dimensions or conceptual associations of *swabhawaya* could be derived in the field by means of various semantic operations. This vague core can be pictured as hanging in a network of associations according to the interview situation or the informant's current state of mind.

Man as a part of nature

It was not possible to find any clear-cut boundary between man and nature in the villagers' use and understanding of the six Sinhala words for nature discussed above, but instead the natural environment and the cultural features intertwined in the answers. This intertwinement of culture and nature is natural in a context where people are living in a close relation with nature. Egnéus and Hettne (1984:26) wrote: 'in most non-western cultures "natural resources" are (or at least they were) part of a larger system, a cosmology, uniting man, God and nature and prescribing the proper relationship between them'.

The explanations of the six words were followed up in semi-structured interviews carried out with a random sample (ten persons) among the respondents of the survey. This started on a more concrete level by asking: 'Can you say one word which means things such as forests, wild animals, trees, birds, grass and flowers?' The objective of this question was to obtain an indication of what concepts were used for such a group of elements, as the expected answer could be corresponding to 'nature' or the 'natural environment'. The answers varied: 'thick jungle', 'big forest', 'four legged animals of the forest', 'all sentient beings' and 'sanctuary'. The following answer illustrates this lack of a common concept corresponding to our concept of nature: 'We call the forest, forest, *kele*; water, water, *watura*; and among the animals there are various types'.

Asked for concepts contrary to or against those used for nature, different aspects of immoral or bad behaviour were given (for example stealing, slaughtering cattle, lack of cooperation). At first it seemed difficult to reconcile these statements with the characterization 'that which comes of itself'. The statements above indicate that human conduct has some influence on the course of nature.

These statements do, however, make sense, although seemingly the farmers were contradicting themeselves. The line of reasoning is as follows. When asked to give a justification for his way of life – that is the morality of his society; a farmer says that it is moral because it is the natural way. Moral for him means 'according to nature'. Nature is used as a justification for his morality. If someone goes against the way of life or the morality, for example, by breaking the law or neglecting to do his duties as a son, then nature is affected negatively by implication. Furthermore, nature seems to be affected positively by moral practices like proper observation of rituals and duties. If nature constitutes the grounds for justifying morality then a violation of morality is also a violation of nature.

All the concepts, more or less equivalent to nature, discussed in the interviews were generally regarded as something positive. According to one informant: 'The forest, *vanantare*, is a gentle, beautiful and valuable thing.' Another informant said: 'Nature, *svabhavadharmaya*, is good, there is nothing bad in nature. It is people who make it bad.' The latter part of the last quotation shows the theme of man as a threat to nature. It was, for example, expressed like this: 'If the forest, *kele*, is cut down and destroyed it is contrary to nature, *svabhavadharmaya*. Even when considering the trees, their value is more than the profit you can make from them. Clearing of forests is like kicking nature.' It should be kept in mind that from the forest also came, for example, the elephants which sometimes destroyed the crop and the forest also housed demons and snakes. However, at a more general level, the attitude seemed to be positive.

Sins are evolving out of poverty

The religious system of the Sinhala peasants of the dry zone is a very complex one. Ames (1964) divided the Sinhalese religious system into two main parts: *laukika* (worldly or profane) and *lokottara* (holy or sacred). The former consists of a magical animistic system of Hindu gods, astrology and demonism, and the latter is referred to as Buddhism and is divided into 'popular Buddhism' (meritmaking) and 'sophisticated Buddhism' (meditation).[6] This complexity is an important aspect to take into account in any discussion of general attitudes towards nature, not least on a broad level such as 'Buddhist attitudes' or 'Eastern attitudes'. Besides the intricate relationship between ideology and behaviour (Callicott and Ames 1989) we have to examine critically the ideology itself. Even though the farmers here are Buddhists it is obviously not sufficient to look into Buddhist environmental philosophy in order to get to know their environmental attitude.

There are many religious rituals and festivals directly linked to agriculture in the villages. These rituals do not, generally, involve the Buddhist monks. 'It is important to recognize that such rituals do not operate in a vacuum; there is always a practical relevance to the on-going life of the community' (Karunanayake 1978:67). Without going into detail with regard to different rituals, the pantheon and so on, we noted that almost all the villagers participate in the rituals and that they generally claim that they have a great faith in them.

In general, it seems that Buddhism has a very limited *specific* impact upon the farmers' choice and use of, for example, industrialized inputs such as chemical fertilizers or other types of agro-chemicals. It should be noted that this does not exclude the considerable general impact that could be traced from Buddhism to most aspects of life. It is 'apparent that what is generally referred to as traditional Buddhism is doctrinal in so far as certain fundamental features of the Buddhist doctrine... inform and infuse lay Buddhist behaviour' (Tennekoon 1981:61).

The farmers are, for example, very well aware of the increased capacity for killing created by the use of industrialized agricultural inputs as pesticides and herbicides compared with handweeding and other traditional methods, and they are also well aware of the existence of living things in soil and water. Concerning the Buddhist doctrine of not killing, we asked if it was a sin to use these inputs. One answer was that the insects in the water of the paddy rice fields were their enemies so they had to be killed or 'the insects will kill us'. More frequently the explanation was that this was killing without 'intention' and therefore no sin. Killing is a by-product of the agricultural practices, and for

---

[6] This division and the relationship between its elements (and, for example, with modern Buddhism), are discussed by other authors as well. See for example: Bechert 1973, 1978; Gombrich 1971; Schalk 1976. See also: Sandell 1987; Andersen 1992. It must be stressed that the present study was not dealing with religion or Buddhism *per se*, but with the way it was expressed from the focus on agriculture and sustainability.

example, killing worms during ploughing is just an unavoidable effect
of the work. 'Herbicides kill more than handweeding, but since there is
no intention to kill, there is no reason for handweeding.' A Buddhist
monk in a village temple said: 'They [the farmers] do not practise paddy
rice farming to harm anyone. It is done without intention, *chetana* [to
harm]. Therefore, it is not a problem'.

A farmer said that many living creatures in the soil died when an
area was burnt for *chena* cultivation, but no sin was committed since
there was no intention to do so. However, he also added that if there
was any sin connected with this, it would be compensated for by all the
animals (for example, birds, elephants, deer and all the unseen animals)
that would get food from the crop. Nevertheless, rituals were sometimes
carried out asking the animals to leave the area before it was burned for
chena cultivation.

A decrease in precipitation due to deforestation, angry gods and bad behaviour

It was a very common opinion that precipitation had decreased over
time, especially since the beginning of the 1970s. There are great local
variations in precipitation, and it has been impossible to verify the
perception of a general decrease. But Basnayake (1985:104) refers to the
frequent droughts in Sri Lanka and discusses the possibility of a drought
cycle beginning in the 1950s and approaching a decline in the 1980s.
Some indication of a decrease can also be traced in the fact that the
mean precipitation at the Maha Illuppallama Agricultural Research
Station, located twelve to seventeen kilometres from the studied villages
was 1,257 millimetres for the period 1970-1979, which could be
compared with a mean of 1,403 millimetres during the fifty-year period
1905-1956. The villagers' perception of a decrease in the precipitation is
even more understandable since the mean precipitation of 1,521 millimetres for the period 1961-1971 was even higher than that. (All these
figures refer to the Maha Illuppallama research station; Sandell
1988:140-141.)

From an agricultural point of view, the precipitation pattern over
the year is as important as the annual sum. The farmers often claimed
both a total decrease and that at present the rains do not come when
due. According to C.M. Madduma Bandara (pers. comm. 1985), an
analysis of 'agriculturally significant rainfall' also tends to support the
farmers' view.

Being such a crucial natural resource in this local context, it is easy to understand that speculations concerning reasons for changes in precipitation are very frequent. The most frequently given reason was the clearing of forests: 'There is no rain because the jungle has been cleared. If there is jungle even a passing rain cloud tends to stay'. Some people said that increased *chena* cultivation (which mainly occurs in young forests) was not a major reason for these problems, because no large trees were felled for this. It was the large trees which blocked the rain clouds, they claimed. Others said that *chena* cultivation was partly responsible for deforestation, and some said that there had been a threefold increase in the areas for *chena* cultivation during the last fifteen to twenty-five years. There seemed to be a vicious circle: less rain –> less paddy rice –> need for more dryland cultivation –> deforestation –> less rain...! That we are here discussing a general problematique is verified by the fact that, according to C.M. Madduma Bandara (1985), the forest covered seventy per cent of the total land area of Ceylon in the year 1900. By 1953 the forest coverage had diminished to approximately fifty per cent and in 1982 it had been reduced to twenty-five per cent.

The lack of large trees is pointed out as being crucial for the decreased precipitation: 'If the wind dashes against that tree, it rises directly, and there it stops the rain clouds in the sky, and then it will start to rain'. Scientifically it is well known that, on a large scale, the forest cover influences precipitation. But to what extent the forest cover, and especially the large trees, influence the local spatial distribution of rainfall in the way that the farmers claim is not known.

Gods and religious rites were the second main explanation for a decrease in precipitation. 'Because we do not pay attention to the Gods, they pay no attention to us.' Nevertheless, almost all of the villagers participated in the ordinary ceremonial rites. But one villager said: 'Even if the ceremonies are performed, it is not done with any faith in them.'

Bad behaviour among the villagers was the third reason given for the perceived decrease in rain, without explicitly linking this to religious rites or Gods. The country in general was mentioned as being involved: 'It could be the government, it could be the people'. When asked about the main types of bad behaviour, the villagers gave examples of general social misbehaviour such as 'crimes, murders, threats' or 'the fact that children do not even look after their parents'. The parallels between human behaviour and environment could be traced in various ways. We could remember the Buddhist theme that the earth has gradually been destroyed through the sins of the people. 'Thus Buddhism maintains that there is a close link between man's morals and the natural resources available to him' (Silva 1987:13). There is generally a pessimistic view concerning precipitation in the future: 'In our estimate the situation will be very unsatisfactory', some villagers said. The present landscape is 'like a desert, *kanthare*'. This is contrasted with a glorious past when 'the tank was as full as if it was overflowing with milk'.

The lost rasaya *(taste of fertility)*

During the interviews concerning agriculture we came across the Sinhala concept *rasaya*. Literally, it means 'taste' or 'good taste' and could be used to praise a good meal. When informants mentioned *rasaya* while discussing soil fertility and nutrients, it was used as a synonym of fertility. But not in a physical sense – tasting with the mouth. An example is the following statement: 'Now the plants do not grow as when we cleared this land [highland]. The *rasaya* was absorbed by the plants'. Or: '*rasaya* will be there when the earth is loosened and when the forest is burned. That is *rasaya*'. Also 'the *rasaya* of the soil in the paddy fields' was referred to.

Linkages between sweet taste of soil and a harmonious relation between Man and Nature is a part of, for example, Buddhist mythology (Silva 1987:11). As examples of farmers physically tasting the soil to judge its fertility have been reported from other countries, we tried to investigate whether or not the concept of *rasaya* used by these Sinhala farmers involved 'soil tasting' to determine the fertility of the soil.

The informants described how fertility could be judged by the amounts and types of plants growing in the area. They also said that the colour of the soil gave an indication. But no one had heard of the possibility of tasting the soil until one day, during an interview with an 87-year-old man who said that 'soil tasting' was possible and that he had heard of it being done. He also gave an example of a well that had been located according to this method. According to him the 'taste is like honey if *rasaya* is very abundant'. He also claimed that *rasaya* is created in contrast to chemical fertilizers that are produced, used and absorbed. He said that *rasaya* is created and generated in the way that the living air, *prana vayuva*, has been created out of the interaction between water, fire, the sun and the moon and comes to the plants. 'It is like inhaling and exhaling.' He also said that if an area is used for *chena* cultivation the living air is collected by the forest and, as regards paddy rice cultivation, the water creates *rasaya*. 'The water provides the paddy rice with food as a mother ... The quality of the water is absorbed by the soil in the paddy rice field.' The story of *rasaya* illustrates that important agricultural knowledge and practices probably have been lost or at least hidden in this region. But it also has a parallel in the common themes discussed by these farmers concerning deteriorating natural resources and scepticism towards industrialized agricultural inputs.

Physical and social adaptation to the package

The following sequence of ideas was common during the semi-structured interviews. Firstly, the irregular use of industrialized inputs (like chemical fertilizers) was motivated mainly by the high costs involved. The need to use the whole package of chemical fertilizers, pesticides and herbicides, with the HYVs, as 'they [the HYVs] need them', was often stated. The non-use of other sources of nutrients or other varieties, which are considered as the 'good old' practices was noticed. Asked why, if the old practices were so good, most answers dealt with the quick effects and the easy handling of the industrialized inputs. This sequence will be somewhat further discussed below.

During initial surveys the following theme arose: diminishing yields with the passing of time due to the use of chemical fertilizers. From a sustainability point of view this was interesting to scrutinize further. The survey and semi-structured interviews indicated a very strong line of reasoning about some sort of deterioration being due to the use of chemical fertilizers. The conflict between high yields of today and long-term problems, in addition to current expenses, was a viable theme among the farmers. None of them argued that the short-term net yield would have been higher without industrialized inputs. 'It is the pesticides and herbicides and the chemical fertilizers which make it possible for us to eat our rice [make a living].' Some farmers even claimed that there were no long-term, negative effects whatsoever: 'Yes, I have heard about the soil or paddy rice getting used to chemical fertilizers, but, those who say that do not have a good knowledge'.

It should be noted that the Agricultural Extension Service offered heavy subsidies, loans and advice for the promotion of the green revolution package (the fertilizer subsidy was withdrawn in 1990). External channels of information were also important: two-thirds of the interviewed were literate and forty per cent of the households in the largest village claimed that they listened to the radio daily.

From a scientific point of view, this line of reasoning, that paddy rice is getting used to chemical fertilizers, is questionable. But if a broader, long-term perspective is applied to 'soil' and if it is discussed in terms of the local natural and social environment, the picture of adaptation to the external inputs seems quite reasonable. Since chemical fertilizers are costly it will not be sufficient with a slightly increased yield, but instead the yield must be so much higher that it exceeds the expenses of the input which involves a higher risk. It could also be hypothesized that the farmers' impression of a decrease in fertility linked to the use of modern inputs could partly be a reflection of the very high potential of the HYVs, if well managed. In other words, the decrease could partly be seen not only in relation to previous yields but in relation to the potential yields.

The good old methods

The traditional practices were generally considered good with regard to long-term effects: 'As nothing happened when using the traditional varieties in the past, nothing will happen now'. The following passage from an interview with an old former irrigation headman (A) and a young man about twenty years old (A1) illustrates some of the lines of reasoning about the choice of agricultural methods (even if the statement that people were taller in the past obviously has to be understood as a metaphor and an idealization of the past). This former irrigation headman (A) was an 'early adopter' of the new practices, which means that he was in a way evaluating his own efforts.

> [After questions about how and when the agro-chemicals and the chemical fertilizers came to this village.]
> ...A1: 'The elders say that with the introduction of chemicals and chemical fertilizers, more diseases had come. The people in the past were four *riyan* (192 centimetres). Very tall people. But as time passed, their strength decreased and the diseases increased. The elderly say it is due to agro-chemicals and chemical fertilizers.'
> Q: 'Are they correct?'
> A: 'That is really correct. The hybrid paddy rice is not as nutritious as the other [old varieties]. No taste. No matter how many tasty curries are made, the rice is not tasty to eat.'

Q: 'Then why did the farmers [start to use the new varieties and chemical fertilizers]?'
A: 'We realized it later, *passene vetahune*. Because of the desire, *asawa*, for income.'
A1: 'Desire for income. It was only realized when looking back.'
A: 'The hybrid system did not originate in Sri Lanka. It was created and proliferated elsewhere, *bo karanawa*.'
Q: 'So what does that mean?'
A: 'It first started elsewhere and was then given to [Sri] Lanka.'
Q: 'What's wrong with that?'
A: 'There is nothing wrong really. When these varieties were cultivated in those countries, they brought a good harvest. Therefore they thought that this should be done in Sri Lanka, too...'

There was obviously a conflict about different characteristics of the new varieties and the old varieties. Some disappointment over the previous adoption, combined with an idealized picture of the past, could be noted as well. Rational arguments too, were often given in favour of the traditional varieties, for example, that the old varieties could stand low management conditions better, which is reasonable.

The quick and easy way

Since some sources of nutrients (like dung manure and green manure) were so rarely used and at the same time considered good, a natural question was why they were used so infrequently? In addition to the arguments of 'adaptation' of the soil and the society to 'the package', farmers often started to talk in terms of 'laziness'. One farmer said: 'Why it is not used? It is the same when we do not use curry leaves around here [for cooking], but use onions and so on bought from other places'. A trader argued: 'People want to do things the easy way. A farmer just asks his son to go to the shop and buy instead'.

There is a low concentration of nutrients in bio-fertilizers (for example, dung manure has a nitrogen content of only around one per cent, compared with forty-six per cent in urea). In practical terms, this means a tremendous difference in the amount of human labour involved in fertilizing fields with different fertilizer inputs, since the studied farming system was mechanized only to a limited extent. Or as one farmer said: 'To fertilize half an acre [about 0.2 ha] a lorry load of dung manure is needed. Instead, about twenty-five kilogrammes of chemical fertilizers which you can take on the back of your bicycle could be used'. Generally, the use of bio-fertilizers needs more planning, forethought and cooperation than the industrialized inputs, preconditions that are counteracted by the deterioration of the traditional village cooperation. Therefore, with regard to the workload necessary before the paddy cultivation, a higher risk is also involved in the use of bio-fertilizers as sometimes no cultivation is carried out due to, for example, lack of water. The following excerpt from an interview illustrates some of the arguments discussed above. The informants were a 23-year-old man (B) and a middle-aged man (B1).

> ... Question: 'Are there other sources of nutrients besides chemical fertilizers? What do you think of dung or green manure for example?'
> B: 'These are not in use in this area.'
> Q: 'What is the reason for this?'
> B: 'Because from those days, *ekale*, people were not accustomed to those. That is why. But in fact we don't need chemical fertilizers in our village. We have dung manure and green manure. We could use these types if people used their brains. But people don't think. They only want to buy chemical fertilizers. But dung manure is more valuable than chemical fertilizers.'
> Q: 'Why are dung and green manure better than chemical fertilizers?'
> B: 'There is a way to make local fertilizers. Dung manure should be mixed with green manure in a certain way.'
> Q: 'Are you talking about compost?'
> B: 'Yes, that is better than chemical fertilizers. Cattle eat grass. Fertilizers are already in the plants, so they remain. Therefore the manure is better than chemical fertilizers.'
> Q: 'How can grass be better than chemical fertilizers?'
> B: 'The cattle don't eat one type of grass but many. Thus they eat all types of nutrients. For example *mukunuwenne* and *gotukola* [leafy vegetables, also eaten by people] contain more nutrients. They have more quality. These are eaten by cattle, and dung is dropped on the ground. That is how it is working.'
> Q: 'Is dung manure better than chemical fertilizers [rechecking]?'
> B: '*Hondai* [Very Good!]'...
> Q: 'Do you use dung manure yourself?'
> B: 'No!'

Q: 'Why?'
B1: 'Because they are lazy. If dung manure was used, how valuable it could have been, *watinewa*...'

There is obviously a striking discrepancy between what is said and what is done concerning the benefits of different sources of nutrients. At the time of the present study, it was easy to recognize that the perspectives concerning the 'good old methods' were not carried out in practice due to various problems, not 'laziness', but mainly technical and structural problems.

The conceptual framework of three ecostrategies

The shaping of environmental attitudes and behaviour is obviously not easy to study. It could be seen from an individual point of view, but also as a process taking place within different groups and within the whole society. The conceptual framework of 'ecostrategies' has been used for discussions of strategies for the utilization of nature employed by individuals or groups (Sandell 1988). 'Eco-' indicates that the man-nature relationship is in focus, and it is not used in any normative way as in, for example, 'eco-development'. The fact that there are often tensions between views (ecoviews) and practices (ecopractices) is an important part of the conceptual framework.

It is common to identify a dichotomy of 'domination' versus 'adaptation' with regard to human views and use of nature. A similar division has, for example, been carried out by Friedmann and Weaver (1979) with the concepts 'functional' and 'territorial' development. In the following, domination will be understood as the principle of trying to adapt nature to man as far as possible. With the help of large-scale technological structures, one tries to free oneself from the local environment, its resources and characteristics. The ecostrategy of adaptation will be understood as an endeavour to adapt to the local context. This strategy of adaptation, however, contains features which are quite disparate, and a division into three main ecostrategies has therefore been suggested (Fig. 1).

Figure 1. The division of ecostrategies into three directions (Sandell 1988:57)

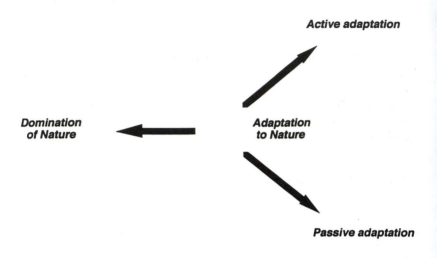

'Active adaptation' indicates an interest in utilizing the human compe-
tence to raise the carrying capacity of a local environment with the help
of technology. This involves the acceptance of changes in the environment and its characteristics. The strategy of 'passive adaptation' does
not involve a belief in any sustainable rise in the carrying capacity and
involves a, more or less explicit, perspective of the need for human
subordination to nature.

All ecostrategies are composed of various elements, and agriculture
is no exception. The main factor affecting orientation along the axis of
domination versus adaptation (passive or active) is the extension of
material, spatial and temporal linkages. The domination inputs are in
the present context linked to industrial society. These inputs are often
produced from non-renewable resources, and with the help of processes
which are large-scale, producing long series of identical products for
large markets. The inputs are meant to be generalized solutions to
similar (but not identical) problems. Examples of such inputs are HYVs,
tractors, chemical fertilizers, pesticides and herbicides.

The passive use of nutrients available in soil and in water, could be seen as a passive adaptation to nature. In the present case study this could be illustrated with the *chena* cultivation. The active use of local resources, such as collecting and increasing the production of dung and green manure and agroforestry (diversification involving different crops for consumption, fodder, timber and fuelwood) according to, among other things, 'conservation farming' methods (Wijewardene and Waidyanatha 1984), could be seen as practices and views close to the active adaptation strategy. This means that an agricultural system is more or less influenced by a domination of a passive or an active adaptation ecostrategy.

A main question in the endeavour for a more sustainable development is to what exent it has to take the adaptation strategy seriously. It could be argued that the main cleavage between a more conventional and a more radical perspective of sustainability is linked to the tension between a domination versus an active adaptation ecostrategy (passive adaptation is hard to combine with any development in terms of increased material welfare).[7] Therefore, the role of local, cultural and physical features will be crucial if an endogenous, active adaptation ecostrategy is chosen. The local environmental philosophy is one important aspect of this, both as a carrier of and a barrier against different development efforts.

With regard to the necessary discussions concerning the possibility of a more sustainable development better adapted to local cultural and physical context, it is important to keep in mind that the two main reasons for the recent greatly improved food supply situation in Sri Lanka (increased yields and extended areas for cultivation) are closely linked to a domination ecostrategy. It is not known, however, what the current situation in Sri Lanka would look like if the same amount of effort had been made in the direction of a more active adaptation ecostrategy. It should also be noted that Sri Lanka's current 'self-reliance' concerning food is externally dependent as regards necessary inputs (for example, financial support, know-how, machines and chemical fertilizers). But it is also important to face the fact that dependence on small regions makes it difficult to even out the imbalances in space and time found in nature. This shortcoming is one

---

[7] With regard to sustainable development see, for example: Brown 1993; Fox 1990; Gadgil and Malhotra n.d.; Naess 1973; Nerfin 1977; Redclift 1987, Sachs 1974; WCED 1987, Wolf 1986.

reason for the interest in local diversity in the utilization of natural resources.

Figure 2. The change in the ecostrategy found in the study area, from adaptation towards domination, mainly manifested itself in terms of ecopractices. The contradiction between stressing the glorious past while further developing local ressources manifested itself as ecoviews (Sandell 1988:177).

The farmers in the studied villages expressed a need for increased yields and therefore the need to use industrial agricultural inputs which to a large extent were not available due to cost and, if used, perceived as being bad for the quality of the soil and for the quality of the food produced. This situation was expressed in terms of being in a 'sandwiched' position. The possibility of a move in the direction of an active adaptation ecostrategy in terms of, for example, better use of local rainfall and active use of local bio-fertilizers was almost solely manifested verbally, not in practice. Instead, there was a strong element of longing for the past, perceived as a situation when no fertilizers were needed, people cooperated with each other and the forest was tall. The latter perspective involved a lack of progressive, active approaches to the use of the local environment and must be considered as an ecostrategy of passive adaptation to natural fluctuations: 'Cannot do anything beyond what the sky does'. In sum, these villages were in a process of transition involving the disintegration of previous norms and practices and with various tensions between ecoviews and ecopractices. Figure 2 illustrates some major elements in the farmers' environmental perspectives related to agriculture.

Ecological awareness from above or from below?

According to Leach's investigation of a similar village in the 1950s: 'Magical hocus-pocus has been replaced by guaranteed prices and the government mill at Medawachichiya railway station. Folklorists may lament, but the modern villager finds himself living in a golden age' (Leach 1971:32). Obviously, this stands in sharp contrast to the picture I found, and in principle, the differences could depend upon: (i) negative effects of the new era have gradually become obvious to the farmers and/or; (ii) lack of reliability or validity of the study carried out and/or; (iii) there were real differences between the villages studied. Because the results were similar in the five villages, because different investigation techniques were used and because the farmers had very articulated explanations and arguments, the first reason seems to be most important, or as a farmer said: 'We realized it later'.

But how could we know that this increased interest in the negative aspects of the new techniques is not a result of influences from the authorities who now show an interest in these aspects of Third World development strategies? This is of course hard to prove since there were such influences present to some extent. For example, the officials of the Agrarian Services Centre were positive about the use of dung and green manure. But at the same time, when we asked the farmers about what the types of fertilizers recommended for paddy rice by the Agricultural Extension service were, out of 156 farmers (in four villages) 138 answered chemical fertilizers. Only one said green manure and two said dung manure (fifteen gave no answer or did not know).

Looking at another important theme – the farmers pointing to deforestation as a main reason for a decrease in precipitation – the possibility for an external influence was there because such information has been available in the area. However, when Tennakoon (1986:144) investigated how various people explained drought, he found that in similar villages as those we have studied, 70 per cent of the villagers mentioned forest destruction as a primary cause of drought. This was followed by excessive use of water (29 per cent) and acts of God (25 per cent). Colonists in the same region placed deforestation third on their list of causes (17 per cent), preceded by acts of God (21 per cent) and 'don't know' (39 per cent) (more than one answer could be given), despite the fact that such people generally are more exposed to official information.

According to the case study presented here, the general impression from the mid-1980s was that there was still not much communication between the two perspectives of 'ecological awareness' from 'above' and from 'below'. Instead the situation was mainly perceived as a dichotomy between: (i) the positive attitude held by the farmers towards traditional management (involving many 'ecological' lines of reasoning) but also associated with 'backwardness'; and (ii) the necessity of using the 'green revolution package' associated with the 'progressive' perspective of more affluent farmers, the authorities and the industrialized world. The recent inclusion of aspects of ecological sustainability in the ideology of authorities was not noticed by the farmers according to this case study. This perspective of 'backwardness' versus 'progressivity' could be illustrated with the following excerpt from the interview with the farmer B1 above.

> ... B1: 'Example, when the tractor man comes he asks for 500 Rs. People don't have money to pay that. Because of that they have to work hard to get a harvest. Foreign methods are very good, very good to follow, but for that we have to be developed, *dijonou* [broad term], first.'

Nevertheless, with regard to the need for being more 'developed', there is considerable evidence for the need of more sustainable development efforts than the conventional strategy concerning the use of natural resources. Therefore we could hopefully interpret the situation in the context of the case study, not as a 'Malthusian trap' (Mikesell 1970:49), but as a transition to an intensified and sustainable use of local resources.

But, even though the environmental philosphy of the farmers, here briefly presented, could hopefully be of some inspiration for the cross-cultural interest in a more sustainable development, it is even more important to remember that '...environmental philosophies that are meaningful and inspiring in nations of the Asian persuasion will have to emerge out of Asian traditions of thought' (Hargrove 1989:xxi). The impression of a deep public concern for the environment seems to be firm in the area studied, a concern which is important to take into consideration when looking for sustainable development strategies for tomorrow. But, the farmers' environmental perspective has, nevertheless, to take its starting point in the crucial balance between the dual need for risk-minimization and a good yield. The real test for any environmental philosophy is, from the farmers' point of view, whether its practical implications inspire confidence with regard to this fundamental need.

References

Allwood, J. 1980. *Antropologisk lingvistik - en projektbeskrivning*. Papers in Anthropological Linguistics, No. 1, Univ. of Gothenburg.

Ames, M.M. 1964. 'Magical-animism and Buddhism. A Structural Analysis of the Sinhalese Religious System'. *Journal of Asian Studies* 23(6):21-52.

Andersen, J.Ø. 1992. 'Sinhalese Buddhist Cosmology and Nature'. In Bruun, O. and A. Kalland (eds), *Asian Perceptions of Nature*. Copenhagen: Nordic Institute of Asian Studies.

Basnayake, B.K. 1985. 'Climatological Drought in Sri Lanka, 1871-1980'. In *Abstract Volume, International Symposium on Concepts and Techniques of Applied Climatology*, March 18-21, A.U. Waltair, India.

Bechert, H. 1973. 'Contradictions in Sinhalese Buddhism'. *Contributions to Asian Studies* 4:7-17.

—— 1978. 'On the Popular Religion of the Sinhalese'. In Bechert, H. (ed.), *Buddhism in Ceylon and Studies on Religious Syncretism in Buddhist Countries*. Göttingen: Vandenhoeck and Ruprecht.

Brown, L.R. (ed.). 1993. *State of the World '93*. New York: Worldwatch Institute (annual report).

Callicott, J.B. and R.T. Ames. 1989. 'Epilogue: On the Relation of Idea and Action'. In J.B. Callicott and R.T. Ames (eds), *Nature in Asian Traditions of Thought: Essays in Environmental Philosophy*. New York: State University of New York Press.

Daléus, E. 1988. *Resource Management in Traditional Farming: A Case Study in the Dry Zone of Sri Lanka*. Linköping Studies in Arts and Science, No. 31, Linköping.

Daléus, E., O. Palm, K. Sandell, S.N. Jayawardena and G.D. Siripala. 1988. 'Management and Environmental Constraints to Rice Yields Within a Village Irrigation System: A Case Study from Sri Lanka'. *GeoJournal* 17(3):401-12.

Egnéus, H. and B. Hettne. 1984. 'The Analysis of Natural Resource Use: A Conceptual framework'. Paper presented at the ISSSR/SAREC symposium, Nov. 5-7 in New Delhi.

Ericsson, E. n.d. 'Naturdefinitionen, tre-betygsuppsats i allmän språkkunskap'. Dept. of Linguistics, Univ. of Gothenburg, Sweden.

Fox, W. 1990. *Toward a Transpersonal Ecology: Developing New Foundations for Environmentalism*. Boston: Shambala.

Friedmann, J. and B. Weaver. 1979. *Territory and Function*. London: Edward Arnold.

Gadgil, M. and K. Malhotra. n.d. *A People's View of Eco-development*. Environmental Services Group, World Wildlife Fund-India, New Delhi.

Gombrich, R.F. 1971. *Precept and Practice*. Oxford: Clarendon Press.

Hargrove, E.C. 1989. 'Foreword'. In J.B. Callicott and R.T. Ames (eds), *Nature in Asian Traditions of Thought: Essays in Environmental Philosophy*. New York: State University of New York Press.

Hirsch, R. 1980a. 'A Study in Swedish Fear Vocabulary'. *Papers in Anthropological Linguistics*, No. 4, Dept. of Linguistics, Univ. of Gothenburg, Sweden.

—— 1980b. 'Ett semantiskt fält för glädje'. *Papers in Anthropological Linguistics*, No. 8, Univ. of Gothenburg, Sweden.

Hirsch, R. and K. Sandell. n.d. 'Eco-views and Ethnosemantics: What We Could Learn from Some Villagers in Sri Lanka about Our Relation to Nature' (ms.).

Johnson, B. and M. Scrivenor. 1981 *Sri Lanka: Land, People and Economy.* London: Heinemann.

Karunanayake, M.M. 1978. 'Mutti-Mangalaya: A Note on the Cultural Ecological Significance'. *Vidyodaya J. Arts, Sci., Lett.* 6(2):67-69.

—— 1983. *Irrigation Systems in Sri Lanka: A Survey.* Dept. of Water in Environment and Society, Univ. of Linköping, Sweden.

Leach, E.R. 1961. *Pul Eliya, a Village in Ceylon.* Cambridge: Cambridge University Press.

Madduma Bandara, C.M. 1985. 'Catchment Ecosystems and Village Tank Cascades in the Dry Zone of Sri Lanka'. In Lundqvist, J. et al. (eds), *Strategies for River Basin Management.* The GeoJournal Library. Dordrecht: D. Reidel Publishing Company.

—— 1987. 'Towards an Optimization of the Use of Local Water Resources in Integrated Rural Water Development'. A Paper Presented at the Working Group on Sustainable Rural Water Development: Nordic Conference on Environment and Development, Stockholm, 8-10 May, 1987.

Mikesell, M.W. 1970. 'Cultural Ecology'. In Bacon, P. (ed.) *Focus on Geography,* Washington DC: National Council for Social Studies.

Myers, N. (ed.). 1985. *The GAIA Atlas of Planet Management.* London: Pan Books.

Naess, A. 1973. 'The Shallow and the Deep, Long-Range Ecology Movement: A Summary'. *Inquiry* (16):95-100.

Nerfin, M. (ed.). 1977. *Another Development: Approaches and Strategies.* Uppsala, Sweden: The Dag Hammarskjöld Foundation.

Palm, O. 1988. *Traditional Lowland Rice Agriculture in Sri Lanka, Nitrogen Cycling and Options for Biofertilizers.* Linköping Studies in Arts and Science, No. 21, Linköping, Sweden.

Palm, O. and K. Sandell. 1989. 'Sustainable Agriculture and Nitrogen Supply in Sri Lanka: Farmers' and Scientists' Perspective'. *Ambio* 18(8):442-48.

Redclift, M. 1987. *Sustainable Development: Exploring the Contradictions.* London: Methuen.

Sachs, I. 1974. 'Ecodevelopment'. *Ceres* 7 (Nov-Dec): 8-12.

Sandell, K. 1988. *Ecostrategies in Theory and Practice: Farmers' Perspectives on Water, Nutrients and Sustainability in Low-resource Agriculture in the Dry Zone of Sri Lanka*. Linköping Studies in Arts and Science, No. 19, Linköping, Sweden.

Sandell, K. (ed.). 1987. *Buddhist Perspectives on the Ecocrisis*. Buddhist Publication Society, Wheel series, No. 346/348, Kandy, Sri Lanka.

Schalk, P. 1976. 'The Encounter between Buddhism and Hinduism in Buddhist Ritual'. *Temenos* 12:78-92.

Silva, L. 1987. 'The Buddhist Attitude Towards Nature'. In Sandell, K. (ed.), *Buddhist Perspectives on the Ecocrisis*. Kandy, Sri Lanka: Buddhist Publication Society, Wheel series, No. 346/348.

Tennakoon, M.U.A. 1986. *Drought Hazard and Rural Development*. Colombo: Central Bank of Sri Lanka.

Tennekoon, S. 1981. *Buddhist Involvement in a Changing Society*. Colombo: MARGA Inst., M/566.

Tilakasiri, S.L. 1984. *The Indigenous Irrigation System at the Village and Liyadda Level*. Paper presented at the workshop on the History of Science and Technology in Sri Lanka, General Reserach Council, Sri Lanka Ass. for the Advancement of Science, Dec., Colombo.

Wijewardene, R. and P. Waidyanatha. 1984. *Conservation Farming*. Colombo: Dept. of Agriculture, IITA Sri Lanka Program.

Wolf, E.C. 1986. 'Beyond the Green Revolution: New Approaches for Third World Agriculture'. *Worldwatch Paper*, No. 73, Washington DC: Worldwatch Inst.

WCED (World Commission on Environment and Development). 1987. *Our Common Future*. Oxford: Oxford University Press.

Ole Bruun

Fengshui and the Chinese Perception of Nature

The intention in this essay is not to go into great detail about the techniques involved in *fengshui*,[1] the Chinese art of placement, which in lack of more precise terms we translate as 'geomancy'. Many similar techniques are practised across East and Southeast Asia. Instead, I shall focus on *fengshui* as a system of statements on the man–nature relationship in an environment of holistic thought. Of particular interest is the use of natural metaphors: how the *fengshui* idiom provides common people in China with a means of paraphrasing relations in the social world, explaining not only hierarchy, social competition and personal success and failure, but also allowing strong anti-authoritarian political statements to be dressed up in a metaphorical language.

There are, nevertheless, good reasons for investigating *fengshui* as a key element in the Chinese approach to nature. Developed from a diffuse vitalism, *fengshui* has a long continuous history dating back several centuries BC,[2] and it was already in the fourth century AD divided into two main schools of thought, Fujian and Jiangxi, emphasizing 'orientations' and 'shapes' respectively (March 1968:261; Needham 1962:242). It bridges classical literary works and public uses, and it seems to have been utilized by all strata of Chinese society (Freedman 1968:8) and taken seriously by many eminent Chinese thinkers (March 1968:1), although Confucianism has repeatedly opposed it as overblown magic. It is spread geographically all over the Chinese world (Needham

---

[1] The Chinese encyclopedia *cihai* accounts of *fengshui* as follows: 'Fengshui, also called *kan yu*. A superstition of the old China. Considers wind directions, water streams and other topographical features in the surroundings of a house or a grave site in order to indicate the inhabitants' disaster or good fortune. Also way of directing residences and graves'.

[2] For a discussion of several theories on the origin of 'Chinese geomancy', see Yoon (1976:245-59).

1962:240),[3] it has been used continuously in Hong Kong, Taiwan and Singapore, and it is currently being seen to increase its influence dramatically on the mainland, despite its strong suppression there since the revolution in 1949.

Premises

Any social scientist who has been working in China knows that the written tradition and the ordinary social life of the Chinese are often far apart. They may even represent separate realities – not in the sense that one is true and the other false, but by both being indispensable to the Chinese social ethos, since the Chinese have continuously preferred to depict their world by means of such contradictions. When we investigate the Chinese perception of nature (*ziran*), these problems are further amplified. The Chinese have a long literary tradition emphasizing the veneration of nature, but we have few means of investigating how this was applied in practice.[4] We should keep in mind that in this field a profound discrepancy may also have prevailed between word and practice, with philosophy being a moralizing agency stressing ideal culture rather than observed reality. A tension between natural philosophy and concrete human interaction with nature must have been felt, for instance between Confucianism maintaining that 'wealth and honour are from Heaven' and common ancestor beliefs and burial rituals indicating how men may alter Heaven's doom.

When dealing with comparisons between literary expressions of nature in China and the West, we run the risk of comparing dissimilar classificatory, or cognitive, spaces for which highly different terminologies are used. In such cross-cultural comparison a basic consideration should be semantics, syntax and noun typology of the

---

[3] Needham, occupied with the Chinese contribution to 'world science', has only treated *fengshui* principles sporadically: 'Purely superstitious though in many respects they sometimes became, the system of ideas as a whole undoubtedly contributed to the exceptional beauty of positioning of farmhouses, manors, villages and cities throughout the realm of Chinese culture' (1962:240).

[4] Several writers, for instance John B. Cobb (1972), stress that the Chinese natural philosophy has not prevented deforestation and destruction of the environment in history.

languages concerned.[5]

The Chinese are known for anthropocentrism in their philosophy and extreme sociocentrism in basic orientations – meaning that by far the greater part of the 'world that matters' is made up by humans and human society. Yet I shall not argue that the Chinese perception of what belongs to 'nature' is totally different from our own. China has a long history of reflections on nature, and many of the concepts derived from 'nature' compare with western terms. We may also speak in Chinese of the 'natural world' (*ziranjie*), 'natural environment' (*ziran huanjing*), 'nature preserve' (*ziran baohuqu*), 'natural resources' (*ziran ziyuan*), 'natural behaviour' (*ziran xingwei*), and even 'naturalism' (*ziran zhuyi*). The term signifying nature, *ziran*, indicates spontaneity, while the natural sciences (*bowu*) refer to the study of the 'abundant matter'.

Nature in a pure, material sense – like untouched ground and landscape, wild animals and life hidden in the depth of the ocean – is probably understood and signified in terms comparable with the West. However, the closer we get to the zone where nature and culture blend, the sharper the differences are in a cross-cultural perspective.

Fengshui

Fengshui operates exactly on the borderline between society and nature. *Fengshui*, meaning wind-water,[6] interprets the influence of natural forces on human constructions, primarily houses and graves. The shape of the landscape and the flow of rivers and canals are of prime importance, since these are the products of the creative forces of the 'winds and waters'. *Fengshui* traces human success and failure, not so much to individual acts, but to the mysterious workings of earthly forces, of which wind and water are only their physical aspects. Such forces are believed to be responsible for determining health, prosperity, position

---

[5] The implications of the Chinese exclusive use of mass-nouns (as compared to count-nouns) on the perception of nature are treated by Chad Hansen 1983, although his interpretation is radical.

[6] In Chinese the term may be seen to denote 'that which cannot be seen and that which cannot be grasped' (Giles 1908:447). Western writers have, according to argument and attitude, labelled *fengshui* as for instance a science (ibid.), as the rudiments of natural science (Eitel 1873), as pseudo-science (Needham 1956:346), as superstition and 'a ridiculous caricature of science' (de Groot 1897:938), and as a cosmological model (Feuchtwang 1974:14).

and fortune in general (Rossbach 1983:1).

According to *fengshui,* man and landscape are linked together in a system of immanent order. Nature, consisting of balanced forces, reacts to any interference imposed on it, and this reaction immediately resounds in man. As in a large organism, everything is interdependent and pulsating with energy, penetrating and embracing every single part. In this thinking, the environment should be utilized thoughtfully, since harmful interference hits back like a boomerang. It raises the wrath of the Green Dragon, or the White Tiger – universal figures to be detected by configurations in the landscape. China's strong attachment to agriculture is evident: nature contains forces, which have both creative and destructive potential, and thus must be turned to the benefit of the agriculturalist. Winds carry hot or cold weather and bring rain. Mild winds are beneficial to the crops, but strong winds are damaging. Water determines the growth of crops; it should be led to the fields and water power can be harnessed.

The basic logic of *fengshui* is straightforward – when the landscape is rich and healthy, humans may prosper; when the landscape deteriorates, people suffer. *Fengshui* states that people are affected by their immediate surroundings, of which, however, some are better, more auspicious or more blessed than others. Every mountain, hill, river, cluster of trees, even buildings and other human constructions such as roads and railways have an effect. But *fengshui* is far from deterministic. It is an active endeavour, concluding that if you change your surroundings, you may change your life (Rossbach 1983:2).[7] The aim of *fengshui* can be said to change and harmonize the environment to improve fortunes.

Fengshui is an art of placement, of selecting the best possible ground and to carefully orientate human constructions according to the flow of natural forces at that particular site. Of utmost importance is catching and balancing the flow of *qi,* the cosmic current. The Chinese term *qi* denotes a fundamental life-giving force, often described as the beginning of everything, and the continuous creative force in shaping the earth and breathing life into its inhabitants. The cosmic *qi* and the human *qi* are not exactly the same: the cosmic *qi* is weather, air, gas,

---

[7] Building on experiences from Hong Kong and writing for an American audience, Rossbach evidently emphasizes the active aspect of *fengshui.* Further emphasis is on its alternative potential, for instance by supporting modern ideas of ecology and harmonizing with nature (1983:9, 19, 40).

invisible forces. The human *qi* includes breath, energy, aura, life-force and manner. *Fengshui* intends to direct the cosmic *qi* in order to stimulate the flow of human *qi*, flowing in a microcosm analogous to the macrocosm of the outside. By contrast to other types of divination, *fengshui* does not involve interaction with gods or spirits (Ahern 1981:50), and its practitioner is not reporting from a world beyond (Feuchtwang 1974:201).

Fengshui has its roots in all corners of Chinese thought. It uses ancient classics such as the *I Ching (Yijing)* – 'Book of Changes', it spans a whole range of philosophical thought from Taoism to Buddhism, and incorporates various aspects of rural divination and magic. It applies the theories of *yin-yang*, Five Elements/Phases, the Chinese calendar and astrology. It stands out as a pragmatic constellation of elements in belief systems in the Chinese world that may have a bearing on human fortune. However, its structural position is at an intermediate level between higher learning and popular beliefs. If the higher learning of late Imperial China encompassed the science of the calendar and the exclusive knowledge of cosmology, and thus was tied to the principles of government, then the application and arts of divination belonged to the lower learning, although used by all. It has been suggested that 'it was through these arts of divination that the cosmology of higher learning was shared throughout the empire' (Feuchtwang 1992:37). The *fengshui* practitioner held a corresponding social position; he was the dubious member of the elite, perhaps only a 'half-educated man from a farmer's family' (Eberhard 1962:230), whose services may be acquired by commoners, and therefore a mediator between two strata (Freedman 1968:9–10).

Thus *fengshui* is essentially public, expressing the collective adherence to a number of complementary belief systems so typical to ordinary Chinese religion and thought: if something has a grain of truth in it, it should not be rejected. And people will make sure that if it has an effect, they will not miss it, according to the Chinese device: 'never slip an opportunity, it may not come again' (*ji bu ke shi, shi bu zai lai*).

Fengshui simultaneously defines the ideal place for habitation and sets up remedies for improving a location that is not optimal, since Chinese society passed the level of unrestrained resources long ago – presumably due to a strong centre-orientation as much as lack of geographical space.[8] Within these shared cultural preferences, choices of habitation are exceedingly limited. *Fengshui* compensates for this: it is pragmatic and positive by making the utmost of one's actual place – it attempts to bring the entire universe to this particular house or grave to exploit its forces. As a science, *fengshui* bridges ends and means: it manipulates the given by turning it into the selected, or at least, places one's location within a hierarchy of possibilities, where it could be more auspicious, but certainly also much worse. It grants recognition to a site for people to settle down peacefully.

It is put to use in a corporate practice, which in our terms covers such diverse areas as practical concern for shelter from the winds and access to water and basic resources, proto-scientific concern for orientations and natural forces, aesthetic concern for a harmony-inspiring environment, religious concern for blocking the influence of evil spirits, astrological concern, and psychological concern for stable, uncontested conditions of life. But in spite of our ability to dissect *fengshui* into a number of components to fit its description within a western rationale,[9] it should not be understood in this way. It is thought of and practised as a corporate whole, by use of elastic concepts covering its entire range of meanings rather than signifying them one by one.

Thinking in images

As a corporate system, *fengshui* operates by use of images. When a *fengshui* specialist investigates a site he reads the environment. He intends to interpret and decode the totality of forces in action at a given place; he may say he employs 'a hundred senses', that he brings 'a hundred phenomena to one' ('hundred' itself symbolizing totality). Over the unity of impressions from a site, he establishes a configuration, a judgement, over its total impact on its inhabitants: good or bad, causing good health or disease, bringing happy or unhappy family life.

The judgement of a site is held against an established frame of

---

[8] Yoon (1976:259) has suggested that 'The idea that deficiences in the auspicious place in geomancy can be remedied (artificially by man) is a later development in geomancy.'

[9] According to March (1968:1) *fengshui* is likely to impress us as a 'silly mish-mash of things better sorted out as physical science, religion, aesthetics, psychology, philosophy, and sociology'.

reference, like placing a matrix over it to check how it fits. This frame of reference tends to be narrowly aligned with an ideal image: the picture of the successful, the powerful, the accomplished within the high Chinese ideal – almost invariably the balanced combination of wealth and social standing.[10]

Although *fengshui* is a corporate body of beliefs, which in our terms range from magical religion to abstract metaphysics, its aim is well-defined and concrete: boundless, inexplicable luck – seen as high position, booming business, quick fortune, money pouring in, the family prospering, sons to continue the line – this is harmony. There are no limits to the forces in the invisible world that may be employed to further one's interests in the visible world, or to the spiritual powers used in the pursuit of material aims.

Since the image of the good may change with new social values, new circumstances, or new experience, so may the ideal *fengshui* in the human environment. If someone living under supposedly bad *fengshui* influence nevertheless gets rich, it is not an anomaly, an exception from the rule. The forces reckoned with are the same, only they have been misunderstood, or misinterpreted at this particular site. Or if a man defies the rules of *fengshui*, like for instance living in a house or a room that anyone knows has bad *fengshui*, but nevertheless becomes successful, the image of that house or room changes with his success. It suddenly becomes a place of beneficial *fengshui*, its image incorporates this new life story, which is an example to follow. It is interpreted in terms of the good *fengshui* being hidden to earlier occupants, who were either unaware of it or unable to exploit it, or ascribed to changes in the environment accounting for the improved *fengshui* – graves being built or moved, new buildings being erected, pagodas, poles, lampposts and mirrors reflecting *fengshui* and the like.

Through extreme flexibility and pragmatism, *fengshui* may remain intact under almost any set of circumstances. It has a high adaptability to a new environment, for instance the modern city. In Hong Kong or Singapore it has developed into a religion of wealth. Anything from private persons to large companies will employ *fengshui* specialists, and incredible amounts of money change hands for advice on the best places for houses, graves, shops, restaurants, banks, hotels and factories. Similarly, in the interior design of private dwellings and offices, no

---

[10] For the importance of this combination in another context see, for instance, Bruun 1993, chapter 8.

efforts are spared by the wealthy to make full use of *fengshui*. In fact, in the modern city, where people have little influence on the layout of streets, buildings and apartment blocks, *fengshui* concerns tend to change from exterior to interior design. Increased attention is paid to the layout of rooms, placement of kitchens, living rooms and bedrooms in relation to directions, and the shapes or groundplans of the houses, which by their similarity to for instance boats, boots, axes or knives may be attributed symbolic powers. Also the neighbouring buildings that can be seen from one's windows, and the positive or negative influence of one's neighbours become important to the *fengshui* situation in the modern city. In Hong Kong mirrors are a common means to reflect bad *fengshui* from unhealthy influences in the surroundings.

New economic activities are easily incorporated into the *fengshui* thinking. The long, straight streets of the city are seen to increase the flow of *qi*, and too strong a flow should be avoided (Rossbach 1983:87). Thus corner positions are often better than the middle of a block, and positions slightly set back from the street are preferred since *qi* can rest there. Parallels to the flow of customers and to outstanding positions catching the eyes of customers are of course part of the symbolism. The flow of water is a frequent metaphor for the flow of money, so large companies and factories may benefit from adjacent rivers since their flow of *qi* will stimulate the flow of wares and money. Premises overlooking rivers or the seaside are also ideal for homes.

Success in life is invariably ascribed to beneficial *fengshui*, provided, of course, that you work for it in the highly competitive Chinese universe. However, if someone neglects his duties to work for an improved position for himself and his household, this may also be interpreted in terms of *fengshui*. Bad or missing *qi* may be held responsible for the insufficient human *qi*, counting for laziness, lack of energy or sickness. What strikes the western observer is that having a simple life as an aim in itself, without seeking material improvement, is exceedingly difficult to fit into the *fengshui* thought as it appears today.

The judgement of the *fengshui* configuration in a given place is intuitively composed by use of multiple sources of information, held against a complex range of beliefs. Various impressions of a place are interpreted, translated, manipulated, or even reversed to fit the demands of the moment. Dominance of either *yin* or *yang* in the surroundings should be counterbalanced, the flow of *qi* stimulated or modified, high and low brought into harmony. The judgement is holistic in the strongest sense of the word, amassing impressions and information to a degree that is at odds with any strict classification of nature. Nature and society represent a continuum of influences, when seen entirely from the perspective of the individual. That *fengshui* is anthropocentric is seen from the various means of compensation that are possible for improving a bad site. The nineteenth-century colonial powers quickly learned that the damage done by building roads that for instance cut across what the local inhabitants saw as a dragon's tail, could be made good by monetary payments. Thus, to the people affected, worsened *fengshui* in the long run was counterbalanced by improved *fengshui* in the present. The Hong Kong and Singapore authorities still pay out considerable sums as compensation for violating people's environment when constructing housing, roads, railway lines and harbours.

However, if it is correct that the ideal *fengshui* situation of a given place can be tried against a ready-made image of the ultimate good, it follows that this image of the good is a communal one. This common image, or picture of the good, is in fact one of the most important aspects of *fengshui*, and maybe an important quality of the Chinese perception of nature, too.

There is a classical story about a man who employed a *fengshui* specialist to determine where he should place his father's grave for maximum benefit to his own career. He employed the best specialist of all. The old master investigated the whole area closely, and when he was ready for his judgement, he took out bow and arrow, and shot an arrow into the air. Then he told the man to build the grave where the arrow fell, whereupon he went away. To make sure that he did the right thing, the man employed another *fengshui* specialist, the second best, who happened to be the son of the old master. The procedure repeated itself. After investigating the site the old master's son also shot an arrow into the air, stating that it would indicate the correct position. The arrow eventually hit the arrow shot by the old master, cleaving it end to end. The man build the grave on this auspicious spot, and eventually became the next emperor.

Such old stories intend to demonstrate the masterly skills of the *fengshui* specialists; that what they were practising was science, which unambiguously points to the one and only correct location for the grave. Eventually, the story says more. It tells us perhaps that if there is only one optimal position for the grave among the countless forces and influences of nature, then there apparently is only one path for the son of the deceased. If *fengshui* is correctly handled, two *fengshui* specialists would not disagree about the grave, the judgement, the impact on the living, and the correct path for this man. His aim was to attain the one ultimate and final position – that of the emperor.

Moreover, in spite of the basic assumption of *fengshui* that the environment bears on human fate, it is not to any significant degree assumed that this environment has a different bearing on different people, or that differing personalities may have different needs with regard to the forces of their environment. There are certainly varying *fengshui* situations prescribed for various types of constructions – graves being *yin* dwellings must have maximum harmony, houses being *yang* dwellings have more practical considerations, and businesses should be placed so that the flow of people and money is optimal. Considerations are for types of constructions, integrated into types of environments – to a lesser extent for types of people. *Fengshui* apparently assumes that human values are known and uniform, and that the natural environment is used for specific ends according to shared values.

When social values change it is assumed that it is not the values of individual people that change, but a common model, an image, that flows and has be to taken into account by the *fengshui* specialist. Thus, in this interpretation, *fengshui* implicitly denotes a profoundly competitive society, with little variation in basic life-aim orientations.

The social discourse

A writer on *fengshui* in Korea, where identical techniques are used, lists the five (the sacred number) most important factors for choosing an auspicious location for a house:

> a. Selecting a favorable house location.
> b. Choosing the direction the house should face.
> c. Determining the spatial organization or form of a house.
> d. Completing a surrounding fence.
> e. Deciding what kind of person should live there.
> From the above five considerations, we can infer that all are about ways to achieve a perfect harmony between man and his environment Yoon:76–7).

Venerating wealth as much as nature, *fengshui* obviously fits badly into the policy of the communist regime of the People's Republic, just as it is at odds with the Chinese collective identity emphasizing modesty and a simple life.[11] Discourse on morality and principles for social regulation have penetrated Chinese writings over the centuries. While the Chinese literary traditions such as Confucianism, the historical records, or Chinese Marxism have stressed ideal culture, *fengshui* is different: It is a raw and unclothed expression of the values of everyday life, but the means of obtaining them is ritualised and 'cooked' (Lévi-Strauss 1969).

As the common Chinese see it, no man is equal to another. He is older or younger than the other, higher or lower placed in the state hierarchy, having his native home in a better or worse location in relation to the centre, and, being himself a man, he is superior to a woman. Likewise with the Earth: no two positions on it rank equal, although their relative rank may be disputed.

Countless incidents are recorded of *fengshui* accusations being raised: against villagers building their houses a bit higher than others', one village accusing another for increasing its tapping from common water canals, one market town against another for attracting too much trade, one port against another for catching all the ships etc. Remedies are always possible – since *fengshui* is a boundless aggregation of 'things that matter'. Much of the flexibility, or plasticity, in *fengshui* stems from the social discourse contained in it. Individual people living in a village will take care not to depart from common rules – a whole range of reprisals are possible, drawing on the *fengshui* idiom: a defiant villager may see his ancestors' graves demolished, his fields and crops hit by accidents, his household experience bad luck. Small wars have been fought between families or between villages on matters relating to 'stolen *fengshui*'.

Although *fengshui* is an instrument of competition, there may also be a muting of competition involved (e.g. Freedman 1968:14). *Fengshui* emphasizes the common fortune of a household as related to the influence of its surroundings. By establishing concepts like the common *fengshui* of a village, it may strengthen a communal identity (e.g. Frazer 1913:170). It clearly follows the pattern of the Chinese identity in stressing own household, own local area, own region, even own nation in a serial conception, and always with a clear inside-outside distinction. But even among relatives it may come to open conflict over *fengshui* matters. Writers tell of brothers competing endlessly in building the

---

[11] For an interpretation of *fengshui* as a medium of expression opposed to the morality and rationalism of Chinese high culture, see Bruun 1994.

most attractive grave for their deceased father (e.g. Giles 1908:447), and such rivalry may even be a built-in tendency in the kinship system (Freedman 1970:178).

A clear symbolism is written into the *fengshui* idiom, under the disguise of which keen social competition is expressed. Its techniques aim at attracting to one's own household the largest possible share of limited and clearly defined values, by means of careful management of own resources and manipulation of common resources. In relation to the highly formalized Chinese public morality and public virtue, *fengshui* is the complementary component. It provides an institutionalized outlet for the expression of village characteristics, for familiarism, for individualism, and even egotism in a society that demands all voices in public to confirm the 'common will' of all and revolve around the theme of the 'common good' (Bruun 1993:221). Moreover, *fengshui* should be analyzed against the background of a culture that inhibits open con-frontation, suppresses expressions of sexuality, cultivates dignity and the observance of 'face'. Similarly, Chinese expressions of nature should be held against the prevalent style of communication in the context of culture.

China has a long tradition of producing nature-related symbols and writing symbols into nature, for instance by infusing social content into landscape painting. A rich 'vocabulary' of symbols, of which many apparently had erotic content (Eberhard 1983:10c), was used in art by means of interpreting natural forms, forces and constellations. A great number of word compounds such as mountain-water (*shan-shui*), mountain-spirit (*shan-jing*) and the Emperor's court-wilderness (*chao-ye*), which all build on extensions of the *yang-yin* pair (antithesis where the first word denotes masculinity and the second femininity), constitute a huge and rather uninvestigated semantic field (ibid.:14). Also in *fengshui* the sexual connotations of *yang-yin* often becomes explicit, when the feeling of liveliness and diversity in the landscape is represented as the coupling of male and female elements (March 1968:258).

If the Chinese literary tradition has a strong moralizing tone, beliefs such as *fengshui* are profoundly anti-authoritarian by defying the social 'Will of Heaven'. They provide commoners with a symbolism to express resistance against exploitation and subjugation, perennial aspects of Chinese civilization. Also, forces of nature could become a symbolism of power. When westerners were met with *fengshui* charges in pre-revolution China (e.g. Eitel 1873:1–2) it may have been due to the fact that their presence was fostering images of inferiority and subjugation among Chinese officials and commoners alike. *Fengshui* charges and social mobilization to support them are the weapons of all. By a pragmatic constellation of anything that matters, *fengshui* expresses the interests of those inside against those outside.

It is an old theme in anthropology that classifications of culture and nature run parallel, fostering discussions as to what came first. Chinese society has been used as an example of such classificatory unity by for instance Durkheim and Mauss, Lévi-Strauss, Foucault and a number of others. And that 'nature' may be drawn in to legitimize, give authority to, or emphasize aspects of social affairs is of course a universal aspect of myths, medicine, religion, cosmology and so on. 'Nature' is frequently used as a metaphor for the inevitable, or what may not be manipulated.

In China, nature is consistently employed as a source of metaphors, a parallel idiom allowing for themes such as 'individual fate', 'individual success and prosperity', 'one's own way' (as in Taoism) and so forth to be played out in public. Since egocentric concepts are unacceptable without the natural metaphor, techniques like *fengshui* frame in nature a social discourse that runs counter to established ideals of social considerations, the will of the collective, the common good of the family, the masses, and the nation.

Comments

It was mentioned in the beginning how in the cross-cultural comparison 'distant nature' may be classified similarly, whereas the classification of the 'immediate nature', being closer to human enterprise, shows profoundly more variation. *Fengshui* is a borderline science, dealing with borderline phenomena between nature and culture. Instead of maintaining a demarcation between the two, it investigates their interaction, and does so for specific purposes. *Fengshui* expresses great concern for the immediate nature, how to bring it to bear positively on human fortune – whereas the distant, the unimportant, the invisible, or just other people's nature are not included in *fengshui* concerns. By implication, *fengshui*, and perhaps with it Chinese cosmology in general, says little about nature as an independent category (but here we must tread cautiously as westerners, seeing an independent nature as our spiritual frame of reference).

China's long tradition of natural philosophy, emphasizing cosmic harmony, has inspired philosophers, scientists, politicians, ecologists, environmentalists and so on all over the world. It has repeatedly been

mentioned as a source of conceptual renewal in the western environmental philosophy and in popular literature. Yet contemporary China
boasts some of the world's most polluted rivers, heavy air pollution,
some of the worst working conditions in her mining and chemical
industry, the laying waste of huge tracts of land, not only affecting her
own territories, but also the lands of other cultures in her periphery.[12]
This is of course an irony. What is the Chinese view of nature anyway
– or what is Chinese history, classical tradition, or present public
practice – except for being concepts of eternal contra-diction when
translated to the world outside? On Chinese beliefs such as *fengshui*
precarious assertions have been made, concerning an inherent Chinese
capacity for nature conservation and environmental harmony.

If we favour comparisons between China and the West, and if such
comparison sees control and domination as key concepts in the West, we
should certainly find exploitation a key concept in China. Chinese
culture optimizes the use of natural powers, even to a degree where the
qi – universal energy – is regarded as a limited resource subject to
human competition. The very life space of humans is limited. An important conception in the Chinese discourse on nature is 'the world that
matters' contrary to 'the world beyond', mostly left unexplored and
unnamed.

In summarizing these notes on *fengshui*, I may come close to
suggesting that in the Chinese view, 'nature' not only contains essential
resources, it is resources *per se*. The world that matters embraces that
untouched nature which has an aesthetic function. Beyond the narrowly
visible, where nature is dressed to fit into a picturesque scenery, nature
only consists of potential resources to be drawn in as culture expands.

The 'credence' that westerners give to 'nature' is apparently unique.
We seem to believe, along with our cosmological transcendence, that
nature exists as an entity separate from society and independent of the
human mind, and that nature has a right to exist without human
interference. We suppose that if mankind was extinguished, maybe
animals or insects would survive, and certainly that nature as a category
would continue to exist. The Chinese prefer not to engage in such
speculations, since they have always operated with human life as

---

[12] For reports on environmental problems and strategies in China see 'The Ruined
Earth' (FEER 1991:39); 'Human Population, Modernization, and the Changing Face
of China's Eastern Pacific Lowlands (CEN 1990:3) and 'Urgent Action Needed on East
Asia's Environment' (WBN 1993).

belonging to the spontaneously self-generating life processes of nature (Tu 1989:68), without beginning or end.

Fengshui is a holism, linked to cosmological immanence. However, all 'holisms' tend to be narrowly oriented towards the aspects of the cosmos that are of immediate interest to man. In one way or another, closed tautological belief systems – such as *fengshui* or Marxism – appeal to the Chinese since they lessen the conflicts with the experienced world and thereby permit human resources to remain intact and unchallenged. They induce only minimum disturbance to human devotion and energy, classified among the basic forces shaping the world.

References

Ahern, Emily. 1981. *Chinese Ritual and Politics.* Cambridge: Cambridge University Press.

Bruun, Ole. 1993. *Business and Bureaucracy in a Chinese City. The Ethnography of Individual Business Households in Contemporary China.* Berkeley: Institute of East Asian Studies, University of California.

—— 1994. (Forthcoming). 'Fengshui and the Chinese Nature. The Revival of Organic Symbolism in the People's Republic'.

CEN (*China Exchange News*). 1990(3): 'Human Population, Modernization, and the Changing Face of China's Eastern Pacific Lowlands'. Washington.

Cobb, John B. 1972. *Is it Too Late? A Theology of Ecology.* Beverly Hills, Calif.: Faith and Life Series.

de Groot, J.J.M. 1897. *The Religious System of China,* Vol.3 (Reprint 1964). Taipei: Literature House Ltd.

Eberhard, Wolfram. 1962. *Social Mobility in Traditional China.* Leiden: E.J. Brill.

—— 1983. *Chinese Symbols. Hidden Symbols in Chinese Life and Thought.* London: Routledge and Kegan Paul.

Eitel, E.J. 1873. *Feng-shui, or, the Rudiments of Natural Science in China.* (Reprint 1973.) Taipei: Ch'eng Wen.

FEER (*Far Eastern Economic Review*). 1991. '"The ruined Earth". Focus on Environment in Asia'. 19 September, p.39.

Feuchtwang, Stephan. 1974. *An Anthropoloical Analysis of Chinese Geomancy*. Vientiane: Vithagna.

—— 1992. *The Imperial Metaphor*. London: Routledge.

Frazer, J.G. 1913. *The Golden Bough*, Vol.1. London.

Freedman, Maurice. 1968. *Geomancy*. Presidential Address 1968. Proceedings of the Royal Anthropological Institute of Great Britain and Ireland, 1968–70. London.

—— 1970. *Family and Kinship in Chinese Society*. Stanford: Stanford University Press.

Giles, Herbert A. 1908. *Strange Stories from a Chinese Studio*. Reprint 1968. Hong Kong: Kelly and Walsh.

Hansen, Chad. 1983. *Language and Logic in Ancient China*. Ann Arbor: University of Michigan Press.

Lévi-Strauss, Claude. 1969. *The Raw and the Cooked*. New York: Harper & Row.

March, Andrew L. 1968. An Appreciation of Chinese Geomancy. *Journal of Asian Studies*, 27(2):253–67.

Needham, Joseph. 1956. *Science and Civilization in China*, Vol.2. Cambridge: Cambridge University Press.

—— 1962. *Science and Civilization in China*, Vol.4, part 1. Cambridge: Cambridge University Press.

Rossbach, Sarah. 1983. *Feng Shui. The Chinese Art of Placement*. New York: E.P. Dutton.

Tu, Wei-Ming. 1989. 'The Continuity of Being: Chinese Visions of Nature'. In Callicott, J.B. and R.T. Ames (eds), *Nature in Asian Traditions of Thought: Essays in Environmental Philosophy*. Albany: State University of New York Press.

WBN (*World Bank News*). 1993. 'Urgent Action Needed on East Asia's Environment'. October 14.

Yoon, Hong-key. 1976. *Geomantic Relations between Culture and Nature in Korea*. Taipei: Chinese Association for Folklore.

S. N. Eisenstadt

The Japanese Attitude to Nature
A Framework of Basic Ontological Conceptions

The major point of this paper is that one of the best ways to understand the Japanese attitude or attitudes to nature is to put them within the framework of the Japanese ontological conceptions. We have of course to bear in mind that these conceptions have, especially in their more sophisticated foundations, never been static, but at the same time distinct core assumptions seem to have been prevalent in many sectors of Japanese society through many historical periods. The paper will analyse some of the basic ontological conceptions, especially the ways in which the relations between what in western parlance is called nature and culture or between the transcendent and mundane realms have been constructed in Japanese society; and how the conceptions have changed the attitude to nature and influenced different patterns of behaviour.

Symbolic immanentism as the core of Japanese ontology

The basic conceptions of ontological reality that have been identified as most distinctive on the Japanese scene in the relevant historical, anthropological and philosophical literature, have been the following: first, a very high degree of mutual embedment of what in western parlance are called nature and culture, i.e., a strong sense of the interrelations between the transcendent and the mundane world, of their immanency, as against the emphasis on a deep chasm between these worlds that can be found in the monotheistic civilizations and in classical Confucianism, Buddhism and Hinduism, i.e. in the Axial civilizations; second, and closely related, a strong emphasis on gods as the continuous regenerators of the world, but not as its creators; third, a dualistic – but of a rather specific, distinct type of dualism – conception of the cosmos which strongly differentiates between purity and pollution, order and disorder; fourth, a commitment to the cosmic and natural (including social) orders, and the concomitant structuring of different arenas of action in which 'nature' and 'culture' are combined according, above all, to these basic dualistic categories; fifth a highly vitalistic conception of life, combined with an activist-pragmatist attitude to the world; and sixth a very strong emphasis on mythical time conceptions as the most important temporal dimension of the collective and cosmic rhythm, and a closely related mythocentric, not logocentric, ontological discourse.

This strong immanental, vitalistic-dualistic-activist approach to natural and social reality has been interwoven with a distinct mode of semantic structuring of the major arenas of discourse. This mode has been characterized by the relative minimization of the importance of the subject as against the environment, by a strong emphasis on relational and indexical criteria (as against abstract, linear ones rooted in principles transcending existing reality) as the regulating principles of such discourse.

The common denominator of these basic ontological conceptions and of the semantic structuring of the major arenas is the very strong emphasis on reality as structured in shifting contexts – and in discrete enclosed ontological entities. Reality is being constructed in contextual as against – in the West – absolutist, often dichotomic modes. Reality is conceived of in terms of a relationship which is perceived as defining that reality and not as a 'thing' or 'object' on the horizon of reality.

The first fully articulated formulations of many of these conceptions of ontological reality can be identified in ancient Japanese texts such as the *Kojiki* (712 A.D.) and *Nihongi* (720 A.D.) – which probably built on earlier less formalized formulations, and which in themselves already constituted an elaborate construction by some cultural groups.

John Pelzel's analysis of these conceptions as found in these texts is very pertinent and we may follow the Lebras' exposition of the major points of Pelzel's analysis (Lebra and Lebra 1986:4-5).

> ... What is said and done by gods who appear in the mythical narratives, especially major gods in the Shintō pantheon, such as the Sun Goddess and her recalcitrant brother, Susano-o, may provide a clue to the nature of Japanese morality...

> Some of the most important characteristics of Japanese thought, especially as contrasted with the Chinese and Western ones, are the relative lack of opposition between (in addition to those mentioned above) gods and humans, life and death, mortal and immortal, order and

disorder, blessedness and misery, wild and tamed, nature and culture. Between these, there is no gulf, no confrontation, no dominance, no contradistinction; instead, one finds continuity, compromise, fusion, and duplication. So too is the relationship between good and evil. Hence we come to learn that the gods do not play the role of exemplary moral actors nor do they take full charge of maintaining a moral order. Moral standards are more or less relative and lack the kind of didactic assertions that feature in the rationally oriented Chinese myths and philosophy. What Pelzel indicates, extrapolating from the early myths compels the Japanese individual as a moral actor, in his consideration of other persons, often worded as *giri* or *ninjō*. If there is anything close to an ultimate standard, it is, we are led to believe, the cleanliness of the actor's heart.

The world of *Kojiki* and *Nihongi* does not exhaust the Japanese sense of morality or worldview, however. Undeniably, Confucianism and Buddhism have had overwhelming impact upon Japanese culture and behavior, and the Japanese sense of morality cannot be captured without considering these. The point is that the long history of religious and philosophical transfusions from the Sinified continent and of the conglomeration of newer beliefs with the earlier 'native' cult (which came to be known as Shintō) has not replaced the pre-Confucian, pre-Buddhist intuitions and sentiments symbolized by the myths. Not surprisingly then, we read about 'the principle of harmony that admits no distinction between good and bad... as operating in today's Japan.'

This Japanese basic ontological conception can be characterized, as Iwao Munakata (1986) has put it, as symbolic immanentist thought (or cognition) ('Symbolische Immanenzdenken'). Or, in the words of Augustin Berque (1987:2-4):

In the Japanese tradition it is impossible to envisage either logos or the subject independently of the world. There is no principle which transcendents reality. And reality is the word of appearances (Erscheinungen) which we have to accept as it is contingent, in the given place and time...

For the Japanese, thus, the world is not something the subject has to impose his logic upon; he has to adapt himself to it. Anyway, both the world and the subject are perpetually changing...

The historical roots and transformations of symbolic immanentism

The 'primitive' or archaic mythological conceptions analysed by Pelzel have been greatly changed in later times, especially through the impact of Confucianism and Buddhism. This has been true both on the purely 'academic' and intellectual or philosophical level, on the level of intellectual and academic discourse, and on the level of the prevalent common sense definitions, conceptions and discourse. The definitions of ontological reality, as they have developed in the various Buddhist and Confucian schools in Japan have greatly transformed the formulations presented in the ancient myths referred to above. At the same time we have seen that many of these Buddhist and Confucian formulations originating from mainland Asia have become greatly transformed in Japan, even on the purely philosophical level, but especially on the level of ideological public discourse and on the level of the unconscious assumptions regulating daily common sense discourse. They have moved, indeed become transformed, in the direction of increased immanentization of the transcendental orientations of these religions and particularization of the universalistic ones. Yet the impact of the transcendental orientations was indeed very great – transforming what could be called, in Iwao Munakata's terms, an archaic world view into a symbolic immanentist one.

Such a world-view or ontology entailed a very high degree of spiritualization and aesthetization of the world, creating many arenas in which dimensions of human sensibility could be articulated, while at the same time these arenas were incorporated within the basic immanentist frameworks.

The persistence of these conceptions of ontological reality has often been identified – rightly or wrongly – with Shintōism, or rather with some basic ontological conceptions best represented in 'Shintō' 'beliefs' or assumptions, with what could be better called underlying native orientations. These orientations were not necessarily identical to some of the more formal aspects of the continuously changing organization of Shintō shrines, or even to what was from time to time represented as the true 'Shintō' doctrine – almost a contradiction in terms – rooted in the second major ontological conception prevalent in Japan, namely that of gods as generators and not as creators of the world. As Fosco Maraini has shown (1960), such a conception – in contrast to that of God as creator, who is outside the world and who created it 'in a silent and terrifying act of the mind' – 'establishes a relation which is fundamentally biological, therefore intimate, simple, warm...':[1]

> Creation establishes clear-cut oppositions, of which God and the world, spirit and matter, soul and body, eternity and time, supernatural and natural, are some examples, and is therefore necessarily accompanied by transcendency in religion and by dualism in philosophy. Generation on the other hand is more naturally connected with synthesis and harmony, with immanence and pantheism in religion, with forms of monism in thought, be it explicit or not. In the West terms such as 'immanence' or 'monism' refer to ideas which are essentially bookish, academic, scholastic; in Japan they refer to the stuff of everyday life, to ideas and attitudes which are so ubiquitous and obvious that one hardly talks about them, they are folklore and common sense, festival and proverb.

> If gods beget the world, then nature is somehow sacred, nature is the ultimate criterion of truth, of goodness and of beauty (1960:52-3).

This basic attitude to the world entailed a certain sanctification of the phenomenal world, of nature, the possibility of sanctification of almost any object. Throughout Japanese history there developed at different levels of discourse, but especially at the more implicit level of common discourse, a very strong tendency to conflate the divine sacred spirits (*kami*) with the phenomenal world.[2]

---

[1] Ian Buruma (1986) has presented a similar picture of this Japanese 'Shintōistic' world view:

> The word Shintō was first coined in the seventh century to distinguish it from Buddhism, called Butsudō. It means Way of the Gods, but it can hardly be called a religion, for there is almost no trace in it of abstract speculation, neither is there much awareness of, or even interest in, another world outside our own. Heaven in the midst of the ancient Japanese was a cozy sort of place full of industrious villagers tending rice-fields. There is no evidence of a system of ethics or statecraft, such as we see in China. The earliest myths are, in fact, typically Japanese dramas revolving around human relationships, liberally spiced with sex. Shintō has many rituals, but no dogma. A person is Shintō in the same way that he is born Japanese. It is a collection of myths and ceremonies that give form to a way of life. It is a celebration, not a belief. There is no such thing as a Shintōist, for there is no Shintōism.

[2] Y. Saito (1985); H. Tellenbach and B. Kimura (1989); D.E. Shaner (1989); W.R. La Fleur (1989). See also A. Kalland (this volume) and F.H. Meyer (1981). For another, complementary illustration of the implications of such immanentist 'Shintō' attitudes, see N. Rosenberger (1992).

The dualistic contextual conceptions of reality, purity, pollution and marginal figures

The strong emphasis on the mutual embedment of nature and culture does not entail the perception of reality as unitary or homogeneous. On the contrary, it entailed a perception of reality as structured in multiple, continually shifting contexts, which above all were organized according to the principles of a basically dualistic cosmology.

Needless to say dualistic distinctions are not unique to the Japanese world-view. What seems, however, to be rather unique or at least much stronger in Japan is, first, that there are basically no attempts to subsume these dualistic categories under overarching abstract unitary principles and linear conceptions of reality. Second, the dualistic principles are not defined as contrasting, but rather as flexible, complementary categories – the movement between which is structured in definite contexts which themselves may be continuously reconstructed, in topological and not in linear modes. As Emiko Ohnuki-Tierney has put it (1987a:130):

> The basically dualistic Japanese universe is a universe that constantly ebbs and flows between two opposite principles: purity and impurity; good and evil; order and its inversion. With opposing forces simultaneously present, it is a universe in which the negative elements are as integral as positive elements.

Third – derivative of the first – is that the distinctions between the different dualistic principles refer to different social and cosmic arenas or spaces and the interrelation between them rather than to different dimensions or 'parts' of the cosmic reality and of the world conceived as distinct ontological entities.

Thus such dualistic differentiation is rather weak as regards transcendent and mundane reality, while it is rather strong with respect to different zones in which 'natural' and 'supernatural' are interwoven. The distinction between the dualistic principles, between good and evil, between purity and pollution, order and disorder, is conceived in Japanese culture, not in terms of transcendental absolutes, but in terms of continuously changing contexts. Again in Ohnuki-Tierney's words (1987c:72-73):

Purity and impurity are classificatory principles that govern a particular context rather than absolute properties. Thus, the classification of an object or being in the universe as pure or impure depends upon what it is being contrasted with. Therefore, while both deities and humans are characterized by the dual qualities of purity and impurity, when deities as a category of beings in the Japanese universe are contrasted with humans, the former become pure in contrast to the latter, which become impure. By the same token, when boundaries are contrasted with the structure consisting of the deity-human dyad, the structure is pure and the boundaries impure.

These basic dualistic conceptions that developed in Japan gave rise to the construction of many arenas or contexts of the universe, of reality, regulated by such dualistic principles. The most important among such dualistic principles are those of *omote* and *ura* (front and back), *honne* and *tatemae* (inner feeling and formal pretence), *uchi* and *soto* (inside and outside, home and not home). Such distinctions between contexts or forces defined according to different principles of the dualistic universe are, especially according to conceptions of purity and pollution, closely related to distinctions between insiders and outsiders – the relations between whom have also to be bridged.

Thus a state of pollution is believed to bring danger, adversity, and misfortune to human beings and a state in which pollution has been entirely removed to bring public peace and prosperity. The belief that purification from pollution can be achieved by the repetition of rituals can be discerned in the Japanese belief system from the time of the *Kojiki* and *Nihonshoki* [*Nihongi*] to the present. It is not too much to say that Shintō places this ritualism at the centre of its belief system, and the usual Japanese interpretation of Buddhism is that it brings salvation to the spirits of the dead, that is, purifies them from the pollution of death.

This ritualism can easily be used in support of political manipulation – for example, to explain a class structure with the imperial court, the outmost in ritual purity, at its apex (Namihira 1987:s71).

Among the social implications of this conception is also the possibility of its being used as a rationale for discrimination.[3] In such a universe the transition from one arena or context to another is of crucial importance. Pollution and purity, just as good and evil, are not conceived as abstract absolutes but in contextual terms. In such transitions, especially from situations of pollution to purity, ritual is of very great importance, as are also many mediatory figures which play a crucial role in the Japanese universe (Namihira 1987).

Such situations of transition are affected by a very great number of figures and forces – gods, spirits, strangers and various mediators. Many patterns of ritual behaviour are focused around different taboos. Many taboos can be violated so long as appropriate rituals restore the original state.

It is such mediating figures pertaining to different rituals of 'purification' who connect the different arenas of the universe, of reality, regulated by different dualistic principles. Among such mediating figures, strangers and visitors are, as Teigo Yoshida (1981:87-91) has shown, of special importance and interest – they are often seen as god-like creatures, creatures which are gods and men alike and who appear especially in in-between situations – such as at twilight. Mediating figures range from the highest to the lowest insiders and outsiders in any natural and/or social context. Many figures – such as for instance the monkey – may perform such mediating functions as deities, ritual scapegoats, clowns and the like (Ohnuki-Tierney 1987a; 1990).

Such mediatory attempts at redemption from pollution, and at bridging the gap between inside and outside, is effected not only by foreigners or outsiders, but also by 'marginal' elements, above all by artists, many of whom, especially the itinerant ones, were indeed very much strangers to the closed villages, but at the same time constituted a constant component of the overall Japanese cultural scene. Interestingly enough, the Yakuza (the Japanese mafia) do sometimes portray themselves as such mediators – as outsiders who claim to be the bearers of the most pristine Japanese values (Raz 1992).

---

[3] 'Thus the concept of pollution, having undergone a number of twists, becomes a rationale for discrimination. The concept of pollution is linked to the logic of the inversion of values and order. This is apparent, for example, ... in the adoption of the attire of *hinin* (the outcasts once called "non-humans") and the strategic use of temples for sanctuary by those involved in the insurrections of the late medieval period. The background to the use of this attire as a symbol of the inversion of order is the structure of religious and social discrimination to which the concept of pollution had been appended.' (Namihira 1987:71).

The potentially redemptive qualities of such marginal elements have also been articulated in the development of certain traditional forms of theatre, especially the Kabuki, and even, as Masao Yamaguchi (1973:337-39) has shown, in the conception of the Imperial house as it developed under the Tokugawa and was portrayed in many Kabuki plays.

Indeed the continuous, in a way central, place of the Emperor within this mediatory universe is one of the most significant features of the Japanese cosmology.[4]

> The emperor was referred to in ancient Japan as Sumemima-no-mikoto (divine messenger's sacred body). He was believed to be charged with the spirit of emperorship, which entered his body in the inauguration ceremony. This spirit ensured the timeless continuity of emperorship, assumed to have existed since the creation of the world and to lie beyond the order of everyday life, essentially wild and untamed. What was essential was the spirit; the emperor remained at the center of authority as long as his body remained the receptacle of that spirit. If the spirit left him, he could be banished or killed.

> The peasant community looked upon the emperor with awe because the behaviour of the imperial family deviated from the norms of peasant life...

> ... After the failure of the Kenmu Restoration at the beginning of the 14th century, the emperor became a largely insignificant and marginal figure. It is of great interest here that the closeness of the emperor to the itinerant entertainers once again became evident with the demise of his political influence. (...) The emperor became the central figure in ritual activities that were basically not much different from performances of other kinds...

> ... Thus, ironically, the structure of the relationship between the emperor and the aristocrats was repeated in the organization of these lower-class entertainers and beggars. (Ohnuki-Tierney 1991:199-215).

---

[4] Yamaguchi, with comment by Moeran, 1987:8-20; see also, Miyata 1987; Yamaguchi 1977, 1983; and Ohnuki-Tierney 1991.

The attitude to nature and life

This conception of the givenness of reality and of the mutual embedment of the different dimensions and of a continual shift between the
different contexts in which reality is structured, has been continuously
promulgated in many rites or rituals which have prevailed, even if in
continually changing ways, throughout Japanese history.

This conception also permeates many aspects of life, of attitudes
and behaviour in Japanese society. First of all, it permeates the basic
attitude to nature, the perception of nature and of 'culture', embracing
social life as a continuum of sorts with nature.[5] One very interesting
and, from the western point of view, really astonishing illustration of
this attitude has been described by P. Asquith, a British primatologist,
in an event she witnessed involving a group of colleagues, Japanese
primate researchers. To follow the Lebras' account of Asquith's report
(Lebra and Lebra 1986:29-33), pp.4-5:

> Describing a memorial service for dead monkeys, this short essay reveals
> the status equivalence (or lack of opposition) between human and animal
> life which entitled the 'souls' of monkeys to the same Buddhist rite as for
> the human dead. Something more may be read into this chapter,
> although it is not the author's point. While showing such humane
> compassion for the dead monkeys, the Japanese mourners apparently are
> not opposed to lethal experimentations on live monkeys. In other words,
> the Japanese while holding a belief in the sacredness of all life, are not
> as extreme as antivivisectionists found in the West. Nor do they find
> suicide morally abhorrent. Their regard for life does not reach the
> dogmatic extreme 'absolute'.

Yet another very pertinent illustration of this conception of life – and
death – in more recent times, but building on some earlier Buddhist
conceptions, is the burgeoning around major temples, as for instance in
Kamakura, of memorials for aborted children, recently very thoroughly
analysed by R.J. Zwi Werblowski (1991) and William LaFleur (1993),
among others.

---

[5] For a very insightful analysis of the Japanese attitude to nature see
Seidenstricker (1989). See also D. Richie, 1992, esp. ch. 1, 2, 3. See also the discussion
by Pelzel 1977, pp. 299-315; Jeremy and Robinson 1989, especially Chapters 3 and 5;
Nakamura 1979; Kuitert 1988; Schaarschmidt-Richter 1980. See also note 8.

One of the most important manifestations of this attitude to life and nature developed within the framework of this complex conception of ontological reality is, perhaps, the Japanese attitude to suicide which has baffled and fascinated westerners. It is not only that suicide is not abhorred and that 'altruistic' suicide, suicide in service of the collectivity, has been fully accepted. Even non-altruistic suicide is often perceived as a quite honourable and legitimate way of protest, and of resolving in an ultimate way the dilemmas and contradictions of different situations one is caught in. It is this legitimacy that distinguishes the attitude to suicide to be found in Japanese society from that to be found in other societies where suicide also constitutes an escape from such contradictions. But in Japan it is not only or just an escape – which, of course, it often is. It is also in a very marked way an honourable way out of the contradictions of life, especially those between the individual's intense internal feelings and social and group pressure, and is seen as a very legitimate culmination of one's life (Pinguet 1984).

The legitimacy of certain types of suicide is rooted in the positive attitude to nature, and in a conception of nature which is not seen as totally opposed to life. It is also probably closely connected to the special place of violence, especially ritual violence, as one way of overcoming the boundaries between different contexts, between different spaces of life and nature. By committing such violence against oneself, one overcomes these boundaries, as well as the boundaries between pollution and purity.

Such attitudes and patterns of behaviour were not always universally accepted. Indeed they often constituted foci of public controversies. But even these controversies fully attested to the fact that such attitudes did constitute a continual theme within the Japanese cultural repertoire.

This conception of continuity between the mundane and the worlds of the spirit is manifest in many varied aspects of life in Japan. One such manifestation is the very important place of ancestors cults in Japan, and the continuity between family cult and those of the wider communities, possibly up to the imperial ancestors' cult, thus emphasizing again the central place of the emperor in the Japanese cosmology (Smith 1974).

In daily life, such conceptions of nature, of the given reality, pervade for instance the attitudes to food, the partaking of which is often seen as a partaking in the sacred (Loveday and Cyba 1985:115-131), the modes of wrapping of various objects, and even patterns of behaviour which seem to signify attempts at preventing or neutralizing pollution (Hendry 1990, 1993; Yoshida 1990).

The impact of such conceptions of the embedment in nature, in a dualistic universe, can also be identified in the conceptions of health and illness in contemporary Japan. Ohnuki-Tierney (1987b) has shown how the attitudes toward illness in Japan – of patients and doctors alike – are greatly influenced by conceptions of the body as defined in terms of this mutual embedment of natural and cultural worlds as well as in terms of the danger of pollution; by conceptions of the fragile boundaries between purity and pollution, between 'us' and 'them,' inner and outer space, and of the necessity to circumvent these by a series of ritual or ritualized actions. These conceptions also inform in many ways the aesthetic sensibility and the modes of artistic creativity in Japan.

The basic attitude to nature also gave rise, in daily discourse, in daily artistic activities as well as in aesthetic discourse, in the construction of gardens or homes, to a very strong emphasis on proximity to nature, on being at one with nature. This attitude was not of course something 'natural', but rather something culturally constructed – but it is a construction which emphasizes the quest for unity with nature.

This conception of the mutual embedment in different contexts of nature and culture, of the continuity, through various mediating figures, between them, can also be found in many Japanese folktales, which often distinguish them from similar tales in other, closely-related civilizations. Thus, for instance, it can be identified in the ending of the folktale of the hare and the woman brought over from China. In China, where the classical Confucian conception with its strong emphasis on the discontinuity between nature and culture was prevalent, the ending of the folktale is tragic, the fox ('nature') dies and the woman ('culture') is separated from it forever. In Japan, the fox, after its death, is incorporated in the form of a shrine, into the woman's household.

The dualistic conceptions, the contextualized conception of purity and pollution and the emphasis on the necessity to overcome pollution by appropriate rituals also pervade the basic ethical conceptions and conceptions of conflict resolutions prevalent in many sectors of Japanese society. As Robert J. Wargo (1990) has shown, acts of conciliation on the part of Japanese companies or of the Japanese government towards Americans or Europeans are not based on conceptions of good or evil, but rather performed as sincere acts of purification (hence often misunderstood by 'westerners').

Vitalism and cyclical conceptions of time

These conceptions of the mutual embedment of 'nature' and 'culture,' of a very strong continuity between them and of a dualistic cosmogony went together in Japan with a very strong vitalistic conception and active-pragmatic attitude to life, and with the potential sanctification of everything pertaining to life, to reality (Maraini 1960:55-57).

It is the combination of this vitalism and active pragmatism, together with a strong commitment to the natural, cosmic and social orders, that distinguishes the definition of ontological reality prevalent in Japan from parallel ones that may be found in many so-called pagan or non-Axial religions which have been characterized by their very strong emphasis on the basic homology between the transcendental and the mundane worlds.

In Japan reality in its multifaceted aspects was not conceived as just given, something to be passively adjusted to. Rather, it called for continuous activity in order to master one's fate. Such a quest for mastering the world gave rise to what may be called ethic or utilitarian considerations as well as to an emphasis on the acquisition of technical skills – all of which could easily break through the limitation of relatively narrow contexts and could indeed help in the continuous restructuring of such different 'contexts'.

Such utilitarian orientations have been very strongly emphasized in the various aspects of practical rationality that developed in Japan throughout its history and the ideological discourse that developed in Japan, especially in the Tokugawa period (1600-1868). These orientations were continually confronted with the strong emphasis on one's obligations to the natural, cosmic and social worlds. Continual attempts were made to contain the utilitarian and achievement orientations within the framework of such obligations. Performance and achievement were usually combined with strong obligations to these worlds or contexts; they were put in the framework of these contexts even if such contexts were continually reconstructed, often through the impact of such pragmatic orientations.

Such reconstruction of these contexts tended to be based on the continuous reformulation of the natural, primordial and/or sacral premises, the first relatively unsophisticated versions of which could be found in the ancient myths.

Last, a very central component of the ontological conceptions in Japan was that of mythical cyclical time order or time dimension. This

conception of time defined time as flowing basically not in a historical
or progressive-lineal direction, but rather in a natural-temporal (above
all annual) cycle, conceived in terms of the analytic principles.

> The Japanese conception of annual time, such as it is, is based upon
> these natural and social realities, the harmony of which the calendar
> expresses. Yet this harmony does not seem to be realized by a regular
> mathematical symmetry, but rather by the constant relations between
> human and divine worlds.... It might also be the constant infusion of the
> divine world into human activities that originated the cobweb-like
> structure of annual time.
>   The Japanese attitude, as it expresses itself through the annual
> conception of time, does not require that a central subject compose the
> unity of time; it is, on contrary, quite satisfied with the extreme mobility
> of the subject on the surface of time. Note the fact that the only purely
> Japanese word for time is *toki*. This word is often used with the same
> meaning as the term *jikan*, which is originally Chinese and literally
> means 'intervals between *toki*'; but *toki* is above all a word close in
> meaning to the French *quand*. (Backnick 1986:52).

But just as with respect to the various utilitarian conceptions, so also
with respect to those of time, there developed in Japan a far-reaching
openness to seemingly incompatible conceptions of the temporal and the
ability to contain them within the framework of continually reformu-
lated and reconstructed mythical ones. Thus, for instance, in the
Tokugawa period, and even earlier, there developed among large sectors
of intellectuals a growing emphasis on some linear-historical time
conceptions, always set within the basic framework of the 'eternal',
'mythical' conceptional themes set within periodic cycles of nature.
Throughout its history there developed in various sectors of Japanese
society arenas in which the linear conception of time – very often
connected with utilitarian conceptions – were predominant (Wilson
1990). But these arenas were relatively segregated, did not spill over into
others, or into the central ones, and were on the whole hemmed in by
the mythical non-discursive templates.

The ontological premises and modes of discourse in Japanese society

The prevalence of these various conceptions of ontological reality in
large sectors of Japanese society throughout most periods of its history

does not mean that the concrete formulations of these conceptions and premises, as promulgated by the major 'Kulturtrager,' were identical in different periods of Japanese history. On the contrary, these formulations were, as we have seen above, continually changed and reconstructed, especially under the impact of 'other' cultures or religions, and later on under the impact of the West. Such reformulations did not, however, entail the abandonment of the basic parameters, premises and orientations analysed above.

The prevalence of these conceptions does not mean, of course – as Fosco Maraini has correctly pointed out with respect to the importance of the Shintō myth in contemporary Japan (Maraini 1960) and as in a different mode Paul Veyne (1988) has shown with respect to the ancient Greeks – that most sectors of Japanese society necessarily 'believed' in these promulgations, or that they were aware of these more sophisticated formulations as promulgated by the Kulturtrager.

Neither does the predominance of these templates mean that all Japanese continuously followed the precepts or norms which were derived from them, that they did not often – as we have seen throughout our earlier discourse – rebel against such norms and looked for some release from them.

What it does mean is that these orientations provided the basic premises, templates or master codes that 'formed' the framework of the universes of discourses and the basic attitudes to the world and modes of thinking that developed in Japan. These premises were in a way taken for granted, hence were even more powerful, in most such discourses. They also greatly influenced, as we have seen, the semiotic rules regulating the major arenas of social and cultural activities. Moreover, these templates were also of crucial importance in shaping the various manifestations of dissatisfaction with the existing order, the modes of protest and rebellion.

These various orientations or premises were promulgated in many of the earlier myths. They became reconstructed and increasingly elaborated under the impact of intensive internal changes and external impulses, giving rise in some periods of Japanese history, especially, but not only, in the Tokugawa period, to a highly sophisticated philosophical discourse (Nosco 1984).

But there did not develop in Japan an overarching dogma which presented, in a series of canonical texts, a well-constructed definition or picture of cosmological reality and of its implication for the mundane world, which could constitute a framework or starting point for continuous philosophical or artistic interpretation, or in other words no strong logocentricism developed there. Accordingly, the continual exposition and construction of textual pronouncement did not serve in Japan, in at least partial contrast to China and Korea, as the basic framework for the construction and interpretation of ontological reality, as was the case in most of the Axial civilizations (Kasulis 1981, Nakamura 1964).

The highly sophisticated philosophical and aesthetic discourse was undertaken within the framework of such mythical conceptions or templates, and it was subsumed under the basic 'mythological' non-discursive tenets or premises.

It is also the combination of the strong conception of the mutual embedment of nature and culture, of the relative looseness of the boundaries between them, of their coming together in different ways and different contexts, and of the weakness of logocentric orientations, that explains some of the most crucial aspects of the famous so-called religious syncretism in Japan. It was not just that Japan 'absorbed', as it were, many aspects and dimensions of Buddhism, Taoism, and in a different vein of Confucianism. This in itself is a phenomenon which certainly is not unique to Japan. What is rather unique is that first, many components of the beliefs and practices of Shintōism, Buddhism, Confucianism and Taoism were consciously brought together in different ways in different periods, without seemingly great concern for their respective boundaries.

Second, and as a sort of mirror image of the former point, was the very successful dilution of whatever principled differences – couched in highly metaphysical and transcendental terms – had existed between some of these religions, especially between Buddhism, Taoism and Confucianism. The theological or ideological boundaries between these religions were blurred to a very great extent, and the boundaries that were constructed between different religious groups in Japan were mostly those within each religion – especially within Buddhism.

Modes of semiotic structuring of discourse: subject and environment; typological structuration

These conceptions of ontological reality and the weakness of a logocentric orientation or focus were closely connected with specific modes of semiotic structuring of discourse as well as with the development of specific modes of semiotic structuration which were prevalent in Japanese society. The most important characteristic of these modes was the relative devaluation of the subject as against environment; the construction of a topological-metaphorical relationship between subject and environment as against the active ordering, structuring or 'mastering' of the environment; a very strong emphasis on indexical as against referential, and on relational as against dichotomous orientations as the major parameters of discourse.[6]

Augustin Berque has very succinctly analysed the relation between subject and environment in the Japanese modes of discourse. To quote him (1986a:100-101):[7]

> In many respects, the subject in general is less important in Japanese culture than in European culture. It is the environment, in the Japanese case, that is more important. This tendency has been aptly defined as contextualism (*jōkyōshugi*). ... The Japanese language, for instance, does not need to distinguish the subject from its environment in a statement like *samui* (both 'I am cold' and 'it is cold'). Nor does it distinguish the subject from the object in a statement like *suki* ('[I] love [you]' or '[I] like [it].

In this conception the relations between the subject and the environment are mediated above all by topological metaphors – and not by linear conceptions.[8] At the same time, this environment is conceived as de-

---

[6] Pelzel makes a similar point when he says: 'principles are properly the servants of reality rather than the reverse' (1977:299-315).

[7] See also, Warda 1977; Foard 1982; Grapard 1982; Faure 1987; Kuitert 1988; Schaarschmidt-Richter 1980, 1984.

[8] Berque defines this topological metaphor in the following way:

> The existing subject can be topologically related to a spontaneous environment instead of actively ordering it around itself; culture may be put on even terms with nature (1986a:102).

centered and polysemic, ambiguous.

> From a medial point of view, the way Man feels about his environment
> bears a close link with the way he acts upon it. Indeed, just as Japanese
> culture does not favor intelligibility over experience, it dislikes symmetry
> and general orientations in the organization of space (Berque 1987:5).

These spatio-temporal conceptions – like the ontological ones discussed
earlier – found their expression not only in works of art but also in
many seemingly mundane matters such as, for instance, the symbolic
arrangements of households, of nobles and of 'simple people,' and the
spatial organization of cities (Lebra and Lebra 1986).

They were all rooted in distinct conceptions of the environment,
based on an immanentist and topographic orientation to nature and to
space, with a relative de-emphasis of centre or centrality; on the
conception of space as embodying the interweaving of 'nature' and
'culture' and as having potentially liminal characteristics.[9] They were
rooted in the specific situational, topological conception of order – where
order is implied by actual position and movement from one place to
another, from one room to the next one – which found one of its major
expressions in the strong emphasis on the rules of form to which we
have referred above.

Indexical and relational modes of discourse

The second major feature of the structuring of the modes of discourse
in Japan is a very strong emphasis on (performative) indexing, as
against referentiality, and on a relational orientation to reality as against
a dichotomal one, on lexical literacy as against grammatical
compositions. Jane Bachnick has analysed these orientations in great
detail (1986, 1987, 1992):

... This metaphorical process works, of course, at the heart of any culture; but
a sense of place (*bashosei*) is particularly pronounced in cultures which, as in the
Japanese case, do not enhance the subject's pre-eminence to the degree
European culture has done (1986a:103).

[9] On conception of space see also Plutschow 1979:269-283.

I will focus on indexing, and indexical meaning, as relevant for approaching Japanese social life. My focus is not only on language, however, but on social life, and I wish to show how these perspectives on language are also perspectives on social life.

.... These two perspectives on language – reference and indexing – can be related to the two perspectives on self and other, as objectified and in practice, which have already been discussed above. Thus the objectified poles of self/other can be related to reference – and a focus on what the participants say. The continuum between self and other can be related to index – and a focus on how the participants anchor and index the 'world' both of reference and of social ties (the other) in relation to themselves. Yet in approaching language, as well as social life, we in the West have focused predominantly on the poles rather than the continuum; on reference rather than index; and on what rather than how (Bachnick 1987:25-34).

The common denominator of these various modes of semiotic mediation, in their close connection with the basic 'immanentist' orientations and the dualistic cosmological principles prevalent in the modes of discourse to be found in large sectors of Japanese society, is, as we have already mentioned above, a very strong emphasis on reality being constructed in contextual as against absolutist, often dichotomic modes. Reality is conceived of in terms of a relationship which is not perceived as a 'thing' or 'object' on the horizon of reality – especially of social reality – but rather as defining that reality. Accordingly, there develops a strong emphasis on reality as being constituted by contextual settings, by a multiplicity of such settings and on the importance of the relations and transitions between such different contexts.

These numerous contexts of action between which people move constantly are not constructed in terms of some general, abstract principles which are beyond reality, organizing it as it were from the outside. Rather, such contexts are constituted in some combination of sacral, primordial or natural terms, which are seen as embedded in the reality they construct, and which are rooted in the conception of the mutual embedment of nature and culture and in the dualistic world conception.

The differences between various contexts of action are usually relatively clear – but at the same time there has developed in most sectors of Japanese society a very strong emphasis on the importance and possibility of shifting between these different contexts according to the inherent parameters of each and of the interrelation between them and not according to 'objective', 'formal', linear, and dichotomous principles. Hence the great importance of liminal situations which structure the transition from one context to another.

The combination of dualistic cosmology with the conceptions of the mutual embedment of nature and culture, and contextual orientations and the 'indexical' modes of structuration of semantic discourse, also provide the basic framework and principles of reflexivity in Japanese culture (Berque 1986b, 1986c; Murakami 1990). Such reflexivity is not based on an evaluation of existing reality on the basis of principles transcending it, but rather on the continuous and rather complicated 'mirror' playing of the different principles inherent in the construction of reality. It is no accident that the mirror plays a central role in Japanese rituals – from the Imperial rituals through many religious rituals and extending into many rituals of daily life (Singer 1987).

> In my interpretation, the reflexive structure consists of the self, spatially expressed as 'inside,' and the other, spatially expressed as 'outside'. The self may be humans or the Japanese as opposed to the other represented by deities and foreigners.
>
> The nature of Japanese deities provides us with an important clue to the structure of reflexivity. They are 'divine strangers' who visit humans periodically from outside and are endowed with dual qualities. Harnessed through ritual, their positive quality is the energy source for revitalizing the lives of people in a settlement. Their negative quality, if uncontrolled, looms as a threat to life. The Japanese self is the mirror image of these deities; it too consists of dual qualities and powers. Or, more accurately, the deities, which are symbolically represented by a mirror, represent the transcendental or elevated self. The transcendental self, which mirrors the other, is equated by purity. Thus the structure, comprised of a set of relations – in : out; human : deity; self : other; secular (*ke*) : sacred (*hare*) – is assigned the character of purity and the boundaries that of impurity (Ohnuki-Tierney 1987c).

These basic conceptions of ontological reality and modes of structuring the universes of discourse in Japanese society have also been closely connected to the templates or codes regulating the construction of modes of thought in Japan, such as those proposed by Nakamura Hajime (1964). It was these codes and templates that have, as indicated above, also greatly shaped the transformation of Buddhism and

Confucianism – and of many western influences in Japan.

It is these indexical as against referential, topological as against linear conceptions of time and space, in confrontation with the basic ontological conceptions analysed above and with the ability to shift from one context to another, to cross relatively easily different demarcated boundaries, that provide the basic frameworks within which the basic attitudes to nature have developed in Japanese society.

The preceding analysis has attempted to put the Japanese attitude to nature within the broader framework of the basic ontological premises and conceptions prevalent in Japanese society. We have already touched on some implications of both these premises as well as of the conceptions of nature for some areas of behaviour – as for instance in the attitudes to health and to concrete familial arrangements. But these premises and conceptions have much wider implications – for instance, among others, for the conceptions of political authority, of Japanese collective consciousness, and/or of the relations of the Japanese to other civilizations. Indeed, many of the features which were often held to be uniquely Japanese are closely related to these premises and conceptions. This is, of course, beyond the scope of this paper, but remains on the agenda for further research.

References

Asquith, P.J. 1986. 'The Monkey Memorial Service of Japanese Primatologists'. In Lebra, W.T. and T.S. Lebra (eds), *Japanese Culture and Behavior*. Honolulu: University of Hawaii Press.

Bachnick, J. 1986. 'Time, Space and Person in Japanese Relationships'. In Hendry, J. and J. Webber (eds), *Interpreting Japanese Society. Anthropological Approaches*. Oxford: JASO Occasional Papers.

—— 1987. 'Native Perspectives of Distance and Anthropological Perspectives of Culture'. *Anthropological Quarterly* 60(1):25-34.

—— 1992. 'Keijime, defining a shifting self'. In Rosenberger, N. (ed.), *Japanese Sense of Self*. Cambridge: Cambridge University Press.

Berque, A. 1986a. 'The Sense of Nature and its Relation to Space in Japan'. In Hendry, J. and J. Webber (eds), *Interpreting Japanese Society. Anthropological Approaches*. Oxford: JASO Occasional Papers.

—— 1986b. *Le Sauvage et L'Artifice*. Paris: Gallimard.

—— 1986c. 'Das Verhaltnis der Ekonoomie zu Raum und Zeit und der Japanische Kultur'. In von Barloewen, C. and K. Werhahn-Mees (eds), *Japan und der Western*. Frankfurt am Main: Fischer Taschenbuch Verlag, Vol. 1.

—— 1987. 'Some Traits of Japanese Fudosei'. *The Japan Foundation Newsletter* XIV(5):1-7.

Buruma, I. 1986. *Behind the Mask: On Sexual Demons, Sacred Mothers, Transvestites, Gangsters, and other Japanese Cultural Heroes*. New York: Pantheon Books.

Faure, B. 1987. 'Space and Place in Chinese Religious Traditions'. *History of Religions* 26(4):337-356.

Foard, J.H. 1982. 'The Boundaries of Comparison: Buddhism and National Tradition in Japanese Pilgrimage'. *Journal of Asian Studies* 41(2):232-251.

Grapard, A.G. 1982. 'Flying Mountains and Walkers of Emptiness: Toward a Definition of Sacred Space in Japanese Religions'. In *History of Religions* 21(3):195-221.

Hendry, J. 1990. 'Humidity, Hygiene or Ritual Care: Some Thought on Wrapping as a Social Phenomenon'. In Ben-Ari, E., B. Moeran and J. Valentine (eds), *Unwrapping Japan*. Manchester: Manchester University Press.

—— 1993. *Wrapping Culture: Politeness, Presentation and Power in Japan and Other Societies*. Oxford: Clarendon Press.

Jeremy, M. and M.E. Robinson. 1989. *Ceremony and Symbol in the Japanese Home*. Manchester: Manchester University Press.

Kalland, A. 1994. 'Culture in Japanese Nature'. In Bruun, O. and A. Kalland (eds), *Asian Perceptions of Nature. A Critical Approach*. London: Curzon Press.

Kuitert, W. 1988. *Scenes and Taste in the History of Japanese Garden Art*. Amsterdam: Gieben.

Kasulis, T.P. 1981. 'Philosophizing in Plato's, and Kukai's Shojin, Philosophy East and West'. In Kasulis, T.P (ed.), *Zen Action, Zen Person*, Honolulu:

University Press of Hawaii.

LaFleur, W. R. 1989. 'Saigyo and the Buddhist Value Nature'. In Callicott, J.B. and R.T. Ames (eds), *Nature and Asian Traditions of Thought: Essays in Environmental Philosophy*. Albany, New York: State University of New York Press.

―― 1993. *Liquid Life: Abortion and Buddhism in Japan*. Princeton: Princeton University Press.

Lebra, T.S. 1989. 'The Tri-Dimensional Space of Hierarchy: The Japanese Nobility'. A paper presented for 'The Ascribed Hierarchy Revisited: Subtle Dimensions', at the American Anthropological Association annual meeting, Washington D.C., November 15-19.

Lebra, W.P. and T.S. Lebra (eds), 1986. *Japanese Culture and Behavior*. Honolulu: University of Hawaii Press.

Loveday, L. and S. Cyba. 1985. 'Partaking with the divine and symbolizing the societal: The semiotics of Japanese food and drink'. *Semiotika* 56(2):115-131.

Maraini, F. 1960. *Meeting with Japan*. New York: Viking Press.

―― 1988. 'Japan: The Essential Modernizer'. In Kenny, S. and J.L. Lehman (eds), *Themes and Theories in Modern Japanese History*. London: Athlone Press.

Meyer, F.H. 1981. 'Fauna and Flora in Japanese Folklore'. *Asian Folklore Studies* 40(1):23-34.

Miyata, N. 1987. 'Weather Watching and Emperorship'. *Current Anthropology* 28(4):13-18.

Munataka, I. 1986. 'Struktur und Wandel der Kulturellen Identität im modernen Japan, Ein vergleichender hermeneutischer Ansatz'. In von Barloewen, C. and K. Werhahn-Mees (eds), *Japan und der Western*. Frankfurt am Main: Fischer Taschenbuch Verlag, Vol. 1.

Murakami, Y. 1990. 'Two Types of Civilization: Transcendental and Hermeneutical'. *Nichibuken Japan Review* 1:1-38.

Nakamura, H. 1964. *Ways of Thinking of Eastern People*. Honolulu: East-West Center Press.

―― 1979. 'The Acceptance of Man's Natural Dispositions'. *The Japan Foundation Newsletter* VII(2):1-8.

Namihira, E. 1987. 'Pollution in the Folk Belief System'. *Current Anthropology* 28(4):65-72.

Nosco, P. (ed.). 1984. *Confucianism and the Tokugawa Culture*. Princeton, N.J.: Princeton University Press.

Ohnuki-Tierney, E. 1987a. *The Monkey as Mirror — Symbolic Transformations in Japanese History and Ritual*. Princeton: Princeton University Press.

—— 1987b. *Illness and Culture in Contemporary Japan*. Cambridge: Cambridge University Press.

—— 1987c. 'Comment' to E. Namihira, 'Pollution in the Folk Belief System'. *Current Anthropology* 28(4):72-73.

—— 1990. 'The Monkey as Self in Japanese Culture'. In Ohnuki-Tierney, E. (ed.), *Culture Through Time: Anthropological Approaches*. Stanford: Stanford University Press.

—— 1991. 'The Emperor of Japan as Deity (*Kami*).' *Ethnology* 30(3):199-215.

Pelzel, J. 1977. 'Japanese Personality and Culture'. In *Culture, Medicine and Psychiatry* 1:299-315.

—— 1986. 'Human Nature in the Japanist Myths'. In Lebra, W.P. and T.S. Lebra (eds), *Japanese Culture and Behavior*. Honolulu: University of Hawaii Press.

Pinguet, M. 1984. *La Mort Volontaire au Japon*. Paris: Gallimard.

Plutschow, H. 1979. 'Space and travel – An interpretation of the travel poems of *Man'yōshū*'. In Nish, I. and C. Dunn (eds), *European Studies of Japan*, Tenterden: Paul Norburry.

Raz, J. 1992. 'Self-presentation and performance in the *yakuza* way of life: Fieldwork with a Japanese underworld group.' In Goodman, R. and K. Refsing (eds), *Ideology and Practice in Contemporary Japan*. London: Routledge.

Richie, D. 1992. *A Lateral View: Essays on Culture and Style in Contemporary Japan*. Berkeley: Stone Bridge Press.

Rosenberger, N. 1992. 'Tree in the Summer; Tree in the Winter'. In Rosenberger, N. (ed.), *Japanese Sense of Self*. Cambridge: Cambridge University Press.

Saito, Y. 1985. 'The Japanese Appreciation of Nature'. *The British Journal of*

Aesthetics 25(3):239-257.

Schaarschmidt-Richter, I. 1980. *Der Japanische Garten, Ein Kunstwerk*. Fribourg

—— 1984. 'Gartenkunst.' In Hammitzsch, H. (ed.), *Japan Handbuch*. Wiesbaden: Franz Steiner Verlag.

Seidenstricker, E. 1989. *The Japanese and Nature, with Special Reference to the Tale of Genji*. In idem, *This Country, Japan*. Tokyo: Kodansha International.

Shaner, D.E. 1989. 'The Japanese Experience of Nature'. In Callicott, J.B. and R.T. Ames (eds), *Nature and Asian Traditions of Thought: Essays in Environmental Philosophy*. Albany, New York: State University of New York Press.

Singer, K. 1987. *Mirror, Sword and Jewel*. Tokyo: Kodansha International.

Smith, R. J. 1974. *Ancestor Worship in Contemporary Japan*. Stanford: Stanford University Press.

Tellenbach, H. and B. Kimura. 1989. 'The Japanese Concept of Nature'. In Callicott, J.B. and R.T. Ames (eds), *Nature and Asian Traditions of Thought: Essays in Environmental Philosophy*. Albany, New York: State University of New York Press.

Veyne, P. 1988. *Did the Greeks Believe in Their Myths?* Chicago: University of Chicago Press.

Warda, M. 1977. 'Symbolism of the Moon and the Waters of Immorality'. *History of Religions* 16:407-423.

Wargo, R.J. 1990. 'Japanese Ethics: Beyond Good and Evil'. *Philosophy East and West* XL(4):499-511.

Wilson, G.M. 1990. 'Time and History in Japan'. *American Historical Review* 85:557-571.

Werblowsky, R.J. Zwi 1991. '*Mizuko kuyō*. Notulae on the Most Important "New Religion" of Japan.' *Japanese Journal of Religious Studies* 18(4):295-354.

Yamaguchi, M. 1973. 'La Structure Mythico-Theatrale de la Royaute Japonaise'. *Esprit* 41:337-339.

—— 1977. 'Kingship, Theatricity and Marginal Reality in Japan'. In Jain, R. (ed.), *Text and Context*. Philadelphia: Institute for the Study of Human

Issues.

—— 1987. 'The Dual Structure of Japanese Emperorship'. *Current Anthropology* 28(4):8-20.

—— 1993. 'Le prototype des echecs dans l'histoire Japonaise'. *Stanford French Review*, Summer.

Yoshida, T. 1981. 'The Stranger as God: The Place of the Outsider in Japanese Folk Religion'. *Ethnology* 20(2):87-99.

—— 1990. 'The Feminine in Japanese Folk Religion: Polluted or Divine?' In Ben-Ari, E., B. Moeran and J. Valentine (eds), *Unwrapping Japan*. Manchester: Manchester University Press.

Brian Moeran and Lise Skov

Japanese Advertising Nature
Ecology, Fashion, Women and Art

In this paper, we will deconstruct the idea of a special connection between women and nature by examining the use of natural imagery in what constitutes a vast market for advertising in Japan: women's magazines.[1] Our aim, in particular, is to look at the way in which the two themes of ecology and nature have been taken up in Japanese women's magazine reportage and advertisements, and to explore these as elements in a cultural discourse of femininity and consumption.

Why *women*'s magazines? Because, firstly, it is generally recognized that in most contemporary societies women are the main consumers of most kinds of commodities (with certain prominent exceptions). In this respect, one might even argue that the study of advertising and media as such is simply a branch of women's studies in general. A second, and more ambivalent, reason for focussing on women's magazines is that there has been a line of cultural thought, including anthropological argument, which assigns women a natural function connected to their biological child-bearing abilities. This has, in passing, been used to suggest that certain social rules are a result of the incest taboo which, as the 'supreme rule of the gift', obliges men to exchange their women so that, further, the whole of civilization is made to rest on women's biology. In its shorthand version, this argument equates men with culture, and women with nature (e.g. Beauvoir 1989; Lévi-Strauss 1969; Rosaldo and Lamphere 1974). It is with this line of thought that we wish to take issue here. Rather than seeing the relationship between women and nature as part of a set of fixed dichotomies, we suggest that it is an open-ended image cluster which includes occasionally contradictory and surprising

---

[1] Brian Moeran would like to take this opportunity to thank Hidehiko Sekizawa and his colleagues at the Hakuhōdō Institute of Life and Living for providing him with hospitality and the authors with access to a wide range of materials on which this essay has been based.

elements, inviting endless variations and combinations.

This is not to suggest that it is impossible or even difficult, in Japan as elsewhere, to find advertisements in women's magazines which make use of the idea of 'woman as nature'. For example, in both reportage and advertising, we find that women are often equated with flowers both visually and linguistically. This can be seen in a split-frame advertisement for Attwood jewellery (Fig. 1). On the left is a heavily contrasted colour photograph of a woman whose black-gloved hands and arms are held across her low-cut bright red dress. Her oiled, raven-black hair is combed back from her high forehead and held in a bun. We see only half her face – one eye, one side of her nose, just over one half of her brightly painted red lips. From her ears hang two large glittering ear-rings, while just above her *décolleté* bosom she wears a matching necklace, with a brooch on what must be a fur coat draped over her right shoulder. There is something about the light on her face and the dappled background which makes it seem as if she is sitting in the shade of a tree in the late afternoon sunlight. To the side of the picture, the headline reads in English: *Petal Power by Attwood*.

This advertisement illustrates two points. Firstly, whereas the anthropological 'woman as nature' argument links women's bodies to childbirth, menstruation, blood and pain, advertising's 'woman as nature' associations tend rather to highlight elegance, beauty and eroticism. Few advertisements present female bodies marked by child-birth or women nurturing children (except in specialist magazines). Even those for panty-liners, tampons and painkillers in Japan are dominated by cosiness, order and cleanliness.[2] This is not to argue that biological functions of the female body constitute an underlying condition which false and glossy advertising prevents women from facing (on the contrary, we often find that women's magazines go very well with periods[3]). Rather, we simply wish to point out that the association of 'woman as nature' is not fixed once and for all, and that we may find supplementary meanings of what it means to be natural in the pages of women's monthly periodicals.

---

[2] This is not necessarily the case with similar advertisements in England or Denmark.

[3] Many Japanese women's magazines, especially those targeted at under-thirty age groups, provide abundant information about the female cycle, fertility, contraception, and sexual techniques – information that young women are unlikely to get from either their schools or their families.

This notion of supplementary meanings brings us to our second point. To the determined semiotician or hard-headed feminist, it might sometimes seem as though there is no *specific* rhyme or reason to the way in which natural images are used in women's magazine advertising. Certainly, this is the line of thought adopted by Williamson who, in her discussion of nature and culture, the raw and the cooked, in English advertisements, argues that 'the precise *meaning* of nature as a symbol, i.e. of "the natural", is less important than the significance of its being used as a symbol at all' (1978:123). But is this really true? It may seem at times as if the relation between a product and 'the natural' conveyed in advertising, and hence the symbolic meaning of that relation, is not so important, but our argument is that this approach is simplistic.

In the Attwood advertisement described above, for example, nature is located in the product *and* in the woman who wears the product. This in itself is not so remarkable, but the point about any advertisement is that it cannot be fully explained 'in itself' as some discrete entity in the way that Williamson and others (e.g. Barthes 1977) have done. Even if we leave out the various ways in which an advertisement can be interpreted by potential consumers, it is still necessary to see it, on the one hand, as part of a campaign (in other words, as one of a series of related advertisements put out by a particular advertiser) and, on the other, as competing with other advertising campaigns for rival products or brands. Every advertisement thus draws on a wide range of images and selling points that exist elsewhere than in the ad itself, so that one of the features of the Attwood advertisement that needs to be taken into account in any explanation of the image of 'woman as nature' used therein, is the way in which a large number of jewellery and accessory advertisers in Japan make use of visuals which place their products in *direct* relation to 'the natural' by photographing them hanging from a tropical flower, encircling a pyramid of sand, or – as we shall later have occasion to see – draped around a cactus.

In other words, nature appears in a number of different ways in advertising – ways which may reflect upon the product itself (its name, its aim, its perceived characteristics), and upon other products with which it may or may not be in competition, or which may be incidental to both product and advertiser. Benetton, for example, makes use of the natural in an advertisement whose visual consists of a close up of a zebra's black and brownish white striped head and, perched on its back just behind the spiky mane, a brightly coloured, red, yellow, blue and green cockatoo. The headline, white letters against a bold green background, reads: *United Colors of Benetton*. Another advertisement in this series also makes use of an image from nature – scattered maple leaves floating on the surface of some water – but the campaign as a whole reveals that Benetton is concerned with something other than nature as such, for we come across other visuals of a black baby at a white breast, the faces of children of different races, and a priest and nun kissing. In other words, the natural is used only when it contributes to the advertiser's corporate image and can be made part of the campaign's overall theme of Benetton's united colours.

An advertisement for Kanebo's *La Crème* uses nature in another way. Its visual consists of a horizontal triptych with the product name and manufacturer written boldly in white against a black background at the top, and at the bottom, on a white diagonal surface, an open jar, its lid unscrewed to reveal a rich pink-tinted cream. The central section of the advertisement itself forms a vertical triptych of three black and white *shōji* paper screens, one of which has been slid open to reveal a shock of red maple leaves. Thus, the central and deepest focal point of the visual in this advertisement consists of a depiction of 'nature' – a depiction whose content changes according to the season of the year (in summer there is a clump of green bamboo). The fact that the 'natural' image itself is framed by an obviously 'Japanese' paper screen, and that the advertisement as a whole has been placed in European (especially French) women's magazines, suggests that the Japanese company Kanebo is more concerned with an image of Japaneseness than with nature as such. In other words, maple leaves and a bamboo grove are made out to be specifically Japanese aspects of nature, itself characterized by strict adherence to what the Japanese proudly call 'the four seasons' (see Moeran and Skov, forthcoming).

Frequently, it is the naming of a product which establishes a relationship between it and some aspect of nature – hence a herb-*cum*-shampoo called Timotei, and a woman lying on sand for a perfume called *Dune* by Dior.[4] Tissot uses a picture of the Matterhorn to advertise its *Rockwatch*, while a Kentucky Four Roses visual of glass, ice

---

[4] The 'sand' theme has been taken up both in fashion reportage, and by other designers such as Gucci who, in his 1992 campaign, clothed his models in fish, animal, and floral printed textiles and placed them in the middle of a desert. Frequently, these ads appeared back to back with those by Dior for *Dune* (e.g. *Classy*, June 1992, and *25 Ans*, September 1992).

cube and a bottle of its whiskey, is accompanied in the background by a vase with four red roses in it. Jaeger plays on its meaning of 'hunter' in German by using the motif of a wild animal on the sweater worn by its model (and thereby plays, too, on the phonetic similarity between *Jaeger* and *jaguar*).

The product-nature relationship may also lie elsewhere, in a perceived (or advertiser's wish-to-be-perceived) characteristic of the product in question. For example, a girl, half naked with a shiny blue-green, scale-like skirt around her hips, stands with her back towards the camera, staring at a blue-green sea. This mermaid-like figure places both hands at the top of her buttocks, turning her body slightly so that the sun catches her tanned back and the viewer has a glimpse of one rounded breast. The headline reads: *Manatsu da yo, haru* (*Spring – It's mid summer*). Both the visual's emphasis on the girl's naked body, sun and sea, and the name of the advertiser (the Tokyo Beauty Center), reinforce the association of nature with health, and the underlying argument that all of us can be 'naturally' beautiful if we treat our bodies well. Other advertisements are similarly designed to emphasize, by reference to the natural, a product's 'healthy' attributes, even when they are not immediately obvious. Carlton cigarettes, for example, has as a visual a (superimposed) stretch of green grass in the midst of an arid valley surrounded by cactus-covered rocky hills. From the centre of the green rises a giant cigarette, while the caption reads: *6 Under*.[5] By claiming to be below a certain tar measurement (6 mg), Carlton uses the natural image of a golf course to comment metonymically (six below par) on the quality of its cigarettes. Similarly, though again differently, with an ad for Japan Tobacco's *Frontier Lights*, where a dolphin is shown balancing on its nose on one of a series of famous buildings round the world (the Eiffel Tower, the Empire State Building, the Leaning Tower of Pisa) (Fig. 2). The headline, *karui* (*light*), clearly refers to the mildness of the cigarette (and one of its presumed healthy attributes). But why a dolphin upside down? Because the Japanese word for dolphin is *iruka* – *karui* spelt backwards in the *kana* syllabary.

Yet other ads show the range of meanings which may be attributed to the natural. *Hunting World*, for example, makes use of a visual of travel bags on the sand nearby camels in an oasis, and is accompanied

---

[5] Where, as here, foreign words are used in headlines or captions, we have chosen – for ease of reading – to transliterate them in their original, rather than Japanese *katakana*, form.

by the caption *Urban Adventure*. Nature here (sand, palm trees, camels) is thus romanticized and placed in the context of a contemporary (sub)urban lifestyle, but the advertisement also echoes, in both its use of the visual and romanticism, a global campaign put out by another manufacturer of travelling equipment, Louis Vuitton (where one visual is of sand, desert, rocks and elephants). Such romanticism can also embrace the ethnic – as in an Emile Pequignet advertisement whose headline, *Natural elegance*, refers to what the body copy describes as a watch with a 'Maasai' ornament designed bracelet.

    In all these examples, therefore, we find a combination of textual and visual imagery which is used to express aspects of nature. In some respects, we are faced with a form of *totemic classification*, in which products of various classes (eg. clothing, cosmetics, alcohol, tobacco and cars) are differentiated from one another through different marketing styles. Furthermore, within each class of things brands are differentiated from one another through sets of imagery which may include natural phenomena. In other words, nature can be used as a means of establishing and maintaining differences among similar products.[6] But, of course, advertisers have to understand and play by the rules if they are to succeed in creating a niche for a particular product in the totemic classification of advertising. Thus advertisers adopt different strategies in order to place their products in certain types of market environment, imbuing them with different aspects of 'the natural' in an attempt to make those products sell.

Eco-commercialism

Another way in which nature has been used recently is in advertisers' focus on ecology and environmental problems.[7] One example of this trend, which came into its own in 1990, is to be seen in an advertisement for *Ozone Community* (Fig. 3). Here, two Japanese girls stand facing each other, their legs slightly apart, arms outstretched against adjoining walls of a room which has been totally covered with yellow paper decorated

---

    [6] Rather than simply totemic groups of *people*, as claimed by Williamson (1978:45-50).

    [7] A fuller discussion of the 'ecology boom' in Japanese fashion and media can be found in Skov (1993).

with Siamese-twin mermaids. One girl wears a black embroidered T-shirt, black trousers, black shoes, black nail varnish; the other a silver blonde wig, white tunic, trousers, shoes and stockings, together with matching silver white nail varnish. To the right of the picture, below the 'black' girl's hand, can be found in blue *katakana* syllabary the headline: *Aquarian age*. In the centre, between the two girls and in black Roman writing, is the name of the brand being advertised. This, apart from the mermaids, is the only visual allusion to nature in the ad, although the headline and the brand name together focus on the havoc wrought upon the environment by industrial capitalism.

A second example of this kind of 'nature-as-environment' advertisement is to be seen in the 1990-1 campaign by Norma Kamali, whose handbags are placed on discs supported by rice plants or leafy vines, as well as in the forked stem of a silver birch tree and surrounded by michaelmas daisies. The headlines that accompany these ads read: *Shizenryū (Naturalism); Koko ni ecology (Here is ecology);* and *Ecology wa fashion ja nai. Ikikata da to omou (Ecology is not fashion. I think it's a way of life).*

As this and other campaigns show, eco-commercialism *was* very much an 'in' thing in Japan at the beginning of the 1990s when, during the last heady months of the so-called 'bubble era' prior to the present economic crisis, a number of corporations went about giving themselves an ecological image. In 1990, for instance, one major securities firm started an environment-related trust fund, while two credit companies launched Japan's first 'green' credit cards.[8] Once again, it was differentiation in terms of totemic classification which ruled this approach to the use of 'nature as environment', although newspapers and business magazines were the prime medium for this kind of advertising. This was reflected perhaps in the fact that what was at issue here was not so much a differentiation between *products* as one between *advertisers*. Large corporations were continually seeking ways of establishing an image that would set them apart from their rivals, and eco-commercialism was one way of doing precisely this. Under such circumstances, it was often the *image* that a company was aware of the environment, rather than the *awareness* itself, which characterized much of the environmental

---

[8] 0.5 per cent of the value of purchases charged to the cards was to be given to wildlife conservation – an idea which was taken up by Visa and Mastercard in the United States in early 1991 (cf. 'The Selling of the Green', *Time*, Volume 138, Number 11, September 16, 1991).

consciousness in both Japanese and Western market economies at the beginning of the 1990s.

This gave rise to certain anomalies with regard to precisely what should be done to save the environment in Japan. Some things – like paper, envelopes, business cards, account books, even receipts – were singled out for recycling, while others were ignored. For example, fruit and vegetables were, and still are, individually wrapped in plastic before being boxed – the argument being that, in Japan if not elsewhere, plastic bags more or less *had* to be used for purchases in stores. This cultural explanation was reinforced in the minds of all concerned when a move by Seibu Department Store to save paper by cutting down on 'unnecessary' wrapping during the *ochūgen* gift giving season proved to be singularly unpopular.[9]

In some respects, then, 'corporate greening' during 1990 was as transparent in Japan as it was elsewhere. One example is that of Suntory Breweries which launched a new beer on Earth Day (April 22). In spite of its advertised claim to be *Thinking about the earth*, Suntory failed to use recycled paper plates in its 'Earth tent' restaurant in Shiodome, downtown Tokyo. Furthermore, the labels on its bottles were made to look as if they were made of recycled paper when in fact they were not. This may be an extreme example of how the ecology *image* was more important to corporations than their actual protection of the environment. Indeed, the only positive, though very limited, step taken by Suntory was to manufacture cans with push-in tabs – a move that merely led to discussion in the press of a problem facing Japanese brewers in general. Should they use beer cans with tabs that remained attached to them when opened, or stick with the metal rings which could be thrown away, even though environmentalists disapproved of the latter? The problem as such was that many Japanese thought that tabs were impure and that their beer, *sake*, or soft drinks would be 'polluted' when they opened their cans by pushing tabs into the drink, rather than by pulling them off.[10]

These snippets of information are interesting for the way in which they relate to such general theoretical issues as purity and pollution. At the same time, however, what was said to have been a cultural problem

---

[9] 'Seibu's save paper campaign unpopular', *The Daily Yomiuri*, July 8, 1990.

[10] 'Corporate greening in Japan termed advertising gimmick', *Japan Times*, June 5, 1990.

in 1990 was no longer so two years later. By 1992, almost every canned drink manufacturer in Japan, regardless of its environmentalist position, was selling its products in cans whose tabs were pushed in, and not pulled off and thrown away as before. In other words, a claimed 'cultural propensity' had been broken down by market forces.

The same might yet be said of packaging. Japanese consumers' predilection for having their purchases double, even triple, wrapped has been criticised for its contribution to the latest environmental crisis in that country.[11] At the same time, however, wrapping in itself has been seen as a 'pervasive ordering principle' (Hendry 1990) in Japanese society as a whole. According to this line of argument, not only do the Japanese 'wrap' goods; they 'wrap' their forms of communication (with honorific and other polite phrases), their bodies (with multi-layers of clothing), even their literary and art forms. In other words, it has been argued that there is a cultural propensity for Japanese to value wrapping of one sort or another – in which case consciousness of certain environmental issues (such as use of paper and plastics in wrapping) becomes that much more difficult to attain.[12] This is to ignore, however, the way in which the packaging of commodities and cultural events is closely controlled by marketing methods and consumerism, which may well override this so-called 'cultural propensity' as and when those concerned see fit.

If corporate greening was sometimes no more than skin deep in Japan, the same could also be said of Japanese consumer reactions to environmental problems at the beginning of the 1990s. A comparative survey conducted by the *Nikkei Marketing Journal* (June 1990) revealed that Japanese consumers were far less willing to make a personal sacrifice and pay for environmental protection than were either German or American consumers, even though they were generally as aware as inhabitants of Frankfurt and New York of the need for such protection.[13] This apparent unwillingness on the part of most consumers to take an active part in saving the ozone layer, rain forest, or (an often non-endangered species of) whale, brings us to the role of advertising

---

[11] See 'False economics', *Far Eastern Economic Review*, September 19, 1991:37.

[12] We should recognize, however, that the whole notion of wrapping – as an explanation of *Japanese* society – is very much part and parcel of strategies used in Orientalism in general.

[13] 'Consumers seek global protection', *The Japan Economic Journal*, June 23, 1990.

and women's magazines in the environmental debate and the use of 'nature-as-environment' images. It is clear that *all* advertising has to respond to important political, cultural and ecological issues in order to work effectively. In this respect, it takes those issues into the public arena of consumerism and, by relating them to corporate images and commodities, broadens public awareness, shifting the focus away from the customary distance imposed by politics to the immediate proximity of people's everyday lives. At the same time, by entering this kind of cultural discourse, advertising serves in some respects to make the issues themselves less political, less powerful symbolically. Thus with eco-commercialism, from the Gordon's gin series of 'green' advertisements and Philip Morris's more insidious 'green' ads for *Superslims* – complete with floral background and surgeon general's warning[14] – on the one hand; to other British ads which (like *Ozone Community* mentioned earlier) played on fears of environmental disaster by making use of such headlines as *Ozone layer* (for the urine on baby's nappies) and *Eau zone* (for a French mineral water), on another; and – on yet a third – to Japanese ads, like those for Norma Kamali, Nihon Kodak and Japan Tobacco, which simply used 'ecology', 'nature', and 'smokin' clean' as gimmicky keywords. Indeed, strictly environmental advertising (such as that for biodegradable packaging) is said to take up less than one per cent of the market, so that during the 'ecology boom' advertisements by companies like NEC (*Saving a tree just takes a little paperwork*) and NKK Corporation (*The latest development in advanced technology: Back to Nature*) would appear to have been – nonetheless important – exceptions, rather than the rule.[15]

At the same time, we should note that environmental awareness took on a rather different tone in Japanese women's magazines, precisely because their subject matter focussed on what might be termed limited issues like detergents and fabrics, as opposed to the more extensive problems posed by Japan's logging, car and chemical industries. Ecology was still the 'in' word in such magazines,[16] but it referred to fashion

---

[14] Both western and Japanese cigarette advertisements make use of (light) green in their colour photographs, but this is usually connected with the idea of 'coolness' in menthol flavoured cigarettes.

[15] See 'False economics', *Far Eastern Economic Review*, September 19, 1991:37.

[16] See, for example, 'Eco-fashions painless way to make "statement"', *Japan Economic Journal*, June 1990; and 'Fashion for the ecologically minded', *Asahi Evening*

trends rather than to the destruction of the ozone layer or the devastation of the rain forests. Everything, from stockings to love,[17] became 'ecological', while 'ecology colours' everywhere were the height of fashion – whether in the 'primitive casual' giraffe blouse in one woman's fashion magazine,[18] as part of an 'avant garde night' in another,[19] or surfacing in a photo-reportage on women's underwear in yet another.[20]

But what happens when political issues are taken up in women's magazines? What is the outcome of the blending of politics and fashion? An answer to these questions may well lie in two photographs accompanying a short description of the ecology boom in *Classy* (July 1990), where a small man cuddled up against a slender young model in her leopard-like clothes. In one sense, it would seem as though the environmental problems are here being depoliticized into little more than eco-commercialism, in that the models hold, or stand beside, the kinds of placards used by those who demonstrate for the protection of wildlife. Similarly, an advertorial for Arbatax suits carried a gratuitous *We love the mother earth* above its brand name, while an ad for Castelbajac consisted of a painting of wild animals by the French designer, accompanied by such slogans as *Suport nature is pure (sic)*, *Save the world* and *Save the nature is always in style*.[21] In other words, women's magazines seemed to resound with nothing but the hollow sound of 'echo' fashion.

But then again, we may ask whether it is reasonable to blame women's magazines for not carrying out political campaigns, since they address a realm of style and consumption which really has very little to do with environmental politics. From this point of view, rather than regretting that political issues are brushed under advertising's carpet, it

---

News, May 17, 1990.

[17] For 'ecological stocking' see *Ryūkō Tsūshin*, Number 323, November 1990; for 'ecological love', see the advertisement for Agnat men's wear, in *Playboy*, September 1990.

[18] 'Taste of Elegance – *natsu-iro no romance*'. In *25 Ans*, May 1990.

[19] *Ryūkō Tsūshin*, Number 324, December 1990.

[20] 'Yume-iro no jikan – *romantic na shitagi*'. In *Non-no*, May 20, 1990.

[21] *With*, October 1989.

is more important to note the ways in which the ecology trend ruffled conventional notions of good taste in Japan. In this respect, allusion to an environmental demonstration is a powerful and unusual setting for a fashion editorial. The model wearing fake leopard clothes and carrying a political placard presents the readers with a new kind of fashion figure in which mainstream consumption merges with counter-cultural styles.

Being natural

It is exactly in this blending of conventional fashion and counter-cultural styles, or rather in the dialectics of mass consumption and individuality, that nature and ecology took on a special meaning in the advertising of the early 1990s. During the fashion's peak a photo-advertorial, *Text Book for Natural Girl*, appeared in the teenage magazine *mcSister*. It was divided into four 'scenes' titled 'Like a man', 'Like in a South of France resort', 'Like an L.A. girl' and 'From the inside of the body, natural'. While the 'natural girl' was advised to wear boy's clothing consisting of jeans, polo shirts, and khaki camouflage trousers, she also found that the South of France was equated with 'pastel colours', L.A. girls' 'natural-ness' with their 'healthiness' and a 'natural body' with drinking mineral water.[22]

What are we to make of this? Does nature in this context refer to anything at all? All the scenes, apart from the last one, associated 'being natural' with something which young Japanese women readers of *mcSister* simply could not be: European, American and male. In this respect, the advertorial was compatible with the view put forward by some of those writing about youth groups and subcultures in Britain: that young people tend to negotiate their identity by way of an inner dialogue with other groups. In studies which have for the most part focussed on young, white, working class men, these 'hidden others' usually refer to young women and to blacks, whose music and style of dress they appropriate and incorporate into their own sense of self (Hebdige 1979, 1988). Similarly, young Japanese women readers of magazines like *mcSister* may try out boyish clothes, together with European and American styles, as a means of coming to terms with

---

[22] *mcSister*, June 1990.

'others' whose presence is clearly felt in their everyday lives.[23] The difference, however, is that the girls appropriate styles 'upwards' from a *subordinate* position whereas working class boys, albeit not from an altogether dominant position, choose to negotiate their identity *vis-à-vis* relatively weaker groups.[24]

Nature, then, has something to do with a sense of self. Behind all the different styles that are, in one way or another, described as natural, and behind all the different advertisements in which nature has been a key visual or word, we may find that 'being natural' provides us with shared connotations which themselves have very little to do with nature 'out there'. Rather, being natural is connected with 'being unrestrained' and 'being at home' – though not necessarily domesticated – in one's surroundings, and thus is very different from the idea of natural as raw, unpolished or unlearned. Being natural is an achieved quality which marks the goal of a feminine learning process (cf. Connerton 1989:88-95). The opposite is not that of being cultured or civilized, but rather being clumsy in the way a woman is when she does not match, or master, her – culturally fixed – surroundings. A woman acts naturally when all signs of effort at achieving feminine behaviour have been erased, so that we find ourselves agreeing with *mcSister* that even the 'natural girl' needs a 'textbook'.

The sense of self was certainly central to the ecology trend since it tended to emphasize 'natural' colours which were close to skin tones or in other ways becoming. An advertorial for make-up, for example, had a colour page of lipsticks, powders and blushers embossed with the English word *Ecology*, while readers were told that 'Browns and oranges that make you aware of "nature" are in this spring'. Here it appeared that 'to be natural, you should use only mascara on your eyes', while 'lipstick should be the colour of your skin, with just a touch of orange added'. The main body of the advertorial's text read:

---

[23] A similar, though slightly simplistic point is made by Rosenberger (1992) who, in her discussion of western images in Japanese home living styles, focusses on generalized social categories such as (the 'aspiring' or 'wealthy') 'class', 'family', and 'individuality'.

[24] The different conditions for men and women in stylistic play and crossdressing are typical of fashion in general: whereas a skirt or make-up worn by a man is often seen as a powerful and provocative subcultural expression, business suits have blended smoothly into women's dress and are seen as conventional.

Another noteworthy kind of make-up is the natural type known as ecology. Ecology is a new trend that espouses a 'return to nature', and is much the rage in the fashion world. Making up your face with colours that suit the skin makes you feel fresh, and in particular you should use make-up that is even 'closer to the skin' than ever. Rather than accentuating the eyes or mouth, you should thus try to develop a technique which makes the natural nuance a plus, with all the colours on your face merged into a single overall tone.[25]

The year that browns and oranges replaced the pale powder and pink lipsticks in Japan, women's individual features rather than fashion conventions came to be the central parameter for choosing make-up. Even though the 'ecology' make-up in 'natural colours' certainly was an element in a successful fashion trend, it also emphasized that make-up was not simply a conventional mask but a means to bring out one's personality. Yet, given that the function of 'ecology colours' was to focus on women's individuality, precisely what made colours 'ecological' was hard to say. They could, for instance, be 'born of nature', which usually meant that a prime colour was given a name which made use of some aspect of the environment to give it an ecological twist.[26] Thus:

Beige the colour of the sand on desert dunes, red brown earth and *azuki* bean colours, plant greens, sea and sky blues. Pure colours are fresher than the earth colours used up until now.[27]

Another aspect of eco-fashion was designers' emphasis on 'nature' in patterns and prints:

Ecology ... is expressed in floral, shell, jungle and other patterns and prints. But the most easily understood aspect of nature is its colours – sand, red earth, mustard, pumpkin yellow, sunset orange, cocoa brown, olive green – all colours that have been squeezed out of natural phenomena, the earth and nature's plants.[28]

---

[25] (*With*, March 1990).

[26] (*Spur*, March 1990).

[27] (*La Seine*, April 1990).

[28] (*Elle Japon*, February 20, 1990).

For all this emphasis on colours, advertising also frequently portrayed models wearing flower prints (Leonard *Sport*), and such animal patterns as dogs (Bryant), wolves (Givenchy), elephants (Mizuone), tigers (Jean-Charles de Castelbajac), and crocodiles (Flandre). At the same time, as if to emphasize the woman-nature relation, women were portrayed *as* animals, for example, in an advertisement for Yoshiki Hishinuma (Fig. 4) which shows five models standing or sitting in dark clothes with muzzle-like frames around their heads. The muzzles – together with the fact that all the women keep their arms close to their bodies – seem to indicate that they are domesticated, tame animals. But at the same time, the fact that the women are wearing muzzles at all makes them also wild and eerie. A similar ambivalence can be found in a two page advertisement for Yohji Yamamoto (Fig. 5) which shows a woman's face merging with that of a cat in such a way that the reader is met by a strange three-eyed gaze which acts as a powerful reflection of her own gaze into the magazine.

Of course, animal motifs, like fake leopard spots and zebra stripes, have been used in women's (and to a lesser extent in men's) clothing for a long time. According to one Japanese fashion magazine which analyzed the trend current at the time, animal prints were originally seen to be 'daring' and 'sexy', rather than 'fashionable' as such. It was the 'sexy' image of the Hollywood star, for instance, in leopard-skin tights which Japanese married women found threatening, since they feared that their husbands would be preyed upon by attractive young women dressed in such clothes. As a result, the feature concluded, the 'animal style' itself took on a connotation of 'badness', excitement and sexuality, so that in the end all women wanted to try it out for themselves. This desire was partially fulfilled with the entrance of the 'safari look' in the 1970s, when women began to wear all kinds of animal and jungle prints, and since then there had been a move towards ridding leopard skin and animal designs of their 'bad' connotation.[29] By the autumn of 1992, when wild animals came once more to prowl the catwalks of Parisian *haute couture* fashion shows, Japanese women were probably ready to publicly express their feline charms – and in so doing hope to be worshipped by men in the same way as the model shown in a Veuve champagne ad the year before (Fig. 6).

As a style the ecology trend set some central issues on the agenda

---

[29] Nishiyama Eiko, writing on 'The influence of the ecology boom', in *Classy*, July 1990.

of women's magazines, in that it first stressed the importance of starting from the individual in choosing colours and styles; then emphasized the importance of being natural in the sense of being at home with, or mastering one's surroundings; and, finally, suggested a way for women to play out their sexuality. As we have seen, the ecology trend was directed at a mass-market, and made a hit there, but it was nevertheless a trend which took the individual as its starting point. This ambivalence was also at the heart of the Norma Kamali advertisement's headline: *Ecology is not fashion. I think it is a way of life.*

Nature in the city

From what we have said so far, it is clear that natural imagery used in women's magazine advertising is not designed merely to place women in a position inferior to both men and culture. On the contrary, we have argued that it creates an individual and private space for women readers. The question then is, how does 'being natural' as a 'way of life' connect with other main themes in magazine advertising? Here we will look at two such themes in particular: the city and art.

One of the tensions that has preoccupied Japanese copywriters, designers and other cultural intermediaries in the postwar period has been a perceived contrast between 'tradition' and 'modernity', country and city (Moeran 1989:138-140). This has meant, briefly, that during the 1970s, much was made in the Japanese media of such keywords as 'nature' (*shizen*), 'tradition' (*dentō*) and 'native place' (*furusato*), epitomized by the Japan National Railways *Discover Japan* campaign in 1970. During the boom in Japan's consumer economy in the 1980s these keywords were replaced by new terms such as 'city' (*tokai*) and 'internationalization' (*kokusaika*) which today, in the 1990s, form the platform from which the new emphasis on 'ecology' and 'nature' has taken off. Thus today the two opposing sets of concepts, through which the media have imagined Japanese society, have now been reconciled, albeit according to the terms of the 'city' (and the consumer economy).

In other words, Japanese advertising of the 1990s no longer makes a contradiction out of 'nature' and 'city', *shizen* and *tokai*. Thus one ad, for Evele Japan, pictures a woman carrying an armful of twigs with leaves, captioned by the headline: *This is where the city's nature is* (*tokai no shizen wa, koko ni imasu*), while another, for the Women's Wear Retailing Association, makes use of a visual of greenery seen through a rain-specked window, and uses the phrase *City Leaves* (*tokaiha*), which puns, through (mis)use of a Chinese character, on the more customary *City-ites* used to portray a fashionable upper-class woman (in crude shorthand describable, perhaps, as a culture-vulture with a Gucci bag). A third advertisement, for Studiov, depicts two women in floral print suits, with flowers as hats, and a pastiche of natural phenomena (butterflies, sea, fish, rock), with a large T-shaped cut-out of a cityscape at the top of the design.

Ads like these address housewives, and when we examine the way in which they connect nature with urban life, we realize that it is precisely through the consumption of fashion items that housewives can escape temporarily from the confines of their home and workplace into the anonymity of the city. For a housewife, the usual separation of private and public is to some extent reversed. The city provides a woman with a personal, private space to which as a well-dressed consumer she can withdraw when not fulfilling her public duties as housewife and mother.

Advertisements which combine city and nature do not just refer to 'the city' as a vaguely defined place or idea: they frequently depict activities that take place in cities (whether Tokyo, Paris or Hong Kong) – like going to the theatre, visiting an art exhibition, eating out at an expensive restaurant, and, of course, shopping. Even so, in ads using natural imagery, women are rarely depicted walking down a shopping street, crossing a busy road, or sitting in a crowded café. The actual inter-subjective space of the city is hardly ever connected to nature as a keyword. Instead, a single model poses in such a way that she stares straight into the camera lens from the abstract space of a studio. In such advertisements, the female body appears as an artefact itself in front of a flattened background – witness the Attwood visual, or an ad for Citizen, where the model appears naked, adorned only in Citizen jewellery and holding in her hands an enormous egg. In this type of advertisement the female body, nature and product actually conflate.

This conflation can be seen more clearly when we compare the visuals of a bracelet draped across a cactus for Mikimoto (Fig. 7), and a necklace superimposed across a woman's body in an advertisement for Quail (Fig. 8). Here the succulent body of the cactus is treated visually in exactly the same way as is the dressed female body, each of which constitutes a substantial background, or raw natural material, against which the ornamental product is allowed to stand out and so present itself in all its beauty. In fact, the Quail advertisement shows this relationship not once, but twice. First, there is the chain of the necklace which crosses, and thus contains, the whole visual. Second, the model is herself wearing a similar chain around her neck. This technique of visual repetition is frequently used in advertising for women – as, for example, in a Hermés advertisement of a woman gazing at Mount Fuji, where the viewer is invited to gaze at the woman gazing at the natural beauty before her. This doubleness draws us into the picture which then appears, not as a realistic natural scene, but as a cabinet of mirrors reflecting our own gaze (see Moeran and Skov, forthcoming).

In this kind of advertising, the female body is thus presented as a piece of nature, in the sense that it provides the raw material for *aesthetic* self-staging. Once again, we are *not* concerned with nature as being in some way opposed to culture. Rather, we are dealing with something that is both malleable and already formed; against the flattened background, the Quail model appears almost as a still-life painting. In other words, just as the female body is similar to nature in ads like this, so is the process through which it is formed comparable to art.

Women, nature and art

Dressing up and adorning the body with make-up, clothing, jewellery and other accessories is clearly the kind of creative process that encourages both advertising and fashion reportages to bring together women and art. This they do in several different ways – either by depicting women in settings that are related to art, such as studios (Max Factor *Duomilia*) or galleries (Edwin *Something*), or by using a real woman artist as a model in a campaign that visually does not allude to art in any way (like Juliette Binoche modelling for Iona). Yet other advertisements show the female body, or the products that a woman uses to adorn her body, as an art object (for example, Nina Ricci's *L'art du temps*), or somehow mirroring an art object.[30]

Such visual use of the female body in art settings raises some issues

---

[30] Art may also be related to eroticism, as in Krizia's *Nature never changes* for its perfume *Moods* – a headline which is translated into Japanese as *koi suru kaori* (*the smell that makes/in which to make love*). This is emphasized by a split visual of, to the left, a painting of Adam and Eve in the Garden of Eden just after the fateful apple has been tasted; and, to the right, a bronzed man in a white vest kiss-biting the naked shoulder of a girl who leans, eyes closed, with her back against him, one pert white breast sharply etched against the dark background.

that have occupied the minds of art historians in recent years. These concern the 'male gaze' (Berger 1972), and the portrayal of 'woman as object' in art, particularly in studies of the nude in western oil painting (Parker and Pollock 1981; Pointon 1991), and this complex has even been seen as the paradigm of women's subordinate position in society. There are, however, important differences between art in advertising and 'real' art. Firstly, the advertising in women's magazines discussed here is directed at women, rather than at men. Thus, even though a lot of sexuality is at play here, it cannot simply be taken to signal women's availability to men. Rather, women's magazines provide their readers with a space for aesthetic self-reflection. Secondly, advertising addresses women as consumers who can actively reconstruct the 'woman-as-object' image on themselves. In other words, while art usually involves two parties in its immediate construction – the artist and his subject or motif – art in advertising encourages women to perform art work on their own bodies. When dressing up, a woman is at the same time her own artist and subject matter.

One example of the way in which women, nature and art intersect in this way can be seen in an advertisement for Tazaki pearls, in which a Japanese woman stands in front of Botticelli's painting of the *Birth of Venus* (Fig. 9). The caption reads: *Ginza de, Venus hohemu* (*Venus smiling in the Ginza*). Of course, the Tazaki ad plays on the prestige of this famous painting, and suggests that those who buy its pearls are, like the model, sensitive women able to appreciate the world's great art works. At the same time, the bodies of the two women in the advertisement are visually linked to each other. Venus is a white goddess, just born from the foaming sea, with her hair blowing in the wind as she stands naked on an open shell. In contrast, the Japanese model is carefully dressed in a white, off-the-shoulder dress, and long white gloves that reach almost to her shoulders. Her hair is held in place with a white ribbon, her face carefully made up, and her throat adorned with a Tazaki (what else?) pearl necklace.

Both women in the visual have at least one hand placed in front of their crotches. But whereas the Goddess of Love is covering both her breasts and genitals in a gesture as if that she has just become aware of her nakedness, the Japanese model has adopted the joined-hands posture in a more neutral, though typically Japanese, gesture of decency. This decency is reflected in the virgin bride-white colour of her dress which, though in contrast to the Venus's nudity, together with her gloves and pearls play on the western woman's pale skin. Thus, the heavenly beauty of the Goddess of Love makes up the background, even the foundation, of the beauty of the Japanese woman. Venus is naked and new-born. As such, she represents a natural stage for the woman in white before her. In fact, the Japanese model covers that part of Botticelli's painting where a female figure, known as the Goddess of the Seasons, is rushing to throw a purple cloak over the naked Venus. According to this visual analogy, the Japanese model has usurped the position of the goddess who dresses Venus, thereby forming and transforming her beauty (anticipating, perhaps, the *haute couturier*'s fashion seasons). Although, as a woman, Venus is naked and unfinished, as a work of art, the *Birth of Venus* is both constructed and composed, and as such presents the epitome of beauty for which a Japanese woman can strive when dressing herself up. Venus, then, is both the starting and finishing point in the art that women perform when making themselves beautiful.

When we take into account the gaze of women readers on this advertisement, we see that the Japanese model dressed all in white may simply be a mediator between the beautiful goddess and the reader's gaze. When we look at the advertisement, our attention is simultaneously taken into the visual and back again to ourselves by means of a cyclical movement – from the Japanese model in white to the naked Venus in the painting, and via the model back to ourselves, the readers of the magazine. Standing in front of this famous Italian painting, the Japanese model represents the means by which the divine beauty of Venus can be made accessible to women consumers. And, as such, she parallels the mediating function of a Tazaki pearl necklace, which is, after all, designed to bring out the beauty that already exists in every woman.

A nature image cluster

In this article, we have discussed various uses of natural imagery in contemporary advertising in Japanese women's magazines from a number of different stylistic angles. We have described the ecology trend of 1990 with its emphasis on earth colours and animal prints. We have shown, too, how nature and city are linked. And we have analysed ways in which art, women and nature play off one another. By collating a large number of advertisements that allude to nature in one way or another, we have been able to put together a cluster of images which

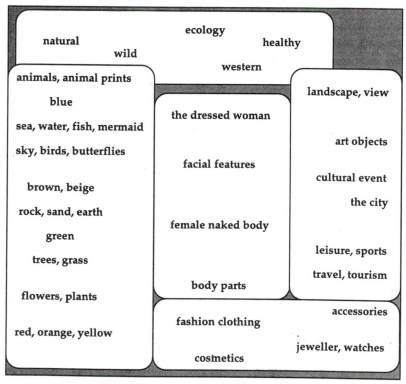

Diagram: The nature cluster in Japanese advertising

illustrates these different types of nature advertising. The interrelated elements of the image cluster are connected with products, the female body, natural elements, colours, background, and style (see Diagram). It should be realized, however, that these categories are adapted eclectically and may not necessarily all be present in any one advertisement. Thus, to take an example, advertisements for jewellery, watches, and accessories all make visual use of natural elements, such as sea, sand, rocks, flowers, and plants with accompanying colour impressions, and in so doing set off the product being advertised – both from other brand names within the particular product category (e.g. Mikimoto from

Nina Ricci) and as a single product category (jewellery) that is distinct from other product categories (watches, accessories). At the same time, they will allude to the female body, either dressed or naked – or to parts thereof (hands, neck, face, lips) – which itself is the focus of attention in advertisements for *other* product categories like cosmetics of fashion clothing, which bring in as their visuals art objects, cityscapes, cultural events, on the one hand, *and* animal prints, being natural and wild, on the other, with *their* own references to ecology, earth, trees, sky and so on. We thus find that there is a constellation of signifiers, by means of which the image cluster outlined here links nature and women both to each other and to the products that they help advertise.

In the extensive field of women's magazines, nature images form a dense cloud of connotations between natural elements, visual styles, body parts and products. What needs to be emphasized is that the relation between these visual and textual elements – for example, jewellery-cactus (Mikimoto), jewellery-woman (Quail), jewellery-sand (Dune, Gucci) – is neither fixed nor systematic, on the one hand, nor subordinated to a specific hierarchy of values, on the other. It is for this reason that we have chosen the term *cluster*, in order to emphasize the openness by which products, colours and styles previously unrelated to nature can be integrated into nature advertising – as epitomized by the ecology style discussed here. A term like 'set' or 'system' of images would fail to recognize that the cluster is extensive and unsystematic in the way that it can combine freely different elements. Furthermore, as we have seen in earlier examples of tobacco advertising, nature advertising is not governed by a particular set of values. Rather, advertising itself can manipulate and subvert any values connected to nature. The nature image cluster is thus extensive and open-ended, generating endless variations on the same themes according to the rules of totemic classification. Thus, for example, Dior's *Dune*, Gucci's models in the dunes, and fashion reportages on 'women of the dunes' relate back to Abe Kōbō's novel, and later film, *Woman in the Dunes*, at the same time as they exist in a creative and informal counterposing of symbols and visual elements, which depend on what is being advertised, who is being targeted, where the advertising is being placed, and how consumers wish to re-interpret what they see.

Material analyzed in this paper has been taken from Japanese men's and women's magazines published between 1989 and 1992.

Figure 1: Attwood

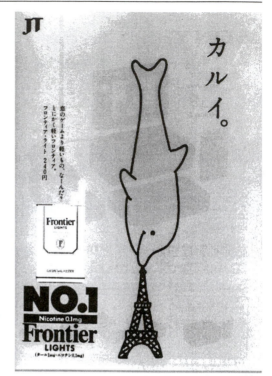

Figure 2: Japan Tobacco (right)

Figure 3: Ozone Community (below)

YOSHIKI
HISHINUMA

Figure 4: Yoshiki Hishinuma (left)

Figure 5: Yohji Yamamoto (below)

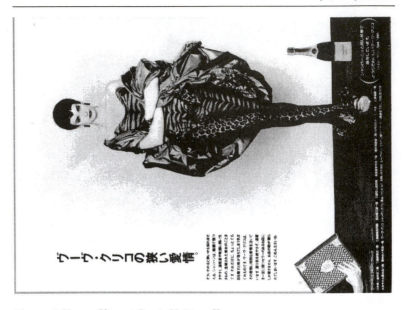

Figure 6: Veuve Cliquot, Louis Vuitton Champagne

Figure 7: Mikimoto

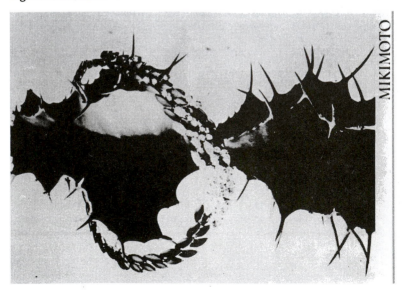

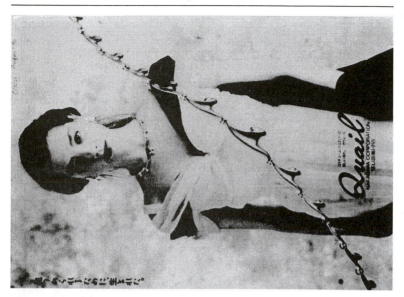

Figure 8: Quail

Figure 9: Tazaki Pearls

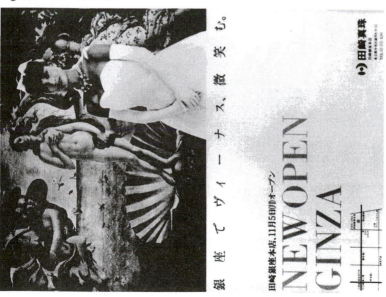

References

Barthes, Roland. 1977. *Image, Music, Text*. London: Fontana.

Beauvoir, Simone de. 1989 (1949). *The Second Sex*. New York: Vintage.

Berger, John. 1972. *Ways of Seeing*. Harmondsworth: Pelican.

Connerton, Paul. 1989. *How Societies Remember*. Cambridge: Cambridge University Press.

Hebdige, Dick. 1979. *Subculture: the Meaning of Style*. London: Methuen.

—— 1988. *Hiding in the Light*. London: Routledge.

Hendry, Joy. 1990. 'Humidity, hygiene, or ritual care: some thoughts on wrapping as a social phenomenon'. In Ben-Ari, E., B. Moeran and J. Valentine (eds), *Unwrapping Japan*. Manchester: Manchester University Press.

Lévi-Strauss, Claude. 1969. *The Elementary Structures of Kinship*. London: Eyre and Spottiswoode.

Moeran, Brian. 1989. *Language and Popular Culture in Japan*. Manchester: Manchester University Press.

Moeran, Brian and Lise Skov. Forthcoming. 'Mount Fuji and the cherry blossoms: A view from afar'. In Asquith, P. and A. Kalland (eds), *The Culture of Japanese Nature*. London: Curzon Press.

Parker, R. and G. Pollock. 1981. *Old Mistresses: Women, Art and Ideology*. London: Routledge & Kegan Paul.

Pointon, Marcia. 1991. *Naked Authority: the Body in Western Painting 1830–1908*. Cambridge: Cambridge University Press.

Rosaldo, Michelle and Louise Lamphere (eds). 1974. *Women, Culture and Society*. Stanford: Stanford University Press.

Rosenberger, Nancy. 1992. 'Images of the west: homestyle in Japanese magazines'. In Tobin, J.J. (ed.), *Re-Made in Japan: Everyday Life and Consumer Taste in a Changing Society*. New Haven and London: Yale University Press.

Skov, Lise. 1993. 'Økologi på mode: Japanske billeder'. *Tendens* 5(2):45–58.

Williamson, Judith. 1978. *Decoding Advertisements*. London: Maryon Boyars.

Arne Kalland

Culture in Japanese Nature

A growing awareness of a worldwide environmental crisis has given rise to a new discourse on the connectedness between world-views and management of natural resources. In particular, the present dominant world-view – which has variably been attributed to Judaeo-Christian influences, the development of the market economy, the rise of capitalism, patriarchal societies (Devall and Sessions 1985:45) or the Scientific Revolution (Merchant 1980) – is seen as the root of the problem facing us today. A dichotomy between nature and culture is seen as fundamental to this world-view, with people separated from, and in command of, nature. Therefore new paradigms in which human beings are seen as part of, and in harmony with, nature are called for.

Inspiration for formulating new concepts and perceptions of man's relation to nature comes from a wide variety of sources, such as native North American cultures and eastern traditions, not least from Chinese and Japanese philosophies. In this regard it will be especially rewarding to analyse the Japanese attitudes to nature because Zen – particularly through the writings of the thirteenth century Japanese master Dōgen – has profoundly influenced the *Deep Ecology* movement (Devall and Sessions 1985:100–101). Zen is said to pervade Japanese attitudes and is given credit for their alleged love of nature (Suzuki 1988).

This paper will offer an alternative interpretation of Japanese relations to nature. An attempt will be made to show that the 'nature-loving Japanese' is to a great extent a misconception, which is created by taking Japanese praise of nature – as expressed in literature and the visual arts – at face value and not as metaphors for something else. It will be argued that the Japanese try to control nature, or 'conquer' it, by processes of taming but without resorting to the nature-culture dichotomy, which Lévi-Strauss (1973) claims is a basic distinction made in all cultures. On the contrary, nature and culture are not always exclusive categories in Japanese. Nevertheless, Japan has faced more severe environmental disruptions than most countries. World-views where humans beings are firmly integrated in nature might be a precondition for an enlightened resource management regime, but it is certainly not a sufficient condition.

Do the Japanese love nature?

Much has been said and written about Japanese attitudes toward nature (*shizen, tennen*).[1] It has been taken more or less as an established fact that they love it. Taking poems, paintings, sculptures, gardens and other artefacts as proofs of this alleged love, scholars and others have been preoccupied with trying to explain *why* the Japanese love nature rather than with testing the validity of this widely-held notion as such. Among the popular explanations is the one suggested by the late Daisetz Suzuki, the scholar who has done more than anyone else to introduce the ideas of Zen to the western world. In his celebrated *Zen and Japanese Culture*, he writes that the 'Japanese love of Nature, I often think, owes much to the presence of Mount Fuji in the middle part of the main island of Japan' (1988:331). Others have echoed this view and claimed that the beauty and perfect shape of the mountain are proofs of the divine character of the Japanese islands (e.g. Idemitsu 1971). Such a view falls within the *nihonjinron* ('Japanese uniqueness') genre of analysis and has little explanatory value as it presupposes the existence of an objective – and thus not culturally acquired – standard of beauty. Such an assumption is, in my view, not warranted.

Closely related to this notion of love is the equally widely-held notion that the Japanese live in harmony with nature, which frequently is contrasted with the quest to 'conquer nature' allegedly found among westerners. 'The Japanese lives too close to nature for him to antagonize her, the benign mother of mankind', writes another authority on the subject (Anesaki 1973:6). Generalising for the whole of the Orient, Suzuki writes that in 'the East ... this idea of subjecting Nature to the

---

[1] There are a number of Japanese terms for 'nature', the most common are probably *shizen* (lit. 'by the way of itself') and *tennen* ('by the way of heaven'). There is a slight difference in nuance between the two concepts. There is a tendency for *tennen* to refer more to concrete objects, as in *tennen shigen* (natural resources), while *shizen* refers more to the abstract, as in *shizenhō* (natural law) and *shizen no chikara* (forces of nature). Both appear as adjectives (natural; *shizen no* and *tennen no*) and as adverbs (naturally; *shizen ni* and *tennen ni*). For a recent discussion of the concept *shizen*, see Tellenbach and Kimura (1989).

commands or service of man according to his selfish desires has never been cherished... Nature has been our constant friend and companion, who is to be absolutely trusted...' (1988:334).

But if these two notions are true, how can we then account for air and water pollution caused by Japanese companies both at home and abroad? How can we explain their reckless stripping of rain forests in Southeast Asia? And why is Mount Fuji – and other national parks – covered with litter after the tourist season? At the more subtle level, why are the trees in a Japanese garden not allowed to grow 'naturally', e.g. without being trimmed by humans? Or is it perhaps the case that the Japanese *used to* love nature and *used to* live in harmony with it, before the original ways of thought – perhaps embedded in Shintō and Buddhist sentiments – were destroyed by bad influences from the West?

Not so. There have been many serious cases of environmental destruction in premodern Japan. Marine resources have been depleted (Kalland 1994) and forests have been stripped (Totman 1989). Writing about forest recoveries in preindustrial Japan, Conrad Totman has the following important point to make:

> Foreigners, and some Japanese as well, often speak fondly of a special Japanese 'love of nature' that can be credited with this early modern forest recovery. To so argue, however, invites the tart query: did they love nature so much less during the ancient and early modern predations? More seriously, to advance this 'love of nature' as an explanation would be to misconstrue terms. The 'nature' of this sensibility is an aesthetic abstraction that has little relationship to the 'nature' of a real ecosystem. The sensibility associated with raising *bonsai*, viewing cherry blossoms, nurturing disciplined ornamental gardens, treasuring painted landscapes, and admiring chrysanthemums is an entirely different order of things from the concerns and feelings involved in policing woodlands and planting trees (Totman 1989:179).

In our attempts to contrast Japan – and the rest of Asia – with the western world we have looked for dissimilarities and ignored similarities. We have overlooked the fact that for millennia the Japanese have tried to conquer nature as much as westerners have done. At the technological level, rice fields have been carved out of steep hills, breakwaters have been built to make safe harbours, bays have been filled in to give additional farm land, animals have been domesticated and fishermen and sailors have obtained more seaworthy boats better able to stand against the wrath of the sea. At the cosmological level, rituals have been performed in order to come to terms with spirits that influence natural forces. In these matters, the Japanese hardly stand out from the rest of mankind.

The Japanese have, like most other people, an ambivalent attitude toward nature, in which their love of nature is only one dimension. But they also fear nature. They have learnt to cope with natural disasters caused by earthquakes, erupting volcanoes, typhoons and floods. But the threat of nature goes beyond this. Many Japanese seem to feel an abhorrence toward 'nature in the raw' (*nama no shizen*, Buruma 1985:65), and only by idealization or 'taming' (*narasu*) – e.g. 'cooking', through literature and fine arts, for example – does nature become palatable and even lovable. In other words, nature can be both raw and cooked, wild and tamed. Torn by destructive and creative forces, nature oscillates between its raw and cooked forms,[2] and in its cooked form nature and culture merge. It is in this latter state, as idealized nature, that nature is loved by most Japanese (cf. Saito 1985).

Taming nature

There is a common belief in Japan that people, animals, plants and even inorganic objects have 'souls', or some inert power. In Buddhist doctrine one takes a holistic view and talks about 'Buddha-nature' in all things,[3] while in Shintō one talks about *kami*, e.g. a supernatural power that resides in anything which gives a person a feeling of awe. But to infuse animals and plants with Buddha-nature or *kami* does not mean that they are elevated to the status of some high-ranking deities, as claimed by Hajime Nakamura (1985:149). On the contrary, as *everything* has Buddha-nature or has the potential of harbouring supernatural powers, all living

---

[2] The oscillation between nature in the raw and cooked forms appears in Japanese myths, as in the struggle between the Sun Goddess Amaterasu and her unruly brother, Susano-o, who destroys her rice-fields. The contest between creative and destructive forces is, of course, a central theme in most religions.

[3] Nishitani sees 'nature' as a process (1982:149): 'Each thing is itself in not being itself, and is not itself in being itself. Its being is illusion in its truth and truth in its illusion. This may sound strange the first time one hears it, but in fact it enables us for the first time to conceive of a *force* by virtue of which all things are gathered together and brought into relationship with one another, a force which, since ancient times, has gone by the name of "nature" (*physis*).'

creatures are on the same level. There is thus not a sharp line, as in much of Judaeo-Christian thinking, between people and the rest.

This has, of course, far-reaching implications for Japanese attitudes but has not induced the Japanese to take a 'no-touch' approach to nature, as is the case with much of the recent ecological movement in the West. It is recognized that it is the nature of things that one organism feeds upon another, creating relations of indebtedness in the process. Although the Japanese do not talk about 'animal rights' (Totman 1989:180), human beings are considered to become indebted to nature when exploiting it. A whale which has been killed is regarded as having given itself up to mankind so that we can live, and in return the whalers have to perform memorial rites (*kuyō*) so that the whale can reach enlightenment, in much the same way as whalers do for their own ancestors (Kalland and Moeran 1992:150–155).[4]

Although there is no sharp distinction between deity, man and beast in Japanese cosmology, there is a clear dichotomy between 'inside' (*uchi*) and 'outside' (*soto*). The inside covers one's social universe. Through extensive flows of gifts and services, people are linked to one another through mutual obligations (*giri*). The inside world is predictable; one knows what to expect from one's relatives, neighbours and friends. The outside world is, on the other hand, threatening. This applies to one's social world as well as to nature.

One interesting Japanese concept in this connection is *yama*, usually translated as 'mountain'. But *yama* can also mean the 'wild' as opposed to the cultivated, particularly in connection with plants and animals, as when people refer to the completely flat pine grove (*matsubara*) along the beach as *yama*. *Yama-neko* is the term both for a wild cat and a lynx, and *yama-dashi* means a countryman. The notion of the wild is also apparent in the term *yama-ke/yama-ki* (lit. 'mountain spirit, mind or heart', which can be translated as 'speculative disposition' or 'a gambling spirit'.[5] Finally, in Buddhist context *yama* has come to mean the temple.

What then do mountains, forests, 'the wild', and temples have in common? They can all be said to be bridges between the inside and the outside (e.g. between heaven and earth, or between this and the spiritual

---

[4] *Kuyō* are also performed for inorganic objects, as for example old needles. It should also be stressed that nature, e.g. plants and animals, might be indebted to benevolent human beings.

[5] *Yama-ke* is written in two characters which alternatively can be read *san-ki*, in which case it means 'mountain air'.

world). *Yama* denotes a zone of transition and is therefore potentially dangerous. It is precisely where most of the malevolent spirits are to be found, as mountains and trees are ideal abodes (*himorogi*) for spirits.[6] The *yama* therefore makes the ideal site for pilgrimages and other religious exercises. But *yama* is not only a bridge between human and divine worlds, it also denotes the outside in opposition to human society, which is inside.

Yama is thus both outside (in relation to society) and the border between inside and outside (in relation to the human and divine worlds), and for this reason – and also probably because of the physical discomfort of penetrating dense Japanese forests – most Japanese do not like to hike through forests and mountains, and if they occasionally do they take great precautions. The trip is turned into a ritual. Whether it is the lone pilgrim or a women's club going on a picnic, the paraphernalia must be proper. The pilgrim should preferably be dressed in white, carry a staff symbolizing the bonze Kōbō Daishi (774–835) and wear a straw hat symbolizing a coffin (Reader 1991:113–114; Statler 1984). By shaking rattles and chanting sutras, pilgrims try to ward off dangerous spirits. The women's club on an outing will most likely dress up in boots, rucksacks and hats, and their noisy chattering and laughter will be just as efficient to warn the spirits as the pilgrim's rattling and chanting.

The borders between the inside and the outside are not absolute but contextual and must be defined from case to case. Frequently the passage from one to the other is punctuated by rituals. When leaving the civilized world and entering forests, pilgrims may toss some dried fish (*iriko*) or salt so as to feed hungry ghosts and thus keep them busy eating. The entering and leaving of houses is also ritualized, and the entrance, being neither completely inside nor outside, is an anomalous zone (Ohnuki-Tierney 1984; Hendry 1987). In Shingū in the Fukuoka prefecture, most of the houses have an altar for the hearth deity Kōjin at the entrance in order to protect the house and its residents. The borders between the village and the outside world are also clearly marked by a series of powerful stones and other religious objects. The village shrine protects the community from bad influences originating

---

[6] For this reason trees are often venerated in Japan, as are mountains. Most shrines are situated in a grove of trees, and sacred Shintō paraphernalia – such as the sprig offered to the deities (*tamagushi*) and the sacred staff *gohei* which both symbolize the presence of deities – symbolize trees.

in the dangerous northeast direction, and the temple and the graveyard protect Shingū from the almost equally dangerous southwest (Kalland, forthcoming).

By infusing spirits into nature, the Japanese also obtain the means of coming to terms with nature by establishing a working relationship with the spirits. This is done by performing rituals in which purification and offerings are a central part. In return, the spirits offer their protection. Harmony and happiness are seen as a 'natural', or original, states of affairs – the Japanese term for healthy, *genki*, literally means the original spirit – but this bliss can easily be destroyed if the balanced reciprocity between man and spirit is lost. Illness and accidents are often interpreted as an attempt by spirits – whether *kami*, ancestors or Buddhas – to communicate their misgivings and sufferings (Kalland 1991). By establishing a relationship of mutual dependency with the spirit world through rituals, the Japanese metaphorically come to terms with nature.

It has been argued that when nature is seen as immanently divine, as it allegedly is in Japan, this leads to a 'love of nature' relationship (Hjort and Svedin 1985:162). But such a world-view can also imply a danger to the environment, at least if nature is preserved because of the spirits residing therein. This can prevent the development of a true concern for nature as such. One may try to adjust to the spiritual forces, as when forces of geomancy (*kasō*) are taken into account in connection with building houses, but it is always possible to remove spirits through powerful rituals from one area of nature in order to utilize the area in question. Before the construction of a house can commence, for instance, a ground-breaking ceremony (*jichinsai*) is invariably performed. Spirits can be enticed to move into shrines so that their old abodes, in nature, can be appropriated. A divine nature is, therefore, by no means a guarantor against environmental degradation (see also Boomgaard, this volume).

There are other means of taming (*narasu*) or controlling nature than working through spirits. One way is to violate nature, as is done when forests are felled, mountains levelled or bays filled in order to create living space. Less destructive to the environment is taming, through making models of nature, such as can be seen in the Japanese gardens and miniature *bonsai* trees, where nothing is allowed to grow according to its programmed genes. Like a witch who tries to control and inflict harm upon a person by attacking a doll substitute, the Japanese gardener or *bonsai* enthusiast can control nature by violating its model.

In these examples the outcome is clearly a cultural product. But unlike the Versaille park, which with its strict symmetry is not intended to be anything but culture, the Japanese garden and miniature tree are meant to give an impression of being natural. They become idealized models of nature, as does fish when eaten in a Japanese meal. Pretending to be raw (e.g. 'uncooked'), it has gone through a highly ritualized process, which in fact can be said to have turned the fish into 'cooked' food (Lévi-Strauss 1969).[7] The Japanese garden, the miniature tree and the raw fish are all used as metonyms for both nature and culture, making nature and culture into overlapping rather than exclusive categories.

Nature as metaphor

With this rather negative approach to nature in the raw, to 'what is of itself', one might wonder why so many Japanese write poems about it. There are several possible answers to this seeming puzzle. First of all, writing about nature is a taming process in itself. Through literature, as well as through the visual arts, people become acquainted with nature, albeit in an idealized form. The Japanese verb *narasu*, which I have translated as 'to tame' can also mean 'to become accustomed to something'. The known is in Japan, as elsewhere, less threatening than the unknown.

Secondly, writing poems is a kind of spiritual training (*shugyō*), on a par with fencing, standing under waterfalls, meditating and other austerities. Thus, when the war lord Date Masamune (1565–1636) could find 'room in his brain to appreciate Nature and write poems on it' (Suzuki 1988:333), this is not – as claimed by Suzuki – necessarily an indication of 'how innate the love of Nature is in the Japanese heart' (ibid.), but must rather be seen as spiritual preparation for war. It is a method of reaching a higher level of awareness. Masamune could equally well have meditated or drunk a cup of tea. Probably he did both as parts of his spiritual training.

Finally, we have to understand much of the writing about nature as metaphors. It is hardly novel to claim that nature can be used

---

[7] Something similar is at work when the Japanese paint an ugly concrete wall green to allude to nature, or when the Umeda underground station in Osaka plays singing birds over the loudspeaker system. The Japanese are quite at ease with this kind of 'synthetic nature'.

metaphorically. Durkheim and Mauss pointed this out almost a century ago in their *Primitive Classification* (Durkheim and Mauss 1903), arguing that we use elements from nature in order to say something about the social (cf. also Hastrup 1989). And as pointed out by Ian Buruma:

> In art and daily life Japanese like to use natural images to express human emotions. Japanese novelists are masters at weaving natural metaphors and images into the fabric of their stories. And letters and postcards written by a Japanese always begin with a short description of the season (1984:64).

Through metaphors we understand the abstract in terms of the concrete (Lakoff and Johnson 1980:112). We try to say something about human emotions – like sadness, happiness, love, anger, frustration and so on – as well as about life – birth, ageing and death – through metaphors taken from a more concrete world. In Japanese culture the natural environment plays a prominant role as a repertoire for metaphors. Although they can be creative and highlight similarities hitherto hidden, metaphors are frequently conventional in that they play on already established similarities, as is usually the case when animals and plants are used metaphorically by the Japanese.[8]

Usually, if not always, animals and plants are stereotyped and given a standardized interpretation. Foxes are smart and badgers are tricksters, while turtles are hardworking, rabbits are easygoing, and carps are intelligent, strong and have – like turtles, elephants and cranes – long lives. Elements from nature are thus introduced in order to underscore a special point; the story-teller uses nature as metaphors for something else.

The same can be found in literature. In *haiku* poetry as well as in *enka* songs special meanings are conveyed by referring to the moon, cherry blossom, mountains, pines, rain and so forth. These all appear in a predictable, or conventional, way and even authors who have hardly been outside the main cities have become renowned for their sensitive praise of nature. The full moon is frequently used as a metaphor for the

---

[8] In an essay discussing the occurrence of animals and plants in Japanese folktales, Mayer (1981) has analysed 3,000 folktales from the Niigata prefecture, featuring 22 kinds of four-legged animals, 35 kinds of birds, 18 kinds of fish, 19 kinds of other animals (including snakes), 17 kinds of insects, 37 kinds of trees and 64 kinds of other plants.

approaching degeneration ultimately leading to death but the moon also symbolizes the transient world; birth is followed by death in an endless cycle. The short transient life is also symbolized by the cherry blossom and even more so by the short blossom of the morning glory. The mountain bridges earth and heaven and the pine tree, with its long life and being an evergreen, might symbolize life's victory over death. Falling rain makes the ideal setting for farewells – as can be seen from the countless number of *enka* texts – and thus serves as a perfect metaphor for tears.

Beautiful landscapes are – like Japanese gardens – ranked in a hierarchy with the three places of Itsukushima, Amanohashidate, and Matsushima recognized as the most beautiful ones. The single most important factor for how many Japanese experience landscapes is whether they have beforehand been told that the landscape is of particular beauty. It might be argued that a landscape only becomes beautiful to the Japanese if something like a tourist board, a national committee or a film manufacturing company, has classified the spot as such, or if it has been praised by some famous poet or painter.[9] Only then, or when it has been designated as a national park, are people attracted to the site, and construction companies move in to build sky-line highways and hotels so that as many people as possible can enjoy the beauty from their car or bus windows and become 'one with nature'.[10] Moreover, experiencing nature in specific ways becomes institutionalized, as when the 'eco-tourist' is told how to appreciate these beautiful spots in the best way – as to view Amanohashidate by bending down and looking between one's legs or to view the cherry blossom while drinking and singing with friends and colleagues, for example. A landscape is thus a catalyst, or a means to evoke certain emotions, and travelling to a famous scenic spot enables the Japanese to partake in a national tradition and to feel a member of the Japanese tribe.

Nature also structures time, and it does so at several levels. Buddhism stresses the impermanence of things, and this has certainly

---

[9] Recognized beauty spots are celebrated in an unending stream of novels, poetry, paintings and gardens. Mt. Fuji, for example, has been painted from all conceivable, and most inconceivable, angles by all kinds of artists and it is praised in literature. Models of the mountains are also important features in gardens, as for example at Kumamoto's Suizenji.

[10] This is indeed very different from the attitude in many other countries where any building activity, as well as motor transport, in a national park is prohibited.

influenced the Japanese and made them more sensitive to seasonal changes in nature. The Japanese take great care to do everything at a proper time. Flower decorations (*ikebana*) and hanging scrolls (*kakejiku*) are adjusted to the season, and nobody climbs Mt. Fuji or goes swimming before the season is properly opened through Shintō rituals (*yama-biraki* and *umi-biraki*, respectively) in which spirits are requested to protect the climbers and swimmers. And the full moon is only worth seeing in September, when moon-viewing turns into a ritual. Other full moons are hardly worth appreciating.

Nature structures time and there are natural symbols for practically all annual celebrations, in *rite de passages* and in separating ceremonial time from ordinary time. I will not make an exhaustive list of plants and animals used in these ways but limit myself to mentioning the plants which are most closely associated with the 'Five Festivals' (*gosekku*) (Casal 1967). New Year decorations make liberal use of pines and we have already alluded to the symbolic meaning of this tree in Japanese culture.[11] Peaches and dolls are symbols for Girls' Day celebrated on 3 March and irises and flying carps are symbols for Boys' Day on 5 May. Besides blooming at the proper time, the peach and iris symbolize the female and male genitals, respectively. Bamboo plays a central role in the Star Festival (*Tanabata*) on 7 July, when bamboo poles adorned with colourful pieces of paper are on display. Bamboo is rich in symbolic meanings and is extensively used in Shintō rituals. In the autumn carefully grown chrysanthemums are exhibited throughout Japan, and this is the remnants of the fifth of the *gosekku* festivals, the Chrysanthemum Festival (originally held on the ninth day of the ninth lunar month). Blooming late in autumn, the chrysanthemum signals the coming of winter, and death, but it is also a metaphor for the sun (Casal 1967:102).[12]

---

[11] A bitter orange *daidai*, which written in other characters also means 'generation after generation', is frequently used together with twigs of pine for such decorations, thus underlining the request for a long life and prosperity of the house.

[12] Casal (1967:102-103) sees the chrysanthemum as a symbol of the sun, with the flower's petals as rays, which might explain why the descendants of the Sun Goddess have a stylized chrysanthemum on their crest. It should, perhaps, be added here that Japanese culture is, like most others, a totemic society in that natural objects, such as animals and plants, are used to classify people. Clans and lineages often have plants on their crests, and each prefecture has a prefectural flower and animal, for example. (See also Moeran and Skov, this volume.)

Conclusion

The Japanese sensitivity to nature has been taken by many as 'love of nature' but, as has been argued in this chapter, this is nature in its idealized form. Matching this 'love' is their abhorrence towards nature in the raw. One therefore seeks to tame, or to come to terms with, nature in various ways, such as through rituals, literature and visual arts. Through such processes, nature appears in a cultivated form (e.g. gardens, miniature trees, raw fish), which then can be used metonymically for both nature as a whole and for culture. Hence nature and culture fail to become exclusive categories in Japan, like in many other societies (see, for example, Goody 1977; MacCormack 1980; Strathern 1980).

But above all nature is used as a reservoir for metaphors. The Japanese like to express themselves in metaphors and a great number of these metaphors are taken from their natural environments. This and the Buddhist concept of the impermanence of all things have certainly caused some Japanese to be sensitive to nature and to changes therein. For those socialized into a certain culture, references to animals, stones, landscapes or natural phenomena might set off a series of associations. Through standardized usages in literature and folktales, metaphors evoke a given feeling in the listener or reader (Berque 1986:105). It is thus possible to transmit a message rich in content by a short *haiku*, as in the following written by Ryōta in the eighteenth century, in which rain, the moon, pines and the season are all important images:

> In the June rains,
> One night, as if by stealth
> The moon, through the pines
> (Suzuki 1988:387)

To take this sensitivity to nature for love masks important points, however. For it matters little to most Japanese whether they observe these changes in a small flower in the backyard or in a vaste nature reserve. The quantity of nature, if I can put it that way, is of no great importance, and nature invisible to an actor – as one located in faraway places – is of little general interest. Many scholars have stressed the particularistic character of Japanese norms and this applies equally well to the environment. It is just as difficult to get Japanese to fight against environmental destruction *per se*, as it is to get them to fight for human rights in distant countries. Only when nature is brought into the realm of the known, e.g. tamed, and there are some immediate personal gains, do most Japanese become interested in protecting nature (McKean 1981; Mouer and Sugimoto 1986:336–337). The persons who are most likely to protect the environment are those with vested economic interests in it, like fishermen, farmers and loggers – or the tourist industry if nature is turned into a commodity for their use. One important lesson we can learn from this is that there is hardly any direct relationship between the Japanese sensitivity to nature and their environmental behaviour.

References

Anesaki, Masaharu. 1973. *Art, Life, and Nature in Japan*. Tokyo: Charles E. Tuttle.

Berque, Augustin. 1986. 'The sense of nature and its relation to space in Japan'. In Hendry, J. and J. Webber (eds), *Interpreting Japanese Society: Anthropological Approaches*. Oxford: JASO.

Boomgaard, Peter. 1994. 'Sacred trees and haunted forests in Indonesia – particularly Java, nineteenth and twentieth centuries'. In Bruun, O. and A. Kalland (eds), *Asian Perceptions of Nature: A Critical Approach*. London: Curzon Press.

Buruma, Ian. 1985. *A Japanese Mirror: Heroes and Villains in Japanese Culture*. Harmondsworth: Penguin Books.

Casal, U.A. 1967. *The Five Sacred Festivals of Japan - Their Symbolism & Historical Development*. Tokyo: Sophia University/Charles E. Tuttle.

Devall, Bill and George Sessions. 1985. *Deep Ecology - Living as if nature mattered*. Salt Lake City: Gibbs Smith, Publ.

Durkheim, Emile and Marcel Mauss. 1903. *Primitive Classification*. (English edition 1963, translated by R. Needham). London: Cohen-West.

Goody, Jack R. 1977. *The Domestication of the Savage Mind*. Cambridge: Cambridge University Press.

Hastrup, Kirsten. 1989. 'Nature as historical space'. *Folk* 31:5–20.

Hendry, Joy. 1987. *Understanding Japanese Society*. London: Croom Helm.

Hjort, Anders and Uno Svedin (eds), 1985. *Jord - Människa - Himmel*. Stockholm: Liber Förlag.

Idemitsu, Sazō. 1971. *Be A True Japanese*. Tokyo: Idemitsu Kosan Co., Ltd.

Kalland, Arne. 1991. 'Facing the spirits: Illness and healing in a Japanese Community'. *NIAS Report*, 1991–2. Copenhagen: Nordic Institute of Asian Studies.

——— 1994. *Fishing Villages in Tokugawa Japan*. London: Curzon Press/Honolulu: University of Hawaii Press.

——— forthcoming. 'Geomancy in a Japanese Community'. In Asquith, P. and A. Kalland (eds), *The Culture of Japanese Nature*. London: Curzon Press.

Kalland, Arne and Brian Moeran. 1992. *Japanese Whaling - End of an Era?* London: Curzon Press.

Lakoff, George and Mark Johnson. 1980. *Metaphors We Live By*. Chicago: The University of Chicago Press.

Lévi-Strauss, Claude. 1969. *The Raw and the Cooked*. New York: Harper & Row.

——— 1973. *Structural Anthropology*. Harmondsworth: Penguin Books.

MacCormack, Carol P. 1980. 'Nature, culture and gender: a critique'. In MacCormack, C. and M. Strathern (eds), *Nature, Culture and Gender*. Cambridge: Cambridge University Press.

McKean, Margaret A. 1981. *Environmental Protest and Citizen Politics in Japan*. Berkeley: University of California Press.

Mayer, Fanny Hagin. 1981. 'Fauna and flora in Japanese folktales'. *Asian Folklore Studies* 40(1):23–32.

Merchant, Carolyn. 1980. *The Death of Nature - Women, Ecology and the Scientific Revolution*. New York: Harper & Row.

Moeran, Brian and Lise Skov. 1994. 'Japanese advertising nature: Ecology, women, fashion and art'. In Bruun, O. and A. Kalland (eds), *Asian Perceptions of Nature: A Critical Approach*. London: Curzon Press.

Mouer, Ross and Yoshio Sugimoto. 1986. *Images of Japanese Society*. London: KPI.

Nakamura Hajime. 1985. 'Japansk kultursfär'. In Hjort, Anders and Uno Svedin (eds), *Jord - Människa - Himmel*. Stockholm: Liber Förlag.

Nishitani, Keiji. 1982. *Religion and Nothingness*. Berkeley: University of California Press.

Ohnuki-Tierney, Emiko. 1984. *Illness and Culture in Contemporary Japan - An Anthropological View*. Cambridge: Cambridge University Press.

Reader, Ian. 1991. *Religion in Contemporary Japan*. London: Macmillan.

Saito, Yuriko. 1985. 'The Japanese appreciation of nature'. *The British Journal of Aesthetics* 25(3):239–251.

Statler, Oliver. 1984. *Japanese Pilgrimage*. London: Pan Books.

Strathern, Marilyn. 1980. 'No nature, no culture: the Hagen case'. In MacCormack, C. and M. Strathern (eds), *Nature, Culture and Gender*. Cambridge: Cambridge University Press.

Suzuki, Daisetz. 1988. *Zen and Japanese Culture*. Tokyo: Charles E. Tuttle.

Tellenbach, Hubertus and Bin Kimura. 1989. 'The Japanese concept of "nature"'. In Callicott, J.B. and R.T. Ames (eds), *Nature in Asian Traditions of Thought: Essays in Environmental Philosophy*. Albany: State University of New York Press.

Totman, Conrad. 1989. *The Green Archipelago: Forestry in Preindustrial Japan*. Berkeley: University of California Press.

Poul Pedersen

Nature, Religion and Cultural Identity
The Religious Environmentalist Paradigm

In the global concern about the environment, appeals to traditional, religious values play a significant role. Throughout the world, people turn to their ancient scriptures or myths in search of ideas and values which can encourage a protective attitude towards nature.[1] It is interesting to note that these efforts to recover an ancient, ecological wisdom very often have a remarkable similarity to the teachings of modern environmentalism.

How should we understand this? Why is concern about the environment so often expressed in religious terms? Why do people link nature and ecology to religion when they could just as well invoke ecological science or common environmentalist recommendations? This is what I shall discuss here. I argue that the appeal to traditional, religious ideas and values – which I shall call 'the religious environmentalist paradigm' – signifies other concerns than just those about the environment and that these are concerns about cultural identity in the modern world. From this perspective, the religious environmentalist paradigm represents an example of forceful cultural creativity.

I shall begin with a few historical observations on the religious environmentalist paradigm and give examples from Buddhism, Hinduism and Islam. Thereafter, I shall discuss the basic claims of the religious environmentalist paradigm, before I argue that its ecological and conservationist representation of nature is a modern creation, a

---

[1] See, for example, the various contributions in Callicott and Ames 1989; Davies 1987; Engel and Engel 1990; Samartha and de Silva 1979; Vecsey and Venables 1980. In this article, I shall – in accordance with my sources – use 'nature' and 'environment' interchangeably. In other contexts, there are reasons to distinguish between the two terms, cf. Evernden 1992; Hepburn 1967; Ingold 1992; Lovejoy 1948; Mocek 1990; Simmons 1993; Williams 1972.

'global ideology of nature'. Finally, I argue that the religious environmentalist paradigm offers an efficient tool for the articulation of local cultural identity as it is linked to the dynamic forces of the globalized modern world.

Nature, religion and ecology: The religious environmentalist paradigm

Historically, it has been quite common to link environmental problems with religion. Floods, droughts, earthquakes, and other natural disasters were, for example, often understood as God's punishment for human misconduct. But it is a recent idea to link environmental problems to religion in the sense that human environmental behaviour is conceived as determined by religious beliefs and values.

We can trace this idea – in its explicit formulation – to an article with the title 'The historical roots of our present ecologic crisis' which the American historian Lynn White published in *Science* in 1967.[2] Here White argued that the origins of the environmental crisis could be found in the fundamental ideas of Christianity, and he based his claim on the proposition that 'what people do to their ecology depends on what they think about themselves in relation to things around them. Human ecology is deeply conditioned by beliefs about our nature and destiny – that is by religion' (White 1967:1205). White argued that the Judaeo-Christian tradition, in contrast to Asian religions, is strongly anthropocentric and founded on a dualism of man and nature. Man is separated from other physical creatures because it is God's will that man exploits nature for his own proper ends, and when science and technology developed their enormous forces, these were used against the interests of all of nature.

How should we, according to White, get out of the crisis? He warned against finding the answers in more science and more technology. Instead, he suggested that we find a new religion with other values, or that we rethink Christianity. He had good things to say about the beatniks whom he considered 'the basic revolutionaries of our time', for they showed 'a sound instinct in their affinity for Zen Buddhism, which conceives of the man–nature relationship as very near the mirror image of the Christian view' (White 1967:1206). He doubted, though,

---

[2] One should note that White says 'ecologic'. This points to the fact that 'ecology' was still not widely used outside specialized scientific communities. It had not yet found its common stable adjective form as 'ecological'. This is quite often overlooked in references to White's article which frequently appear as '...ecological crisis'.

that Zen could take root in the West. Therefore the solution was to rethink Christianity and he suggested a starting point for this in the teachings of Saint Francis of Assisi whose profoundly religious sense for the spiritual autonomy of all parts of nature gave hope for a new rethinking and re-appreciation of our nature and destiny. He ended his article by proposing Francis as a patron saint for ecologists.[3]

White's article is a fine example of the right message at the right time. It is interesting to note that the well-known Zen Buddhist scholar Daisetz T. Suzuki published a paper in 1954 with the title 'The role of nature in Zen Buddhism' (Suzuki 1954) in which he anticipated many of White's ideas without anyone paying attention to it. But in 1967 much had changed and White hit a receptive audience. By associating religion with nature and ecology, by criticizing hard core ideas of Christianity, and by speaking favourably about Asian religions, he captured the countercultural *Zeitgeist* of the 1960s. White's article was widely read and discussed and was reprinted in many anthologies. It became a classic in the environmentalist literature with a global audience and was probably the most important single contribution to the religious environmentalist paradigm.[4]

The 1960s were not only countercultural, they were also anti-capitalist, anti-colonial, anti-imperialist and anti-Western. In these turbulent years, White's and others' criticism of Western religion, science and technology – in combination with a strong and positive interest in native American and Oriental religions – became part of the political confrontation between the West and its critics. Against this background, the religious and ecological ideas found their way to the Third and the emerging Fourth Worlds where they echoed a growing political and cultural self-consciousness. During the last twenty years Native Americans, Australian Aboriginals, Hindus, Buddhists, Muslims and many others have presented their religious traditions as authentically ecological and conservationist and, today, the religious environmentalist paradigm has its well-established position in the global environmentalist discussion.[5]

---

[3] This suggestion was not new. In 1960, the zoologist Marston Bates said that for Christians who loved nature, 'St. Francis of Assisi rightfully is their patron'. In 1980 the Vatican officially declared St. Francis the patron of ecologists. Cf. Nash 1989:93.

[4] For an overview, see Nash 1989:89ff. and related comments in White 1973.

[5] For examples, see Atisha 1991; Dwivedi and Tiwari 1987; Manzoor 1984; Momaday 1976; Nasr 1990; Swain 1991 and contributions in Engel and Engel 1990.

The following examples of the religious environmental paradigm closely follow White's seminal ideas in their emphasis on religious values and beliefs as determinants of human environmental behaviour and in their more or less openly expressed assumption that the West is responsible for the present environmental crisis.

Buddhism

In his paper 'The Tibetan perception of the environment' (1992) the Tibetan Buddhist Karma Gelek Yuthok, says that the Tibetans have lived in perfect harmony with their natural environment for more than three thousand years.[6] 'The secret of this historical success', says Yuthok, lies 'in the spiritual and ethical traditions inherited by the people of Tibet' (Yuthok 1992:1). What is important here is that Tibet's entire spiritual and ethical traditions are directed towards the fulfilment of a meaningful human life where man is 'a genuinely humble, wise and compassionate guardian of all living beings through embracing the paths of love, compassion, altruism, wisdom, and self-perfection' (1992:2). Tibetans respect the physical environment as a sacred common heritage of all worldly beings and give no moral right to exploit and destroy man's fellow beings and the natural resources (1992:3).

The environmental crisis is, Yuthok claims, a direct offspring of the scientific and industrial revolutions with their unchecked materialism which was superimposed over the spiritual and ethical values of society. As such, the environmental crisis represents an ethical breakdown (1992:4). But, in Yuthok's opinion, the Tibetan religious and ethical traditions were not affected by this. In Tibet, the national ethical and cultural traditions contained essential measures for the safeguard of the environment, so it was not necessary to formulate numerous specific laws and rules for its protection. This is also the reason why Tibetan scholars had no need to focus exclusively on the subject. In fact, for a Tibetan, the environment and its protection is not 'a new question to think about' (1992:4).

The Tibetan way of understanding the environment has been valid and sound, says Yuthok, and today it is 'attracting the world's attention more than ever before' (1992:7). He concludes his paper with the hope

---

[6] Yuthok (1992) includes the period of the pre-Buddhist Bon-religion in the Tibetan religious tradition.

that 'the wisdom of spiritual traditions will finally remedy the delusion of materialism' (1992:7).

Hinduism

In his article *'Satyagraha* for conservation: Awakening the spirit of Hinduism' (1990), the Indian Hindu O.P. Dwivedi outlines the environmental ethics of Hindu religion. Human beings and other living creatures were created by God who has absolute sovereignty over human and non-human life. All living creatures, human as well as non-human, have the same right to existence. 'Human beings have no special privilege or authority over other creatures; on the other hand, they have more obligations and duties' (Dwivedi 1990:205).

Important aspects of Hindu theology, the belief in God's incarnation in various animal species and the belief in the cycle of birth and rebirth where a person may come back as an animal, form the basis of the strong conservationist concern which is often expressed in the ancient Hindu scriptures as very precise and direct recommendations and prohibitions of certain kinds of behaviour, all for the welfare of the environment. In this way, plants and animals were protected, and there was a warning against the pollution of air and water. To Dwivedi, it is obvious that 'Hindu scriptures revealed a clear conception of the ecosystem' (1990:205ff).

Dwivedi claims that the ancient Hindus knew about sustainable development. He sees the caste system as a social mechanism for the creation of an 'ecological space'. The hereditary division of labour of the caste system regulated the exploitation of natural resources by reducing the competition among the various social groups of India. With fixed occupations, people knew that if they depleted the natural resources in their own space, they would not survive economically or physically because no one would allow them to move to other occupations. From this perspective the 'Hindu caste system can be seen as a progenitor of the concept of sustainable development' (1990:208).

In this way, says Dwivedi, the religious values of Hinduism acted as sanctions against environmental destruction. The situation changed, however, during the seven hundred years of first Muslim and later British cultural dominance, which undermined the traditional Hindu value system. The foreign influence 'greatly inhibited religion from continuing to transmit ancient values which encourage respect and due regard for God's creation' (1990:210f.). In addition to this, Hindu culture was in the twentieth century affected by the materialist orientation of the West (1990:201). Dwivedi has, though, some hope for the future, for he detects in the two Hindu countries, India and Nepal, a revival of respect for the ancient cultural values enshrined in the Hindu scriptures (1990:211).

Islam

In his article 'Islamic environmental ethics: Law and society' (1990), the Arabian Muslim Mawil Y. Izzi Deen (Samarrai), emphasizes that Islamic environmental ethics is based on the clear-cut legal foundations which Muslims hold to be formulated by God, and that legal instructions have been revealed in such a way that the conscience approves and acknowledges them to be correct (Izzi Deen 1990:189).

The conservation of the environment in Islam is based on the principle that God created the world and that all living things were given different functions which were carefully measured and meticulously balanced. But all this was not created for human use alone, and therefore humans have a responsibility for God's creation. God entrusted humans with the duty of protecting the environment.

Islam asserts that life is maintained with a balance in everything. Humans are not the owners of the world but the maintainers of the due balance and measure which God provided for them and for the animals that live with them. From this assertion, says Izzi Deen, may be deduced a 'theory of the sustainable utilization of the ecosystem', and he suggests that the relevant verses in the Qur'an are 'an elaboration of the concept of sustainable development' (1990:194).

Islam emphasizes the need for sustained care of all aspects of the environment as it can be seen from its influence on the formation of individual Muslim communities and the environmental policy of Muslim states throughout the history of the Islamic faith. Since the time of the Prophet Muhammad, Islamic rulers have protected the environment by regulating access to utilize certain areas (1990:196).

Protection of the environment in Islamic countries should be based on Islamic belief and environmental awareness. Islam's values are those without which neither persons nor the natural environment can be sustained (1990:192). An imported law, says Izzi Deen, cannot work because 'it cannot be made morally binding upon Muslims' (1990:191).

The religious environmentalist paradigm: A critique[7]

The religious environmentalist paradigm is based on two claims. The first is that traditional religious ideas and values play a decisive – or even determining – role in human environmental behaviour. The second is that traditional religious ideas and values express an authentic ecological awareness and a strong conservationist commitment which are similar to those of modern environmentalist concerns. In spite of their theologically different backgrounds, Yuthok, Dwivedi, and Izzi Deen seem to agree on these two claims, at least in respect to their own particular faith. However, there are two good reasons to reject the claims of the religious environmentalist paradigm. Firstly, they rest on a simplistic and untenable idea of how values and behaviour are related, and secondly, they are anachronistic projections of modern phenomena onto the screen of tradition. Let us look at these arguments in turn.

Do values determine environmental behaviour?

The religious environmentalist paradigm presents us with the well-known problem of how to conceive of the relationship between norms and actions. When Yuthok, for example, claims that the Tibetans for millennia have protected the environment, he argues that the Tibetans' recurrent behaviour patterns can be explained by their shared religious values. Here, we must assume that these values constitute a set of norms – standards or rules which state what people should or should not do under specific circumstances – and that such norms have an inherent ability to bring about action by themselves.

We should be most sceptical about such explanations which assume that values and norms directly determine behaviour. Holy and Stuchlik have convincingly argued that we must conceive of the relationship between norms and actions as problematic and that we need to clarify how norms relate to actions by stipulating 'some mediating motivational mechanism through which [norms] can be brought to bear upon actions, either summoning them or restraining them' (Holy and Stuchlik 1983:83). We can do this by thinking of action in relation to its goals, that is some future state of affairs to whose attainment the action is

---

[7] Below, I shall address the basic claims of the paradigm. For a discussion of particular cases, cf. Harris 1991 and Huber 1991.

oriented. To introduce the goal of the action presupposes the existence of an agent, which can only be a particular individual. When we treat the relationship between norms and actions as problematic, we must account for actions by the goals they are intended to attain and at the same time assume that people have goals or intentions and behave purposively so as to obtain them (Holy and Stuchlik 1983:83f.).[8]

This has some important consequences for how we should understand the relationship between values or norms and actions. To invoke a norm – or to disregard it – is in itself an action with a specific goal. It follows from this that 'norms do not bring about behaviour by themselves but are brought to bear on actions by the actors in the course of their attainment of specific goals' (Holy and Stuchlik 1983:85). This means that we cannot make statements about the specific relationship between values or norms and actions without taking into consideration the goals of the actions.[9]

We can now see that it is far too simplistic when the religious environmental paradigm makes values work directly on the individuals, summoning or restraining their behavioural repertoire. We must reject the idea that behaviour can be predicted from values, and that values can be deduced from behaviour. Values as they are expressed in, for example, scriptural statements about the sacredness of trees, water, mountains, cows and so on, will not tell us what people really do to their environment (cf. Tuan 1968). Likewise, we cannot take environmental behaviour as evidence of specific values. If some people did not harm the environment, this need not imply that they were motivated by a strong conservationist commitment. They could be – environmentally speaking – harmless creatures for quite other reasons that had nothing to do with values, but which related to demography and technology (Johnson 1989).

I do not say that values are unimportant for the way people relate to their environment. The problem is, however, to account for values in that relationship. To do so, we need another kind of work than that inspired by the religious environmentalist paradigm: a detailed empirical investigation into the social life of values with an analysis of how

---

[8] Holy and Stuchlik argue against the objections to the assumption of the intentionality of behaviour.

[9] Obeyesekere (1981:110ff.) emphasizes this perspective when he says that values or 'cultural ideas are being constantly validated by the nature of subjective experience'.

values are invoked in people's practical lives. Quotations from the scriptures are not enough.

Anachronism

There is a peculiarly modern ring about the claim that traditional religious ideas express an authentic ecological awareness and a strong conservationist commitment. No Buddhist, Hindu, or Islamic scriptures contain concepts like 'environmental crisis', 'ecosystem', or 'sustainable development', or other concepts corresponding to them. To insist that they do is to deny the immense cultural distance that separates traditional religious conceptions of the environment from modern ecological knowledge. Fredrik Barth (1987) has important comments to offer on this problem of anachronism, and though they are made in a New Guinea context, they have a strong, general relevance to the study of perceptions of nature.

When the Baktaman – horticulturalists and one of the Mountain Ok groups of Inner New Guinea – weed their taro gardens, they pile the uprooted weeds around the taro plants. We could think that the Baktaman do this because they have a kind of ecological understanding of the benefits of mulching, for example that it enhances the humus content around the taro plants or that it inhibited weed germination and growth, etc. If we asked the Baktaman why they do it, they would answer, 'Because taro likes the smell of rotting vegetation'. Barth emphasizes the difference between these to explanations. 'In the context of this particular praxis', he says, 'the Baktaman idiom seems an adequate way to depict a certain agronomical technique' (Barth 1987:68). Our ecological interpretation, on the other hand, is of quite another order. It

> attempts to relate the phenomenon to a number of more general relationships, and various sciences that treat the chemistry of matter, life processes, etc. – in other words to an elaborate tradition of knowledge built on consistency, generalization, deduction, experiment and measurement (Barth 1987:68).

The Baktaman do not think about taro growing in this sense, and it would, as Barth says, be absurd to celebrate them as if they had a covert knowledge of ecological science, no matter how expert horticulturalists they be. What separates us from the Baktaman is that we belong to different traditions of knowledge, traditions with different conceptualizations of the environment. It is also this – as I shall argue below – that separates us from the ancient Buddhists, Hindus, Muslims and other 'ancients'. The search for the ecological correctness of distant ancestors makes them too similar to us. It produces historical distortion, misunderstanding, anachronism. It is a projection of modern conceptualizations and concerns onto the screen of tradition.

Ecology and the modern representation of nature

We should not reject the idea that traditional religious values may reflect conceptualizations of the environment, but these are not identical to our modern ecological and conservationist understanding of nature. I shall now argue that this way of relating to nature is closely connected to key features of modernity.

Our ecological vision of the environment is global. It involves a strong sense of the interconnectedness of all things in nature, of local events with global consequences. Our ecological understanding of nature transcends particular localities and turns our attention to the *total* environment. Our environmentalist concerns parallel this wide perspective with an understanding that environmental degradation is often caused by human activity and with a strong emphasis on our responsibility to all of nature.[10]

Our knowledge and understanding – our representations – of nature are interpretations, that is, social and cultural constructions (Bird 1987:255). The global, ecological representation of nature was created in an observational and conceptual context which is radically different from that of the traditional, religious representation. From this perspective it would be absurd to compare, for example, ancient Hindu warnings against air pollution with modern concerns about the greenhouse effect. To clarify this difference we should look, first, at the observational and, second, at the conceptual context of the creation of the modern ecological representation of nature.

Environmental changes should have a certain scale and pace in

---

[10] This is the ideal of the ecological vision. I need hardly mention that this is not what people do.

order to be observed and associated with human activity. Changes that took place over centuries or millennia would hardly make much impression within the individual's lifetime (Ponting 1991:74). Only frequent, sudden, and dramatic changes which could be linked to human exploitation of nature could provide the observations necessary for a deeper understanding of the role man played in environmental degradation. Such rapid and large-scale changes appeared with growing frequency throughout the world from the beginning of the western colonial expansion (Grove 1990, 1993).

In looking for the conceptual context of the global, ecological representation of nature, I refer to Anthony Giddens' suggestions concerning the globalizing processes of modernity (1990). Most relevant here is the intimate connection between modernity and the transformation of time, place and space. In the pre-modern world, time reckoning always linked time with place. It was impossible to say what time it was without referring to a locality or a regular natural phenomenon. With the invention and spread of the mechanical clock and with the worldwide standardization of time and calendars, time became an object of uniform modes of measurement. It became an 'empty', or global, time, deprived of its local referents (Giddens 1990:17).

Modernity also separated space from place. In pre-modern societies space and place largely coincide because the spatial dimensions of social life are, for most of the population, and in most respects, dominated by 'presence' – by localized activities (Giddens 1990:18). Modernity increasingly builds up a global or 'empty' space above or beyond the localized place. There is a strengthening and expansion of relations between 'absent' agents who are locationally distant from any given situation of face-to-face interaction. Places or locales become thoroughly penetrated by, and shaped, in terms of social influences distant from them:

> What structures the locale is not simply that which is present on the scene; the 'visible form' of the locale conceals the distanciated relations which determine its nature (Giddens 1990:19).

The conception of the global space found its clear expression in the creation of universal maps, where perspective played little part in the representation of geographical position and form. Space had, as Giddens says, become 'independent' of any particular place or region (Giddens 1990:19).

There is a close conceptual relationship between this notion of global time and global space, which was created by modernity, and our modern global, 'ecological space', where any locality, any ecosystem, links up with other localities, other ecosystems, to disappear as privileged places into the network of relations which all together make up the global environment, the biosphere. Ecological representations of nature belong to a conceptual framework of globality and are therefore fundamentally different from traditional representations of nature with their predominant localized focus.

The global ideology of nature

The strong worldwide inclination to associate nature with ecology and conservation, I shall call 'the global ideology of nature'. To understand the formation of this ideology we should do more than just point to the global conceptual structure which links ecology to modernity. We need to clarify how the ideology was worked out in real life. To do so, we should study the social organization of knowledge about nature – in its widest sense – in order to trace how particular ideas, values, beliefs and practices become salient features in relation to nature.

Many of our beliefs, ideas and practices are part of the common-sense and taken-for-granted aspects of routine daily action which we do not consciously reflect upon. Ideology differs from these by being a creation of reflective consciousness. Ideology is a particular organized selection of beliefs, ideas and practices *within* an ensemble of cultural ideas or wider cultural terrain, and it is made a matter of conscious reflection (Kapferer 1983:19). The formation of ideologies is a social and political process which involves often conflicting interests and interpretations. But most important, it is a process of cultural creativity because it transforms pre-existing beliefs, ideas, and practices by objectifying them and by changing their contexts. This is what happened with the formation of the global ideology of nature and which the religious environmentalist paradigm exemplifies so clearly. It was the fusion of beliefs, ideas and practices from various and originally unrelated cultural ensembles or traditions into a unified ecological and conservationist global vision of nature.

In this perspective, an ideology is in a very literal sense worked out, and to understand its formation, we should look to its work places. One important driving force in the formation of the global ideology of nature was the work of scientific, conservationist, political, and – most recently – religious organizations. The efficiency of these work places is related to the global, institutional reflectiveness of modernity, where knowledge about social practices, including relationships to the environment, is constantly and systematically examined and changed in the light of incoming information about those very practices. In this way, social practices and conceptions are continuously being reconstituted by objectification and recontextualization (Giddens 1990:55ff., 1991:20). We can in the activities of these work places trace a continuous development from a localized engagement to globally coordinated action, from the Commons, Open Spaces and Foot Path Preservation Society in England 1865 to World Wide Fund for Nature (WWF) today, from the isolated studies of naturalists in the nineteenth century to Unesco's Man and the Biosphere Programme, and from the British Act for the Protection of Seabirds of 1869 to the Rio Declarations on Environment and Development of 1992.[11]

In the 1970s and '80s, religious and conservation organizations began to cooperate and created a global network of participants from many faiths (cf. Engel 1990). Let me give a few examples. In the mid-1970s the World Council of Churches started a programme with the purpose of studying how the spiritual insight from Asia and Africa could contribute to a more harmonious and responsible relation between humanity and nature. The programme involved meetings with scholars from various faiths, including Buddhists, Christians, Jews, Muslims, Hindus, and African scholars on African traditional religion (Samartha and de Silva 1979).

In 1983, four Islamic specialists from the King Abdul Aziz University, Jeddah in Saudi Arabia, prepared a *Basic paper on the Islamic principles for the conservation of the natural environment* (Ba Kader et al. 1983). It was published jointly by the Meteorological and Environmental Protection Administration of the Kingdom of Saudi Arabia and the International Union for Conservation of Nature and Natural Resources in Switzerland.

The most wideranging alliance between conservation and religion was created by the WWF, which is the world's largest private nature conservation organization. As part of the celebrations of its twenty-fifth

---

[11] Very little research has been done on the history of ecology and environmentalism – from an anthropology or sociology of knowledge perspective, but Grove (1993); MacCormick (1989); Boardman (1981) and McIntosh (1985) bring useful information on the institutional background.

anniversary in 1986, there was a large meeting arranged in Assisi which culminated in an interfaith ceremony, where religious leaders from five of the world's major religions addressed their own faithful with declarations on the importance of religious values for the conservation of nature (WWF 1986:1). After the Assisi meeting, the WWF established a global network on conservation and religion.[12] In 1990, eight religions had joined the network, including the Baha'i faith, Buddhism, Christianity, Hinduism, Islam, Judaism, Sikhism, and Jainism (Brown 1990:1).

With these global links between conservation and religion, important institutional conditions for the efficient propagation of the religious environmentalist paradigm have been created. Religion is exposed to and accommodated within the global ideology of nature, because the articulation of religious identity has transcended its traditional local setting and must confront global issues (Pedersen 1992:155). It is impossible to imagine that a representative of some religion should say, 'My kingdom is not of this world, so nature doesn't matter!' That would, indeed, be heretical in a world where the ecological cause of nature and conservation has entered the realm of uncontested values like happiness and motherhood.

Religion, nature and cultural identity

Let me now return to the question I raised at the beginning of this article. How should we understand the urgent appeals to traditional, religious values in the global concern about the environment? One answer is, obviously, that people are genuinely worried and try to create a sound environmental ethic on the basis of their own cultural resources. From a pragmatic point of view, it is not surprising that people attempt to make their beliefs and values relevant to important contemporary issues and that this results in considerable reinterpretation of tradition. But we should be aware that there are other concerns involved – concerns about cultural identity in the modern world, and in particular as they appear in the Third and Fourth Worlds.

The religious environmentalist paradigm was invented in the West less than three decades ago. It echoed the strong current of criticism and

---

[12] The activities of the network can be followed in *The new road. The Bulletin of the WWF Network on conservation and religion* which has been published by the WWF since 1986.

protest against the West and, as it spread to the Third and Fourth Worlds, it became linked to global issues of political and cultural dominance.

The historical and cultural background for this is the global transformations of the post-colonial age with the decline of western cultural hegemony and the changes of the social organization of culture, which opened the way for self-conscious political and cultural movements and identities which represent alternatives to modernity and the developed world (Friedman 1992a, 1992b).

Without implying that culture was ever a territorially bounded entity, we can safely say that today culture is less localized than it was before. In one sense, culture has become globalized and constituted within a global flow of ideas, people, capital, information etc. (Appadurai 1990). With this change in the social organization of culture, cultural creativity can rely on an expanding supply of resources. But in spite of the globalization of culture and the brute economic and political facts of the world system with the shifting of centres and peripheries, culture has never lost its local focus. To the extent that there is a global culture, it is a 'culture of cultures' (Sahlins 1993:21).

It is here, at the junction between the global flow of culture and the efforts of local peoples to assert their own significance in the world, that the appeals to traditional, religious values become linked to the creation of cultural identity. Their assertion is structured politically by opposition to the West. Modern and globally circulated ideas about nature are appropriated and merged with the local cultural repertoire into an invented tradition of a glorious ecological past. People create a differentiated cultural space which separates them from that materialist and modernist West that they hold responsible for the environmental crisis and that in many cases was their colonial oppressor.

By offering to the world what they hold to be their traditional, religious values, local peoples acquire cultural significance. When they speak about nature, they speak about themselves. They demonstrate to themselves and to the world that their traditions, far from being obsolete and out of touch with modern reality, express a truth of urgent relevance for the future of the Earth. This achievement, with its foundation in appeals to imagined, traditional religious values, represents a forceful cultural creativity which would not have worked by the invocation of 'pure' ecology or environmentalism.

References

Appadurai, A. 1990. 'Disjuncture and difference in the global cultural economy'. In Featherstone, M. (ed.), *Global culture*. London: Sage Publications.

Atisha, T.P. 1991. 'The Tibetan approach to ecology'. *Tibetan Review* (February): 9–14.

Ba Kader, A.B.A. et al. 1983. *Basic Paper on the Islamic Principles for the Conservation of the Natural Environment*. Gland, Switzerland: International Union for Conservation of Nature and Natural Resources.

Barth, F. 1987. *Cosmologies in the making*. Cambridge: Cambridge University Press.

Bird, E.A.R. 1987. 'The social construction of nature: Theoretical approaches to the history of environmental problems'. *Environmental Review* 11(4): 255–264.

Boardman, R. 1981. *International Organizations and the Conservation of Nature*. London: Macmillan.

Brown, K. 1990. 'Jains to be the eighth faith in new alliance'. *The New Road* 15:1.

Callicott, J.B. and R.T. Ames (eds). 1989. *Nature in Asian Traditions of Thought. Essays in Environmental Philosophy*. Albany: State University of New York Press.

Davies, S. (ed.). 1987. *The Tree of Life. Buddhism and the Protection of Nature*. Geneva: Buddhist perception of nature.

Dwivedi, O.P. 1990. '*Satyagraha* for conservation: Awakening the spirit of Hinduism'. In Engel, J.R. and J.G. Engel (eds), *Ethics of Environment and Development*. London: Bellhaven Press.

Dwivedi, O.P. and B.N. Tiwari 1987. *Environmental Crisis and Hindu Religion*. New Delhi: Gitanjali Publishing House.

Engel, J.R. 1990. 'Introduction. The ethics of sustainable development'. In Engel, J.R. and J.G. Engel (eds), *Ethics of Environment and Development*. London: Bellhaven Press.

Engel, J.R. and J.G. Engel (eds). 1990. *Ethics of Environment and Development*. London: Bellhaven Press.

Evernden, N. 1992. *The Social Creation of Nature.* Baltimore: Johns Hopkins University Press.

Friedman, J. 1992a. 'Narcissism, roots and postmodernity: The constitution of selfhood in the global crisis'. In Lash, Scott and J. Friedman (eds), *Modernity and identity.* Oxford: Blackwell.

—— 1992b. 'The past in the future: History and the politics of identity'. *American Anthropologist* 94(4):837–859.

Giddens, A. 1990. *The Consequences of Modernity.* Stanford: Stanford University Press.

—— 1991. *Modernity and Self-identity.* Stanford: Stanford University Press.

Grove, R. 1990. 'The origin of environmentalism'. *Nature* 345:11–14.

—— 1993. 'Conserving Eden: The (European) East India Companies and their environmental policies on St. Helena, Mauritius and in Western India, 1600 to 1854'. *Comparative Studies in Society and History* 35(2):318–351.

Harris, I. 1991. 'How environmentalist is Buddhism?' *Religion* 21:101–114.

Hepburn. R.W. 1967. 'Nature, philosophical ideas of'. In *The Encyclopedia of Philosophy*, vol. 5, ed. P. Edwards. London: Collier-Macmillan.

Holy, L. and M. Stuchlik. 1983. *Actions, Norms and Representations.* Cambridge: Cambridge University Press.

Huber, T. 1991. 'Traditional environmental protectionism in Tibet reconsidered'. *The Tibet Journal* 16(3):63–77.

Ingold, T. 1992. 'Culture and the perception of the environment'. In Croll, E. and D. Parkin (eds), *Bush Base: Forest Farm. Culture, Environment and Development.* London: Routledge.

Izzi Deen (Samarrai), M.Y. 1990. 'Islamic environmental ethics: Law and society'. In Engel, J.R. and J.G. Engel (eds), *Ethics of Environment and Development.* London: Bellhaven Press.

Johnson, A. 1989. 'How the Machiguenga manage resources: Conservation or exploitation of nature?' *Advances in Economic Botany* 7:213–222.

Kapferer, B. 1983. *A Celebration of Demons.* Bloomington: Indiana University Press.

Lovejoy, A.O. 1948. '"Nature" as aesthetic norm'. In Lovejoy, A.O. (ed.), *Essays in the History of Ideas*. Baltimore: The Johns Hopkins Press.

MacCormick, J. 1989. *Reclaiming Paradise*. Bloomington: Indiana University Press.

McIntosh, R.P. 1985. *The Background of Ecology*. Cambridge: Cambridge University Press.

Manzoor, S.P. 1984. 'Environment and values: The Islamic perspective'. In Sardar, Z. (ed.), *The Touch of Midas. Science, Values and the Environment in Islam and the West*. Manchester: Manchester University Press.

Mocek, R. 1990. 'Natur'. In *Europäische Enzyklopædie zu Philosophie und Wissenschaft*, vol. 3, ed. Hans Jörg Sandhühler. Hamburg: Felix Verlag.

Momaday, N.C. 1976. 'A first American views his land'. *National Geographic*, 150(1):13–18.

Nash, R.F. 1989. *The Rights of Nature*. Madison, Wisc.: The University of Wisconsin Press.

Nasr, S.H. 1990. 'Islam and the environmental crisis'. *Islamic Quarterly* 34(4): 217–234.

Obeyesekere, G. 1981, *Medusa's Hair*. Chicago: University of Chicago Press.

Pedersen, P. 1992. 'The study of perceptions of nature. Towards a sociology of knowledge about nature'. In Bruun, O. and A. Kalland (eds), *Asian Perceptions of Nature*. Copenhagen: Nordic Institute of Asian Studies.

Ponting, C. 1991. *A Green History of the World*. London: Penguin.

Sahlins, M. 1993. 'Goodbye to *Tristes Tropes*: Ethnography in the context of modern world history'. *Journal of Modern World History* 65:1–25.

Samartha, S.J. and L. de Silva. 1979. 'Foreword'. In Samartha, S.J. and L. de Silva (eds), *Man in Nature: Guest or Engineer*. Colombo: The Ecumenical Institute for Study and Dialogue.

Simmons, I.G. 1993. *Interpreting Nature. Cultural Constructions of the Environment*. London: Routledge.

Suzuki, D.T. 1954. 'The role of nature in Zen Buddhism'. *Eranus-Jahrbuch* 22:291–321.

Swain, T. 1991. 'The Mother Earth conspiracy: An Australian episode'. *Numen* 38(1):3–26.

Tuan, Y. 1968. 'Discrepancies between environmental attitude and behaviour: Examples from Europe and China'. *Canadian Geographer* 12(3):176–191.

Vecsey, C. and R.W. Venables (eds). 1980. *American Indian Environments: Ecological Issues in Native American History*. New York: Syracuse University Press.

White, Jr., L. 1967. 'The historical roots of our ecologic crisis'. *Science* 155:1204–1207.

—— 1973. 'Continuing the conversation'. In Barbour, I.G. (ed.), *Western Man and Environmental Ethics*. Reading, Mass.: Addison-Wesley Publication Company.

Williams, R. 1972. 'Ideas of nature'. In Benthall, J. (ed.), *Ecology. The Shaping Enquiry*. London: Longman.

WWF 1986. *The Assisi Declarations. Messages on Nan and Nature from Buddhism, Christianity, Hinduism, Islam and Judaism*. Gland, Switzerland: WWF International.

Yuthok, K.G. 1992. 'The Tibetan perception. of the environment'. Paper presented to the Sixth Conference of the International Association of Tibetan Studies, Fagernes, Norway.

List of Contributors

Peter Boomgaard. Director of the Royal Institute of Linguistics and Anthropology (KITLV), Postbox 9515, NL-2300 RA Leiden, The Netherlands.

Ole Bruun. Former Research Fellow at the Nordic Institute of Asian Studies, Njalsgade 84, DK-2300 Copenhagen S, Denmark.

Graham E. Clarke. Associate Professor at the University of Oxford, Queen Elizabeth House, 21 St Giles, Oxford, OX1 3LA, England.

S.N. Eisenstadt. Professor Emeritus, Faculty of Social Sciences, The Hebrew University of Jerusalem, Mt. Scopus, Jerusalem 91905, Israel.

Arne Kalland. Senior Research Associate at the Centre for Development and the Environment, University of Oslo, P.O. Box 1116, Blindern, N-0317 Oslo, Norway.

Jeya Kathirithamby-Wells. Professor of Asian History, Department of History, University of Malaya, Kuala Lumpur, Malaysia.

Are Knudsen. Research Associate at Chr. Michelsen Institute, Fantoftvegen 38, N-5036 Fantoft, Norway.

Brian Moeran. Swire Professor of Japanese, Department of Japanese, The University of Hong Kong, Pokfulam Road, Hong Kong.

Poul Pedersen, Associate Professor at the Department of Social Anthropology, Århus University, Moesgaard, DK-8270 Højbjerg, Denmark.

Klas Sandell. Lecturer at the Department of Social Sciences, University of Örebro, P.O. Box 923, S-701 30 Örebro, Sweden.

Lise Skov. Ph.D. Research Student at the Department of Sociology, The University of Hong Kong, Pokfulam Road, Hong Kong.

Stephen Sparkes. Ph.D. Research Student at the Institute and Museum for Anthropology, Fredriksgate 2, N-0164 Oslo, Norway.

Birgitte Glavind Sperber. Senior Lecturer at Ribe State College of Education, Simon Hansens Vej 1, DK-6760 Ribe, Denmark.

The Nordic Institute of Asian Studies (NIAS) is funded by the governments of Denmark, Finland, Iceland, Norway and Sweden, and works to encourage and support Asian studies in the Nordic countries. In so doing, NIAS has published more than one hundred books in the last twenty-five years, most of them in co-operation with Curzon Press.